second edition

Doing Cultural Anthropology

second edition

Doing Cultural Anthropology

projects for ethnographic data collection

Michael V. Angrosino
University of South Florida

WAVELAND

PRESS, INC.

Long Grove, Illinois

For information about this book, contact:
Waveland Press, Inc.
4180 IL Route 83, Suite 101
Long Grove, IL 60047-9580
(847) 634-0081
info@waveland.com
www.waveland.com

10-digit ISBN 1-57766-464-7
13-digit ISBN 978-1-57766-464-2

Printed in the United States of America

8   7   6   5   4   3   2

This book is dedicated
to the memory of Julia G. Crane—
inspiring teacher, generous mentor, and good friend

Contents

Acknowledgments

I am deeply grateful to Thomas Curtin, the Anthropology Editor of Waveland Press, who has been a faithful supporter of *Field Projects in Anthropology* for many years, and whose insightful comments about a possible new edition of that handbook led directly to this new endeavor.

All the contributors to this volume deserve special thanks for responding to my call for chapters in a timely and efficient manner, and for producing such readable and useful essays. I also thank my students at the University of South Florida whose experiences and expressed needs in doing ethnographic research have shaped my approach to the material. I acknowledge the clerical and editorial assistance of Petra LeClair.

Most of all, however, I acknowledge my great debt to Julia Crane, my teacher, mentor, colleague, and friend of more than three decades. Although she was unable to participate directly in the preparation of this book, her approach to the learning of ethnography, her knowledge of and unflagging enthusiasm for field research, and her affection and respect for students shaped my outlook. In a very real sense, this book is her production as much as it is mine and the contributors'.

Introduction

Michael V. Angrosino

ETHNOGRAPHY

The English word "ethnography" derives from Greek and literally means the description of a people and its way of life. In contemporary social science, ethnography refers both to a process of research and to the account (usually in writing, but also possibly on film) that results from that research.

The tradition of producing descriptive accounts of the customs and practices of different peoples goes back to classical antiquity—the histories of the Greek Herodotus and the Roman Tacitus are enlivened by such details. Accounts of "exotic" people published by travelers, soldiers, merchants, and missionaries were mainstays of popular literature for many centuries, but it was not until the nineteenth century that attempts were made to systematize the research process that gave rise to these representations of other ways of life. At that point, ethnography became associated with the new discipline of cultural anthropology—indeed, it became the foundation for that new science, concerned as it was with the comparative analysis of the peoples of the world and their cultures. In fact, the greatest insight of cultural anthropology was the concept of culture itself—the idea that people's behaviors, beliefs,

1

interactions, and material productions were not random, but rather formed a "complex whole" that was meaningful, logical, more or less consistent, and worthy of respect on its own terms. And such a concept of culture required the careful and objective collection and analysis of the many details of cultures around the world so as to better understand how those details came together to give substance to culture.

Nineteenth-century ethnographies were originally produced on what is sometimes referred to as a "notes and queries" model. That is, amateur observers (those who, like the travelers and missionaries of previous times, were actively involved with people of different cultures) provided information on demand to scholars seeking to piece together accounts of unfamiliar cultures. For example, Lewis Henry Morgan, one of the founding fathers of anthropology in the United States, constructed a groundbreaking ethnography of kinship systems based on material sent to him by globetrotting non-anthropologists responding to specific questions posed by Morgan at his desk in Rochester, New York. But by the turn of the twentieth century, two models of "direct" ethnography had come into fashion. The first was the systematic ethnographic survey, in which teams of scientists went out to collect as much information as possible about large sections of previously undocumented parts of the world; this approach was modeled on the natural-history surveys of unexplored lands that had been undertaken by nineteenth-century scientists. (Darwin's famous *Voyage of the Beagle*, in the course of which he refined the principles of the theory of evolution, was just such a natural-history survey.) Of greater lasting influence, however, was the intensive study, which usually involved a single researcher living in a single indigenous community for an extended period of time. This approach, typically associated with the pioneering work of Franz Boas in the United States and Bronislaw Malinowski in Britain, has remained the hallmark of cultural anthropology, and has also been adopted and adapted by scholars in the fields of sociology, social psychology, cultural geography, communication, epidemiology, education, and business.

That social scientists representing these diverse disciplines use the ethnographic method demonstrates its value for answering questions about human communities and institutions. Ethnography is distinguished from other ways of conducting social research (e.g., the experimental design) in that it is conducted in "natural" (as opposed to laboratory) settings, in which the behavior of people in everyday situations is followed as it happens—there is no attempt to control any of the variables that might affect that behavior. Ethnographers refer to this natural setting as "the field." The process of doing ethnography is therefore often called "fieldwork." The naturalistic approach implies an inductive analytical strategy; that is, explanatory theories grow out of the experience as it is observed in real life (in contrast to the classic experimental design, in which some general theory generates specific hypotheses, which are then tested under controlled circumstances).

DATA-COLLECTION TECHNIQUES

Ethnography may be thought of as a general strategy for conducting research, the end-product of which is some sort of description of a group and its beliefs, behaviors, and material goods. But ethnography is not, in and of itself, a way to gather information. There are, in fact, many techniques that may be employed to collect data in the course of ethnographic fieldwork. Ethnographers typically use multiple techniques in the field. No data-collection technique is without its limitations and potential biases, so that the more of them that are used, the more chance there is to cancel out those limitations and come up with a reasonably objective overall portrait. Interviewing and observing are the fundamental ethnographic data-collection techniques, but any means of gleaning information that contributes to a description of a people and its way of life can be considered appropriate to ethnographic fieldwork.

THE PHILOSOPHY OF THIS BOOK

In 1974, I was invited by Julia Crane, who had been my dissertation advisor and under whose guidance I had conducted my first fieldwork outside the United States, to co-author a book on ethnographic methods. In those days, there were relatively few courses in ethnographic methods, and most of those in existence were geared to graduate students in anthropology and sociology. We believed, however, that even beginning students in those disciplines could profit from an understanding of ethnography. We agreed that every student, when presented with a body of substantive material such as might be found in the textbooks and lectures associated with introductory survey courses, should ask first of all: "How did s/he come to know this?" In other words, by what process of research did a scholar establish that this or that purported fact or interpretation was worthy of being passed along to those learning about the material?

We nonetheless realized that there was little impact in simply telling students that, for example, Crane learned about 200 years of labor-migration patterns in the Dutch West Indies by an analysis of census records. It would be much better if students were able to experience for themselves what it would be like to work with census records—even if only in the limited context of a small practice exercise—so that they would have a better understanding of and appreciation for what a fieldworker has to go through in order to come up with the material presented so succinctly in a textbook or lecture.

Our book, *Field Projects in Anthropology: A Student Handbook* (1992, Long Grove, IL: Waveland Press), therefore took the form of guided exercises in the more prominent data-collection techniques, based on the philosophy of learning-by-doing. The book has gone into three editions, and has been translated into other languages as well. It has proven to be a durable and, we hope, useful tool that has introduced beginning students to the enjoyment of using ethnographic fieldwork as problem solving; it has also been helpful to more advanced students looking to brush up their skills before launching into more elaborate field research projects. The book has been used as a text in formal courses in ethnographic methods (and there are now many more of them— and in disciplines beyond anthropology and sociology—than was the case back in the 1970s) and as supplementary material in introductory surveys. Over the years, the literature on ethnographic data collection has grown enormously, some of it sharing our learn-by-doing philosophy.

It is now time to revisit the material in the *Handbook*. Some of the data-collection techniques that were popular with researchers in the 1960s and 1970s and were therefore featured prominently in that book are no longer quite so common (e.g., componential analysis). Others that seemed somewhat marginal to ethnographers then have become increasingly important (e.g., standardized surveys). Our treatment of some techniques has been rendered obsolete by advances in technology (e.g., still photography). And new aspects of the study of culture that were literally unheard of two decades ago (e.g., those dealing with communities that exist only in cyberspace or whose complexities can be studied only with up-to-the-minute computer applications) have now moved to center stage. A simple revision of the *Handbook*, then, would clearly not do. Julia Crane and I decided that instead of trying to write a new version of the book, I would edit a collection of essays by an invited panel of colleagues and friends—successful and innovative ethnographic researchers all—each addressing an ethnographic data-collection technique in which they had specialized. In this way, the expertise of various people actually doing current research would be brought to bear on the topic of field research.

Despite this change in organization, the underlying philosophy of the book remains unchanged. Each chapter is built around an exercise/project that readers can undertake to better see for themselves how basic textbook and lecture information is collected and analyzed by ethnographic researchers.

THE PLAN OF THE BOOK

Each chapter in the book begins with the author telling about a particular research project with which he or she has been involved. Although that project almost always involved multiple data-collection techniques, the author demonstrates why particular research questions were effectively answered employing one particular technique. He or she then goes on to present a brief history of that technique—how it developed, in what kinds of research contexts it has been applied. Next, he or she walks readers through a step-by-step discussion of how the technique is typically carried out. A very important part of this discussion entails the ethical implications of research. The primary ethical responsibility of any ethnographic researcher is to respect the dignity and privacy of those being studied; each data-collection technique presents its own particular challenges to the fulfillment of that ethical imperative. In each chapter, students are reminded to seek their instructors' guidance with regard to any specific ethics requirements that might apply in their own setting (e.g., rules about informed consent that might be monitored by a university's institutional review board). Each chapter ends with a suggested guided project for readers to follow.

The chapters are not written as scholarly treatises, and there are no footnotes (although each chapter includes a very brief and highly selective list of recommended follow-up readings). The aim is to give readers just enough information to appreciate the technique and its potential for use by social scientists, and then to go on to practice it for themselves. The exercise projects are written so that even students in beginning survey courses can work them, although instructors in more advanced courses can certainly suggest ways in which they can be modified to suit the needs of students with more background. Although almost all of the contributors are anthropologists, the projects are written in such a way that they can be applied by students of any other discipline that uses the ethnographic method. Most of the projects are designed to be completed by a single student, although a few seem to work best as team efforts. It is highly unlikely that any one student could possibly complete all the exercises in a single academic semester; the instructor will have to decide how many, and which ones, to assign in any given course.

One further disclaimer: there is a very wide assortment of data-collection techniques available to the contemporary fieldworker, and this book does not attempt to cover all of them. But a student who becomes comfortable with the fundamental methods that are dealt with herein will certainly have developed an effective repertoire that will remain the heart of any subsequent field research, and upon which other creative and innovative methods can be built.

The book begins with a chapter by Tierney on participant observation, perhaps the most traditional, most widely revered, and most widely misunderstood approach to conducting ethnographic research. Presentations of two other very traditional techniques (the genealogical method by deRoche and the life history interview by Angrosino) follow. The chapter by Redfern-Vance takes note of the fact that these traditional techniques usually result in a massive amount of undigested narrative data (as opposed to easily sorted and analyzed quantitative data) and suggests some innovative ways to make sense of such material. A chapter on the use of archival records (including census data) by Rodriguez and Baber follows. This group of essays on traditional methods ends with Nanda's discussion of the uses of museum resources as an adjunct to ethnographic fieldwork.

The next six chapters deal with variously formalized, quantitative approaches that were not always necessarily part of the tool kit of traditional ethnographers, but that are very important to contemporary researchers (Borman, Puccia, McNulty, and Goddard on the study of formal organizations; Price on standardized observation; Baer and Weller on survey questionnaires; Rees on demographic analysis; Bryant on focus group reserach; and Bird on applying visual methods).

Two essays follow that bring ethnography into the age of electronic communications. Bird and Barber describe doing ethnographic research online with communities formed by Internet chat groups. Wolfe and Hagen discuss the potential for using powerful, sophisticated computer modeling to analyze complex bureaucratic structures (although their suggested exercise allows readers the feel of such research on a scale amenable to simple calculations).

The last of the project chapters, by Berger and Ellis, is organized very differently from all the others. In recent years, the social sciences have been caught up in a thorough critique of their traditional methods, theories, and assumptions—a critique that often goes by the generic name "postmodernism." The basic proposition of postmodernism is that the objective reality so assiduously sought by social scientists is something of an illusion—the perceptions of even the most highly trained scientific analysts are inevitably shaped by their own situations (their gender, social class, racial or ethnic background, sexual orientation, and so forth) to the extent that all generalizations about social processes are essentially constructions that tell us more about the people who construct them than they do about the external reality they purportedly describe. Because that now-questionable objective external reality has for so long been encoded in standard expository scientific prose, postmodernists advocate the use of alternative means of presenting ethnographic reality—e.g., using the devices of fictional literature to describe social and cultural settings—and a more explicit insertion of their own identities into the analysis of those matters. The chapter by Berger and Ellis itself is written as a kind of "alternative" writing exercise; it is presented as a story, with dialogue and vividly described characters. The key elements of the other chapters (explication of authors' research projects, definitions of the methods used, guided exercises, suggestions for further reading) are included, but they are all woven into the larger narrative, rather than set out as explicit chapter subheadings. As a result, the student will not only receive instruction on how to construct an "alternative" narrative account of cultural process, but will also have a model of the process in the way the chapter itself is written and presented.

The book's final chapter is not a project, but an invitation—an encouragement to participate in an ethnographic field school, particularly one that takes students into another culture for an extended period of time (usually a summer session) under the supervision of a faculty mentor. In this chapter,

Wallace discusses the benefits of participating in a field school and provides some helpful and practical advice on how to find a suitable school and get the most out of the experience. It is our hope that by completing some of the exercises in the rest of the book, students will come away with an appetite for more. The organized field school might well be an effective way to get that additional exposure to the sometimes frustrating, but always enlightening and personally enriching, enterprise of ethnographic fieldwork.

1

Becoming a
Participant Observer

Gerry Tierney

A RESEARCH PROJECT

When I was a graduate student, the time came when I had to think about my dissertation research project. I knew that I wanted to design a project that would give me some insight into the daily lives of homeless people and I realized that the only way I could delve into those lives would be to live in the field. I had done some preliminary research in a homeless shelter in New York City, but ultimately decided to conduct my research in Anchorage, Alaska, a city where I had lived for twenty years and which I considered my home. When I was an undergraduate at the University of Alaska–Anchorage, I became interested in the indigenous people living in the metropolitan area. One of my professors, Linda Ellana, took me on a tour of the infamous Fourth Avenue area, the Skid Row of Anchorage, a street packed with seedy bars. Dr. Ellana was an expert on the Alaska Eskimos; she had lived in native villages and understood the value of experiencing the lives of people in their own setting. But she stressed the importance of understanding what is going on in your own backyard before thinking about going off to exotic places, as traditional anthropologists were supposed to do. She made me realize how fortunate we were to have indigenous people right in our backyard.

That night on Skid Row gave me many insights into a world that was previously hidden from my view, a world that was surprisingly viable, populated by people who were managing to survive despite great odds. That experience convinced me that whatever research I ultimately undertook, it would have to include participant observation in the daily lives of the people I wanted to study. And so I returned to Anchorage for my dissertation research.

PARTICIPANT OBSERVATION AS A TOOL OF ETHNOGRAPHIC RESEARCH

When I began my Fourth Avenue research I felt confident in my training in the skills of social research. On the other hand, I was frightened about entering this world. I would not be passing through, as was the case in New York, nor would I be there only for a brief tour under the supervision of a knowledgeable professor. I would be there essentially on my own for an extended period of time.

At first, my primary activity was just hanging out. I was usually quite comfortable doing so and I watched every little thing, always listening to the sounds of the street, a world that was slowly opening up to me. Through these means, I built some trust among the people and gained their cooperation in helping me learn about them and their activities. The only time I felt uncomfortable was when the tables were turned and people on the street took to watching me and asking me a variety of personal questions. During the first few weeks it became clear to me that I was the oddity on the street and that I was being observed and scrutinized with as much intensity as I myself employed while watching them.

Engaging people in conversation took a little more time, but it too eventually became an everyday activity. In this manner, I was able to begin hearing about my informants' views. I was also able to develop relationships with people that enabled me to interview them about aspects of their lives. One woman, an Eskimo, became a particularly good informant. She shared her life history with me, although she occasionally reminded me that there were some details of her life that she did not want published. ("This is for your ears only," she would tell me from time to time.) She was a woman with a rare and engaging sense of humor. She would frequently annoy me when she would announce in a voice loud enough for everyone in the shelter to hear, "Watch it! She writes." She did so with a twinkle in her eye and a hearty, infectious laugh. We developed a relationship based on mutual respect and trust. Being a participant in as well as an observer of the lives of people means that one has a responsibility to protect the integrity of those with whom one interacts.

My goal was to describe the everyday activities of a group of homeless people, with a focus on women. I wanted to know everything I could about the individuals who inhabited Anchorage's Skid Row. I wanted to know what it felt like to live in public places, how people could survive in such a seemingly hostile environment, and how they managed to get some enjoyment out of life all the same. These goals required not only an understanding of research methodology, but also a particular mind-set, a desire to see the world from the insiders' perspective. It is no accident that participant observation is the strategy used most often by ethnographic researchers to uncover the world views of people from cultures other than their own. While participant observation is certainly not necessary for all kinds of social research projects, it is an important technique for anyone hoping to develop relationships with, and not merely gather information from, those under study. In addition to hoping to write a scholarly dissertation, I wanted to be in a position to make some recommendations for the improvement of services to the homeless. I knew that my suggestions would have greater weight if I had lived through the relevant experiences so that I had a deeper understanding of and appreciation for the needs that the people themselves expressed.

I knew that I could not hope to see the everyday world of Skid Row women from their own perspective unless I shared that world with them over the course of time. To be sure, I was not able to participate completely, as some of the activities engaged in by street people are illegal and dangerous, especially for a woman. Nevertheless, the participant observation that I could do opened up the world of the homeless for me. In many ways, it is a world very much like my own, a world in which people have to be innovative, skillful, and clever if they want to survive. But the specific challenges to their capacities were ones that I had to learn about from the inside.

PARTICIPANT OBSERVATION: A BRIEF HISTORY

Prior to the nineteenth century, people interested in learning about foreign cultures had to read the second-hand accounts of missionaries, merchants, or other travelers. Many of these observations were ethnocentric, biased in favor of the culture from which the travelers came and tending to characterize foreigners as primitive or backward.

One of the first important observers of a non-Western culture to attempt to participate in that culture and understand it on its own terms was Henry Schoolcraft, a government agent working among the Chippewa Indians of the upper Great Lakes region in the 1820s and 1830s. Most Indian agents of that era had little interest in or respect for the native cultures, but Schoolcraft was cut from a different cloth. He learned the Chippewa language and lived in the villages and ultimately shared his intimate, encyclopedic knowledge of the culture in a series of books that detailed the history, traditions, customs, language, and social institutions of the people. He became a friend of many people in the villages, and on occasion found himself in the position of a political advocate who argued on behalf of Indian causes.

Although Schoolcraft was not a trained anthropologist, his work among the Chippewa illustrates the major aspects of what was to become formally recognized as the participant observation approach to ethnographic research. Participant observation is not simply a matter of living in close proximity to the people one wishes to study; after all, traders and missionaries often lived among the Indians, but made little or no effort to understand their culture in all its complexity. Participant observation is not just the collection of data, but a way of thinking about the people from whom one collects those data. It is also a way in which one perceives one's own position in relation to the people and the culture one is studying. Cultural relativism is a philosophical position that goes hand in hand with participant observation; its major premise is that no culture is superior to any other, and that each culture must be understood and evaluated in its own terms. Later in the nineteenth century, anthropologists in both Britain (e.g., Bronislaw Malinowski) and the United States (e.g., Franz Boas and his students, among whom perhaps the most famous was Margaret Mead) formalized the participant observation strategy and the principle of cultural relativism and made them the centerpieces of scientific ethnographic research.

PARTICIPANT OBSERVATION: THE PROCESS

The Skills of a Participant Observer

When I first read that some of the major skills involved in participant observation were watching and listening, I knew that this mainstay of anthropology was well suited not only for my project, but also for my personality. I am a patient person in most respects and I enjoy interacting with a variety of people. Before I entered the field, however, I really did not appreciate the importance of interacting with and getting along with people who, it turned out, would be active participants in my project. My training had always emphasized the activities of the researcher; I had to learn through experience that people from other cultures are not pliable puppets performing for me as a researcher; they are living human beings who quite often demand something in return from the researcher.

One of the biggest shocks for me in the field was the realization that I would have to spend a prolonged period of time living among people so seemingly different from me. I was not really prepared to deal with my own foibles and negative characteristics, but I had to do so—unless I understood myself better, I could not hope to bridge the perceived gap between myself and the people I was learning about. Fieldwork based on participant observation is a two-way street: just as I had expectations of the people (that they would share their experiences with me and honestly answer my questions), so they had expectations of me (to be honest and forthcoming about myself and my motives).

When you live for an extended period of time with people who seem to be very different from yourself, it is a good idea to watch out for feelings of superiority. While feelings of unease, suspicion, even a bit of hostility are only natural, they must be dealt with forthrightly and consciously set aside, lest they color the research in unwanted, negative ways. Indeed, the process of building rapport took up the bulk of my time early in the project, as I had to learn not only what the people I was studying were like, but also what *I* was like. People did not always want to be bothered by my silly questions and I had to learn that my own agenda, as important as it was for me, was not the only agenda that had to be acknowledged and dealt with.

As I reflect on my field experiences, I realize that another important aspect of fieldwork for me was that I was somewhat naïve. Some anthropologists go so far as to advocate cultivating naïveté. I am not sure one can consciously do so; perhaps it is sufficient simply to use the naïveté with which most of us come equipped and not try to overcome it or overcompensate for it. A certain degree of humility is required to do so. It is not, after all, easy to be in the position of one who appears to be constantly in the dark about even the simplest situations. Putting yourself in the position of the student, letting insiders teach you about the intricacies of their culture, is sometimes difficult, but in the end it pays off. You may, of course, have more "book learning" than they (i.e., you will almost certainly have read the available literature on the culture before beginning your fieldwork), but you cannot hope to see the world as they do if you constantly impose an "I know better because I read the book" attitude on every encounter. In my own case, the street people had long since learned that university types tended to be haughty, arrogant, rude, useless, and not very bright about survival on the streets. They frequently told me that nothing good ever came from one of the seemingly countless studies conducted on the streets of Anchorage. My willingness to be humble made me a much more acceptable presence.

It is also important to cultivate a sense of humor, which can help you put yourself and your work in an appropriate perspective. Extended fieldwork can be tedious at times, exhausting at others. Appreciating the ludicrous or incongruous aspects of the work can be a great blessing. When I was on the street in Anchorage, I learned how important a sense of humor was for the native people who became my friends. I was raised in a somber, puritanical, Irish Catholic household in Massachusetts. My sense of humor was never allowed to blossom; indeed, any kind of levity was looked upon with a great deal of suspicion. Early in my research, however, an Eskimo man pointed out that I never laughed out loud. He observed that I would smile and say, "That's funny," which he thought was very peculiar behavior. When I saw myself through their eyes I realized how strange I must have seemed and I made real efforts to lighten up and share a good laugh with my friends.

One additional skill is necessary for a good participant observer: writing. It is most important for you to write down, sometimes in excruciating detail, all your observations. Doing so has become much easier since the advent of computers, but it still takes time, discipline, and organization to sit down and write at length, every day. So if you do not like to write, or think you are not a very good writer, be sure to take time to practice before you enter the field.

The Stages of Participant Observation

The first step is to decide on a topic. Doing so may sound simple, but because it is a great, big world, and anything human in it is fair game for an ethnographer, it can be difficult to narrow your focus down to something you can actually do. One good way to begin is to read about projects carried out by other researchers; you may wish to duplicate one of them in your own area, or you may wish to follow up on some suggestion an author has made. It is important to read as much as possible so that you can identify gaps in the literature, trying to fill in some area of knowledge not already well established. For example, when I began immersing myself in the literature on homelessness, I was struck by the fact that almost all of it dealt with men; there were surely homeless women, but we knew very little about them at that time. Choosing a topic and choosing a site for research are linked processes. In my own case, my prior interest in Alaska natives confirmed my decision to study homeless women in Anchorage rather than in New York.

Selecting a site is not, however, the same thing as gaining entrance. One does not simply show up somewhere and commence participant observation. It is usually desirable to have some trusted person or institution in the community you want to study help introduce you to the people. In my case, I decided to contact a homeless shelter and inquire about the possibility of serving in some capacity as a volunteer while I conducted research. The director of the shelter responded favorably. Nevertheless, my first day in the field was still stressful and anxiety-provoking. It was a very cold January day, and since the shelter did not open until late afternoon, I thought I would just hang around on Fourth Avenue to observe. You might think that a person who had lived most of her life in Alaska would have known better! It is just too cold to be outdoors in January. So I found a fast-food restaurant located right across the street from Skid Row. I drank a lot of coffee and ate a lot of French fries that day. I also felt depressed and wondered what I could have been thinking of to put myself in this awkward position. I found myself gazing off to the beautiful, snow-capped Chugach Mountains, and wondering, "What am I doing here?" I had some doubts about my ability to carry out the project. Anthropologists refer to such emotions as "culture shock."

Things did not get much better once I finally got to the shelter. The director was not on the premises when I arrived, and no one else seemed to know who I was or what I was doing there. So I just sat there trying not to look conspicuous. I continued to be plagued by feelings of inadequacy. Finally, a woman who worked in the kitchen approached me and graciously invited me to join her for a cup of coffee while she prepared the evening meal. She saved me from the stares of all the people entering the shelter and she eventually became one of my best friends. She was a Roman Catholic nun who was the only paid female employee providing direct services at the shelter. She was also the only advocate for women at this particular shelter— a role that, alas, led to her abrupt dismissal just a few months later.

And so with a great deal of frustration, I began what would be a field experience of six months' duration. This first day was not typical of the days that followed, but the major problem became quite clear to me on that day: I would have to interact with these people at the shelter on a daily basis and participate in their daily activities. It was a frightening prospect because I was not at all sure I had what it would take to complete the project.

One of the most difficult aspects of the work was a lack of privacy: I was almost always surrounded by people. After people got over the novelty of seeing me hanging around all the time, they began to treat me like an insider. On one level this sounds like a good thing, but it was troubling in some ways, in that I was treated like many of the women on the street—that is, as a person targeted for sexual abuse. Being a street woman meant that you were subject to a daily diet of sexual jokes, advances, inappropriate touching, harassment, and other forms of abuse at the hands of a variety of males—not just homeless men, but also men who were supposed to protect and serve them, such as police officers and social workers. It was important to have a sense of myself and to set limits about what I could, or would, participate in.

Although scientific research is expected to be objective, participant observation of necessity introduces a degree of subjectivity into the process. When you spend a considerable amount of time in the field with people, you grow close to certain individuals. One woman in particular was very intelligent; without her assistance I would not have understood much of what went on in the shelter and on the streets. This woman, Mariah, was not just an "informant," but a friend. Over the years when I return to Anchorage, she always throws her arms around me to welcome me back. I would not have been able to have conducted my research without Mariah; she may not always have understood why I wanted to be part of their lives, but she was always most generous in sharing herself with me. Participant observation is always a joint effort and it requires mutual trust and respect.

In warmer weather I would be on the streets until about 1:00 AM, at which time I returned to the shelter to write up my recollections of the day's activities. I carried a little notepad in my pocket at all times and I would frequently write down key words or phrases that I would use in the evening to remember as much as possible. It would usually take a few hours to write up even relatively brief daily notes, which would then be used to write more expanded commentaries after a week or so. At times I thought I was drowning in minutiae, but when I was finished with fieldwork and began to write my dissertation, I was very happy that I had tried to record every last detail.

That final write-up—whether it is a dissertation, or a more limited course assignment—entails more than writing; it is a process of thought and reflection as well. There is a lot of organizational work that needs to be done, as your notes are likely to be very extensive. You need to decide how to categorize the notes so that you can efficiently retrieve data on particular topics.

YOUR PROJECT

This project needs to begin early in the semester, as participant observation requires more than one or two visits to a site. It might take some time just to set up the project and obtain permission to work with the people you are interested in studying.

In choosing your topic, do not undertake fieldwork in a situation that makes you nervous or uncomfortable. This first project should be enjoyable. If you do not deal well with conflict or aggression, you may want to avoid fieldwork in a jail, police station, or even a homeless shelter. If you cannot stand the sight of blood, a hospital emergency room is not for you. If you are unsympathetic to organized religion, fieldwork in a church, synagogue, mosque, or temple might be unpleasant. On the other hand, those settings might be perfect for you, depending on your interests or emotional resources. Remember that even sites as apparently mundane as laundromats have made for very interesting ethnographies—use your imagination in selecting both a topic and a site. Some examples from my own students include observations in tattoo parlors, fire stations, and diners. Some of my students are older, working individuals who conduct research associated with their jobs or their children. For example, one student conducted fieldwork in her son's computer science lab at a local secondary school. She not only provided the school with a detailed study of computer lab use, but also included recommendations for increased usage.

Depending on the site you have selected, you may need to contact someone in the environment to see if you would be welcome to hang out there. Some settings selected by my students (e.g., a day-care center) required very formal permission; others are more flexible, although it is always helpful to have someone who is already a trusted insider in that community be the one to introduce you to the others. If you choose some sort of service agency (e.g., a soup kitchen), you should consider volunteering some of your time, so that you are giving something back to both the staff and the clients and not simply hanging out selfishly doing your own thing. By all means, consult with your instructor regarding your school's norms for informed consent in projects such as this one.

Be prepared for some culture shock the first time you enter the field. Even if the place is familiar to you, you will be seeing it and interacting within it in very different ways. Whatever feelings of discomfort you may experience, try to remain as courteous as possible. Keep in mind that the people you are living/working among are providing you with both time and information. They are sharing part of their life with you, and without them you would have no project. Strive, therefore, to treat them with all due respect. An important part of showing respect is being honest about why you are there and what you are attempting to accomplish. If some people choose not to cooperate, do not take it as a personal affront; simply work with those who are more willing to interact with you.

Be sure to keep good notes. Depending on your personal preferences (and your resources), you may do so on index cards, a pad or notebook, or a Palm Pilot. Do not, however, spend all your time in the field with your nose buried in your notes. While you are in the field, use the cards or pads or other devices simply to jot down brief, simple reminders. You can flesh out these comments when you have some time to yourself. Do not put off that task, however, as you will lose many important details if you wait too long to transform the quick field note into a more circumstantial description.

Your final report should include a map of the environment you have been studying, as well as a detailed narrative description of the site. Do not take too much for granted (even if you are studying a very commonplace site); write your description as if for an audience of readers who are not familiar with the setting at all. You can then go on to write an interpretive analysis of what is going on in the environment, based in part on your own readings (how does this material conform to what I have read about other similar settings? how does it differ? why?) and on what your informants tell you about their own insights into their experiences. For example, one of my students chose to observe a local mosque; what particularly struck her was the way in which gender roles were played out in worship services and this aspect of the culture formed the core of her analysis.

Your report may also include photographs or sketches (if you have obtained the people's permission to use them), transcriptions of interviews, or materials pertinent to the site under study (e.g., brochures produced by a civic organization). By all means feel free to include any insights you have gleaned about your own personality in conducting this research.

A FEW SELECTED READINGS FOR FURTHER INFORMATION

Angrosino, Michael V., and Kimberly Mays de Pérez. 2000. Rethinking Observation: From Method to Context. In *Handbook of Qualitative Research*, 2nd ed., ed. Norman K. Denzin and Yvonna S. Lincoln, 673–702. Thousand Oaks, CA: Sage.
Jorgensen, Danny L. 1989. *Participant Observation: A Methodology for Human Studies.* Newbury Park, CA: Sage.

2

Exploring Genealogy

Constance P. deRoche

A RESEARCH PROJECT

Many years ago, I was looking for a field site where I could do research for my doctoral dissertation. I was not planning to focus on family and kinship. Rather, since my undergraduate days, I had been interested in economic development and social change. One day, a friend came to visit. He spoke about his home community, "Benton" (a pseudonym), a former fishing village that now found itself about 27 kilometers (about 17 miles) from a major heavy-industrial park. I was interested. With about 1,500 residents, the village was small enough to allow a single, novice researcher to work effectively. It was also accessible, lying just off a highway that passes through Nova Scotia's Cape Breton Island. Language proficiency would be no stumbling block, since the residents were fluent in English, though they were Acadian (people of French origin who live in three eastern provinces of Canada). Moreover, my friend and his family would provide an entree into the community, helping a stranger like myself to establish rapport. I was *very* interested. After spending the summer of 1971 exploring the site, I was confident that I had found the ideal place to work.

Activity at the industrial park had begun in late 1959, with the construction of a pulp-processing plant that opened in 1962. By the summer of 1971, three more large-scale heavy-industrial plants were in operation, and by 1973 two of the park's plants had been expanded and thousands of construction jobs had been created. In the end, more than 1,200 nonseasonal steady jobs (most of which were available to locals) had been produced, as had employment for about a thousand seasonal pulp-cutters. Villagers were expecting another phase of growth that would place them in the orbit of a prosperous industrial center.

I wanted to discover how the industrial boom was affecting Benton, but I quickly realized that I would first need to know about previous conditions. Village history proved to be more complicated than I had thought. Benton *had* been a fishing village, but that was for only a few decades after its settlement in the mid-1800s! For nearly a century thereafter, villagers had pieced together a living by combining migrant labor, small-scale commercial forestry, occasionally available local employment, and subsistence production. As things turned out, I devoted a great deal of time to reconstructing past patterns of both paid and unpaid work.

While industrial development had brought a certain measure of prosperity to the region, it was clear that villagers had previously had to struggle hard to make ends meet. In fact, the industrial installation was, in part, the product of government policies that aimed to stimulate economic development in poor regions. Those policies were the Canadian version of the "War on Poverty" that was being waged at the time under President Johnson in the United States. In the 1960s social scientists were engaged in lively debates about the causes of poverty. Anthropologists were becoming increasingly interested in examining poverty not only in third-world societies but in industrialized ones as well. In particular, a work by anthropologist Oscar Lewis provoked a major controversy. Lewis had studied impoverished Mexicans and Puerto Ricans, as well as poor Latin immigrants in New York City, and he perceived similarities among them. He concluded that in materialistic, achievement-oriented societies, economic deprivation led to the development of a "culture of poverty." The poor, he suggested, developed certain values and world views that kept them from prospering.

Anthropologists were also becoming more consciously aware of the relationships between the small communities they studied and the larger social worlds in which those relationships were embedded. Lewis's critics argued that the culture-of-poverty approach largely ignored the ways that poverty served the interests of advantaged people, as well as how poverty was produced by self-interested decisions made by powerful people. They felt that, in trying to account for poverty, Lewis overemphasized poor people's habits of mind and underestimated the significance of conditions over which the poor had little control. In short, it seemed as if Lewis was blaming the victims for their own plight. As a result of these criticisms, anthropologists declared war on the notion of culture of poverty. Charles Valentine was among Lewis's most prominent challengers. When he published his major critique of Lewis, in a book called *Culture and Poverty*, Valentine was teaching anthropology at Washington University in St. Louis, where I was studying. That book had a significant impact on me. I had also worked as a research assistant for anthropologist Alvin Wolfe and sociologist Lee Rainwater, both of whom were critical of the culture-of-poverty view. Under their direction, I worked on a project that was funded by the Office of Economic Opportunity. Many of the people we interviewed for that study were rural migrants who had come to St. Louis in the hope of improving their lives, but who found themselves living in material squalor. In addition, my parents were peasant immigrants from an impoverished region of southern Italy who had worked hard and lived frugally in order to send their children to university. In short, when I entered the field, I was already pretty skeptical of any explanation that seemed to blame the poor for their deprivation. What I discovered in Benton confirmed that skepticism.

I had also heard of the "brain-drain" thesis—that is, the idea that the most talented and motivated people tend to leave impoverished regions for places that offer greater opportunity. This notion seems to make sense, at least superficially, and it could have been made to fit my own experiences. However, it also suggests that poverty is mainly the result of characteristics of the poor themselves, and my graduate studies had left me feeling that this thesis was simplistic. So as I learned about the importance of labor migration in Benton, I became interested in assessing the role of brain drain in that community. I discovered that the genealogical charts (or family trees) that I was constructing were quite helpful in this regard, although I had not begun working on them for that purpose.

GENEALOGY AS A TOOL OF ETHNOGRAPHIC RESEARCH

When I started my study, collecting genealogical data seemed to be the natural thing to do. Anthropologists had always studied small communities in which kinship was important. Kinship was a core element in anthropology curricula even in the 1960s. Moreover, it did not take me long to realize that a thick web of kinship ties connected the residents of Benton to one another. Neighbors were often relatives, since extended kin tended to cluster on inherited land. Kin were in frequent contact and were expected to help each other whenever called upon to do so. Some married couples still lived in three-generational extended households, in dwellings that they would inherit (if their siblings had already moved along to households of their own). So, it made sense to construct genealogies in order to systematically document an important type of relationship among residents. Soon after arriving in Benton, I had drawn a rough physical map of the village, cataloguing households and recording the names of villagers who lived in each. By cross-referencing gene-alogical data, I was able to spatially map kinship relationships.

I had been informed that the great majority of villagers in Benton were descended from a few families that had settled the village. Establishing links to village founders was not especially important for charting current, active rela-tionships. The village kinship system was essentially North American in form: that is, bilateral (recognizing descent broadly, on both the mother's and father's sides of the family) but generationally shallow (tending to be restricted to two or three generations of actual ancestors). In Benton, most people knew a bit about their family heritage, and everyone knew that "we're all a little related here." However, the circle of effectively recognized kin went no further than those who shared grandparents. Nevertheless, genealogies *were* useful in reconstructing village history. They led me to identify and to catalogue, in an organized way, past residents about whose lives I could inquire. Constructing genealogies gave focus to my work with sharp-witted elders (especially one woman who had been born in the 1880s) who acted as "key informants" about past work practices and migrant destinations. I asked villagers for data about ancestors' birth and death dates (some of which I was able to check against census and parish records, and which proved surprisingly accurate). Thus, I was able to generate retrospective, but systematic and concrete, data about how people in different time periods made a living, and where they did so. Genealogies helped me identify those natives who had left the village for good. By asking where expatriates had settled, I could confirm generalizations about where villagers had gone in search of employment in various periods. Genealogies also revealed that a substantial proportion of natives had perma-nently settled elsewhere, and allowed me to notice that, by counteracting nat-ural population growth, relocation allowed the village to remain small and personalistic, a social condition that was valued locally. It also reduced pres-sure on family land that was used for small-scale subsistence farming and peri-odic commercial forestry. In short, permanent out-migrants unwittingly did an economic service to their kin and, in a sense, a social service to all villagers.

As my work proceeded, I realized that recurrent short-term labor migra-tion was characteristic of virtually all those who continued to make Benton their home. Most villagers had begun migrant careers in their mid-teens. Upon marrying, young women left the paid workforce for housekeeping (under arduous conditions) and an array of physically demanding subsistence-farm-ing activities. Men, however, continued to engage in seasonal migration until age forced them to retire, except when, on occasion, local construction jobs were available or when job-market conditions in larger society were bad (as in the Depression of the 1930s). In fact, villagers seemed to have an uncanny ability to find work in distant centers. In large measure, this was due to "chain" migration: relatives or friends who were living elsewhere would pass along word about work opportunities, or help villagers secure specific jobs. Some men maintained ties to employers who would call them to work on fish-ing vessels or construction projects, and would also sometimes ask them to recruit other workers. Often, though, groups of men would go, on "guess work," to places where job prospects seemed bright. Destinations changed as economic growth sites shifted. Men also learned "tricks" to increase their chances of being hired, such as carrying well-used tools to suggest they had a wealth of experience. They spoke proudly about the conditions they endured at work camps and about the gusto with which they applied themselves to job tasks. Very few people whom I interviewed expressed anxiety about finding work, despite its uncertainty. In fact, those who were "nervous" about it suffered mild disrepute. The villagers' apparent stamina, courage, creativity, and ability to cope with employment insecurity made a strong impression on me.

In short, these people were not, by any means, fatalistic, distrustful, complacent, work-shy, or lacking in self-esteem. I began to wonder whether their pattern of "circular" migration (i.e., going away and returning home) was actually a sign of character strength. Maybe circular migrants were more self-assured and more prone to risk-taking. Perhaps the brain-drain proponents had it all backwards. I thus became interested in knowing how villagers differed from expatriates. Since most expatriates returned to visit relatives periodically, especially in summer, I was able to speak to a few. They seemed unremarkable. Unfortunately, it was impractical to attempt to survey the expatriate population, since it was spread across the country and beyond its borders. However, genealogical data again came to the rescue. I was able to discover that every sibling set contained both expatriates and local residents. No family line seemed especially ambitious about sending its members away permanently to make good elsewhere. My research suggested that, on the whole, expatriate men had not distinguished themselves in occupational terms, although the very few with outstanding levels of educational achievement found no appropriate local work until the industrial period.

As I generated genealogies, I not only asked villagers about the location and occupation of their expatriate kin, but also inquired a bit about the spouses of these expatriates. The data revealed that marriage patterns exerted a heavy influence on residence. Village exogamy (the practice of taking a spouse from outside Benton) greatly decreased the likelihood of settling back at home. When a man married a woman who had grown up in the host community (that in which he was working), the couple was most likely to settle there. Those whose spouses were from neighboring villages might set up their households there or in Benton. But men who married exogamously were unlikely to settle in Benton, because they were prone to periodic migration that would typically separate them from their wives and children; and, since there were no prescriptive residence rules (i.e., norms defining where or with whom a couple *should* reside), women preferred to establish households where they themselves had kin. In fact, when brides from Benton accompanied their migrant husbands, their first pregnancy typically drew them home to the care of their mothers. In short, kinship data suggested that resettlement decisions were not merely a sign of a drive for economic achievement. They confirmed that the brain-drain thesis was indeed too narrow.

THE GENEALOGICAL METHOD: A BRIEF HISTORY

Collecting genealogical data is as old as anthropology. Lewis Henry Morgan, a founding father of the discipline, sent questionnaires about kinship to missionaries and government agents who were working with Native Americans during the latter half of the nineteenth century. Much of the debate about kinship systems in that era was based on indirect fragments of information and on wild evolutionary speculation. In 1910, however, W. H. R. Rivers wrote a pivotal essay, "The Genealogical Method of Anthropological Inquiry," that described and promoted the systematic collection of genealogical data. Rivers argued that the method could be used to elicit information about kinship terms (the pattern of names applied to types of kin); rules of descent, marriage, and residence; migration; and religious practices. The essay served as a guide for generations of anthropologists (especially in Britain) who undertook firsthand field studies. Some ethnographers used genealogies as a way of discovering rules that guide, and thus pattern, behavior. Others became more interested in how people, as active agents, use the rules to promote practical interests, seeing rules more as products of behavior than as rigid producers of behavior.

Despite different theoretical perspectives, however, kinship was of paramount interest in anthropology for many decades. In fact, in 1949, when George Peter Murdock published his major work on kinship systems, he called the book *Social Structure*. That choice of title may appear odd to you, as it did to me when the book was assigned as a text in my graduate kinship course. (I had been a sociology student in my undergraduate days.) But it makes more sense when we realize that, historically, anthropology was much more focused on relatively isolated small-scale (non-state) societies than it is today. In such societies, kinship played an important role in structuring all sorts of social relationships, and hence was essentially the equivalent of the entire social structure.

Today, the world is getting smaller, and communities are ever more integrated into larger-scale political and economic institutions. Formal government has taken over many functions once served by kin groups (e.g., education and military defense), and corporations, not families or descent groups, organize economic life. Kinship has largely become a private matter, particularly in North America. People also have become more mobile; they often leave home and family to take jobs, for which they are hired as individuals. They may find themselves living in communities where they are surrounded by strangers, and are likely to establish meaningful relationships with neighbors or coworkers to whom they are not related. In short, kinship, especially in urban industrial settings, *seems* pretty unimportant. It certainly cannot tell us all we need to know about how whole societies are organized or how they work. It is thus hardly surprising that the genealogical method of inquiry has lost its centrality in anthropology's methodological tool kit. It is, for example, rarely or barely mentioned in introductory texts, which do, admittedly, give only brief attention to research techniques. Indeed, my point can be underscored by telling you how this chapter came to be written: when invited to propose a topic for the present volume, I suggested three possibilities. Genealogy was *not* my favorite of these. The editor encouraged me to opt for it *because* he did not expect other contributors to offer to write on the subject, though he thought it deserved coverage. Certainly, I hope I have proven him right by exemplifying how genealogy can be used to explore a broad range of themes beyond kinship itself.

Genealogy can be useful in the twenty-first century, and not only in small, rural communities like Benton. Though anthropological studies of kin-based, localized communities are now less common than they once were, kinship ties continue to serve as a significant resource in many *urban* neighborhoods (especially poor ones) in the industrialized world, as well as in underdeveloped nations. Moreover, migration is, if anything, more common than ever. Today, we speak about our postmodern world in which populations disperse and geographical boundaries dissolve. Anthropologists have become interested in social networks (connections to people who themselves have few, if any, relationships with one another) that readily cut across space. While these networks may not be restricted to kin, kin are certainly significant components of them. Kin networks form an important channel through which resources flow. In short, while genealogical data cannot catalogue all, or perhaps even most, of the relationships that are important to people, kin connections should not be ignored by social researchers. So long as we understand the limitations of the genealogical method—and depending on the social processes we want to explore—genealogies can still contribute to anthropological research.

It is worth noting that although the method may have lost its centrality in anthropology, many members of the general public are now taking up genealogy as a hobby. People's interest in reconstructing their own family trees may reflect their concern about losing touch with their roots in an increasingly rootless society. Even if you are a nonmajor, you may find it useful to learn how to collect genealogical data and construct usable genealogical maps (kinship charts) in order to satisfy your personal curiosity.

THE GENEALOGICAL INTERVIEW: THE PROCESS

Although some genealogical data are available in documents, such as parish records, even amateur genealogists will typically want more than can be found in archives. In anthropology, the family tree or genealogical chart is just a way of organizing and compactly illustrating information that goes well beyond identifying ancestors. To find out about active, ongoing relationships among ordinary folk, genealogical researchers need to conduct interviews. Since the genealogical interview is, in its basic form, like any other indepth interview, much of what follows is general advice. Some of my comments will, of course, be specific to investigating genealogy.

Some social science is undertaken to test formal hypotheses (that is, very strict, explicit statements about how certain specific factors are related to one another). Ethnographers do not typically operate this way. However, any type of research needs a focus, so you will have to identify a theme that can be invested through interviewing. In doing so, think of questions about family relationships that you might enjoy exploring. Genuine curiosity is a great boon to good research. Perhaps you have read about a practice that interests you, such as arranged marriage. You might want to know if the custom is changing among immigrants in your community. You might wonder if younger people have begun to have a greater say in the matter or to actually choose their own spouses. Although professional researchers typically develop their topical foci by studying "the literature" (that is, other professionals' writings), ideas can come from other sources too, such as items in the news. For example, you may have heard a news story about how people tend to favor charities that serve a need that is felt by someone who is closely related to them. Personal relationships also can be a source of inspiration; you may know someone from a community that follows an interesting practice, like arranged marriage. Alternately, your own personal experiences might suggest a topic. Your family may have started using e-mail, or bought a long-distance telephone plan. This may lead you to wonder if these devices are changing the way people communicate with relatives who live at a distance. You could ask someone to compare how news flowed within the family before and after it started using new technology. Perhaps your family frequently talks politics at the dinner table, making you wonder whether people tend to vote for the same political party as their kin.

After you have selected a general topic, you should work at bringing it "down to earth." That is, think through your concepts and figure out how they pertain to real-life behaviors and situations. For example, if you are wondering whether social status impacts family interaction, you will need to understand what "social status" means to you. How will you identify it in the real world? Perhaps you will want to find out if relatives who have better paying, more prestigious jobs tend to mix more with one another than they do with kin whose work is less well rewarded. Irrespective of where your thematic idea originated, you should do some pertinent background reading. If your focus is social status and kinship interaction, read a bit about "social stratification." Think about how you would categorize the class position of the respondent and her/his kin. Search the library to find out what others have written on the topic. However, use your reading only as a guide; do not let it lead you to prejudge your results.

Once a researcher has a clear and concrete thematic starting point, the process of selecting appropriate respondents can begin. A respondent must represent the population or circumstance about which you want to learn. If you decided to investigate the above-mentioned theme, you would need to choose a respondent with relatives who are in different social-class positions. In general, select someone for whom the interview will not be a burden, who has the time and capacity to speak to you, and who is interested in doing so. Your own friends or relatives may be the most ready choices. Working with someone you already know is convenient, but note that it can be awkward to switch from a personal relationship to a professional one for purposes of the interview. Friends or relatives also may assume that you already know much of what they have to say, and so might omit useful information. Therefore, it might be better to work with someone to whom you are not so close.

When you have selected a potential interview participant, you will need to contact that person to briefly explain your project and to request their involvement. Describe the general theme of your study rather than the results you expect (e.g., "I want to learn about family ties among immigrants" rather than "I want to show that people retain strong family ties even when they live far apart"). If you reveal presuppositions, you may encourage people to tell you what they think you want to hear. You will also risk making them defensive if their experience is not what you anticipate. People can be sensitive to the implication that they have not lived up to their family obligations or have given preferences to kin in situations that society does not condone (e.g., "nepotism"). You must avoid distressing those you interview. Social researchers, including those who are students, have serious ethical obligations to those they study. Major professional organizations (such as the American Anthropological Association or the Society for Applied Anthropology) have published codes of ethics, and many discussions of ethical principles are available. Suffice it to say here that you must offer respect and protect the personal integrity of anyone you interview. This includes a duty to get "informed consent," which means that when you ask someone for an interview, you must tell her/him about your goals and the uses to which your data will be put. Some colleges and universities require researchers to get such permission in writing. Be sure to find out about your institution's policy before proceeding.

Most people enjoy talking about themselves and their kin, but your respondent may want to know how much time you will need. You can explain that the time commitment will depend on how much the person has to say, but warn her/him that you will likely need a few hours, and may even ask to make a return visit. You might also explain that you will construct a family tree as a way of organizing the information that the respondent is generously providing. You can show your gratitude by offering to give her/him a copy of the tree when it is completed, since many people enjoy having them.

Write a short list of questions about the factors you want to explore. These will get you started, and lead the way to other questions, which build upon answers already provided. The point of *ethnographic* interview is to stimulate communication. You do not want to evoke either vague generalities or very brief responses. So your questions should be fairly concrete but open-ended. It is also important to avoid technical terminology. For example, if you plan to study "economic reciprocity," you should not suppose that the respondent knows the term or, if he does, that he shares your definition of it. Rather than asking, "Does your family engage in reciprocal exchanges?" you would be wise to ask about whether and how your respondent's kin "help each other out from time to time," or "share things." If they do, you can ask about what they exchange, under what circumstances, and how often. But do not become too wedded to your preestablished questions. Prepare yourself for surprises, since people's actions rarely fall neatly into categories that suit the researcher. For example, if you plan to use genealogy to study migration, you will want to know where your respondent's relatives reside and when migrant kin left home. You may ask, "When did your oldest brother leave home?" only to find that he has come and gone several times! Genealogical interviews are relatively structured, since they catalogue a specific set of relationships. However, take advantage of anthropology's open, flexible approach to interviewing, which encourages researchers to add queries, modify them, throw off unproductive ones, and take up unanticipated themes that are meaningful to the respondent.

Review the alphabetic abbreviations that anthropologists use to denote primary kinship connections. This shorthand will help you when taking notes during an interview, as well as when you actually draw a kinship chart. Standard abbreviations include the following: M = mother; F = father; D = daughter; S = son; B = brother; Z = sister; H = husband; W = wife. These symbols can be combined to precisely designate other kin. For example, you can distinguish different biological relationships that English speakers put into the same category, such as "aunt," who could be either your MZ or FZ. (You might also use the term for your MBW.)

When you actually meet your respondent, devote a few minutes to casual chat that will put both you and the respondent at ease. Briefly review your research, and get informed consent. Be sure to ask the respondent for permission to tape the session, since being recorded inhibits or embarrasses some people. While taping is extremely helpful, you should not let your reliance on it make you passive, even if you have checked your equipment and know it is in fine working order. If you become inattentive, you will likely dampen the respondent's enthusiasm. You will also miss gaps in the data, ambiguities in answers, and opportunities to ask follow-up questions. I also recommend that my students always take a pencil and note pad with them, not only as a back up to taping, but also to jot down ideas for further inquiry.

There is no strict optimal sequence to follow in generating data, so long as you remain systematic and thorough. Depending on the respondent's schedule and the size of her/his kin network, you may want to spend one session simply identifying kin relationships, and return at another time to ask about patterns of interaction or exchange. It may, however, be more efficient and less confusing to ask your whole array of questions about each relative in turn. Be sure to find out about the specific linkages that connect each relative to the respondent (e.g., FBD) as well as the particular cultural kin term that the respondent uses to refer to such a relative (e.g., "my first cousin"). The latter is especially important if you are interviewing someone from a non-Western culture. You can also get personal (first) names and use them in the interview to ease communication.

There is a difference between actual ties of descent and marriage and those that are culturally recognized and socially significant. Note that your job is *not* to document every knowable relative, but rather to discover how your respondent recognizes kinship and acts toward kin. If you interview an English-speaking North American, you will quickly realize that there are no clear and distinct boundaries between kin and non-kin. "Close kin" fade into "distant" ones who, in turn, fade off into non-kin. Let the research discover where your respondent "draws the line" between kin and non-kin, or between different degrees of kin. Your respondent may indicate these distinctions explicitly as you catalogue her kin. In addition, the patterns of behavior that she describes will tell you about the distinctions she makes. For example, your respondent may claim to have no special relationship to any of her cousins. But as you ask about patterns of interaction, you might discover that, during special holiday seasons, she always hosts her first cousins, but not her more distant ones. Remember that your job is to figure out how your respondent thinks and acts with respect to kin, rather than to urge her to accomplish the impossible task of producing a "perfect" kinship chart with every conceivable relative neatly in place. So, do not worry about gaps in your respondent's knowledge. In fact, they can be useful indicators of culture, as when North Americans find it difficult to name their great-grandparents.

Eliciting genealogical data can lead you onto some sensitive moral ground. For instance, a respondent may be embarrassed about having been "born out of wedlock" or having had an "illegitimate" offspring. Or a couple may be shy about admitting they have a "common law" partnership. An interviewer must be sensitive to signs of discomfort from respondents, and must respect their privacy. If your respondent seems uncomfortable, offer to move on or to turn off the tape recorder while discussing the sensitive material. It is also possible for respondents to discuss perspectives and/or practices to which the interviewer morally objects. Should this happen in your interview, remember that your job is to understand the other's perspective. To do so effectively, you should adopt *methodological* relativism. This stance does *not* require you to become amoral (which is neither possible nor desirable). Rather, it means that you must manage your own emotional responses in order to avoid inhibiting your respondent or closing your mind. It is permissible to express your viewpoint politely, and even to respectfully ask challenging questions that will enhance your understanding of the respondent's position. But, you should not actively condemn or belittle your respondent's lifestyle.

Your interview session should end much as it began, with a short period of casual conversation. Take advantage of this time to do the following: thank the respondent; reiterate your offer of a copy of the family tree you compile; and request another session, if need be. As soon as possible thereafter, ensure that you have properly labeled, and protected from erasure, your tape(s). To safeguard your respondent's privacy, use a pseudonym or initials in labeling, and keep the recording(s) in a safe place.

Interviewing yields a surprising amount of data, which you will need to organize carefully. You start by writing up a "table of contents" of each tape. Label each segment that pertains to a specific relative using the alphabetic symbols, as well as the person's first name or initials (to avoid confusion where there is more than one relative of the same type). Also, indicate where the segment lies on the tape, using minutes and fractions thereof. For example, MB, Bill R., 5.5–8.7. Ethnographers generally make precise computerized transcripts of their numerous tape recordings, which they then analyze (examine for patterns), often with the aid of specialized software. In a specifically focused project of limited scope, which yields a few hours of tape, it is possible to analyze the data simply by carefully listening to, and taking notes on, the recordings. As you do so, you should pay attention to any ambiguities or apparent errors, about which you should consult your respondent.

Review the graphic symbols that anthropologists use to chart relations. In brief, we use a triangle to indicate a male; a circle for a female; and a square for a person whose gender is unknown, or for a child whose gender is irrelevant to the research question. An equal sign denotes marriage, or socially recognized union. A horizontal line is used to connect siblings, and a vertical line to connect parents with their offspring. A dashed line indicates the adoption of children or siblings. A slash mark through the equal sign indicates divorce, while a slash mark through one of the figures indicates that the person is deceased. Your respondent is conventionally labeled "Ego," the person to whom everyone else on the chart is related, but you might consider eliminating the term in the chart you give your respondent, since the word can have negative connotations. For more detailed instructions for drawing a kinship chart, consult the manual written by Ernest Schusky or check the Internet tutorials that are listed at the end of this chapter.

Draw the chart by hand, unless you are very skilled in technical graphic design. Using graph paper can help you keep all members of the same generation on the same plane. Depending on the size of the kin network you identify, your chart could become quite wide. It is best if you draw your chart on one continuous sheet. You may have to tape together sheets of graph paper to accommodate all the figures. Devise a system of graphics that serve as codes for any further information that is relevant to your topic. Symbols for individuals can, for example, be colored or filled in with line patterns to indicate some characteristic or condition (e.g., use green to indicate all those who left the village in order to find employment). If you need to convey more information than a simple set of graphics allows, you can number each individual, and cross-reference each to a set of notes. For example, your project may be about how kin help each other out. You may have discovered that a relative, such as Ego's oldest brother, helped her get a job and fixed her car twice in the last year, while she, in turn, painted his house. Suppose that this brother is relative number 8 on your chart. The corresponding note 8 can then contain a short description of these service exchanges. For example:

    8. → helped get job in 2005; twice fixed car in 2005
         → painted house in 2005

Feel free to be creative and design whatever system works to convey information efficiently and clearly. Whatever system you use, however, be sure to provide a legend (i.e., a list of each graphic symbol and its meaning). For example, here I used → to mean help provided to Ego.

YOUR PROJECT

Using your knowledge (e.g., from previous courses), your experience, and your imagination, choose a topic that can be investigated through the genealogical method. Although you might ideally need a number of respondents to help you answer your research question, remember that this project is just an exercise designed to help you practice the data-generation technique. After thinking through your ideas, and ideally doing some topical background reading, write up a brief statement of the theme you want to explore, and explain why you have chosen this topic. (Be sure to properly cite any writings from which you drew.) Use clear, simple, ordinary language, since the statement will serve as a guide when you explain your purpose to your respondent.

Write up a short set of pertinent, open-ended questions that will get your interview started. Then identify and contact your respondent, inform him about your research, and find a mutually satisfactory time and place for the interview. Review the alphabetic abbreviations for primary kin before you meet your respondent. When you meet, start out by chatting. Be sure to confirm consent (orally on tape or through a signed form, depending on your institution's ethics regulations) and also ask for permission to tape. Then attentively conduct an interactive interview that encourages your respondent to speak freely on your theme.

Make sure that your tapes and notes are properly organized and indexed, review the graphic notations used in drawing kinship charts, and then draw a chart based on the information generated in the interview. Devise a system of codes for indicating pertinent information (either graphically or using numbered notes), and add these to your kinship chart. Write up a legend for your codes. If you have used only graphic markers on the chart itself, place the legend in a corner of your chart. If you have used numbered notes, place the legend at the top of your note page. If your respondent accepted your offer of a copy of the chart, be sure to deliver it. Write up a commentary containing any information to supplement or clarify your coding.

Your report to your instructor should include: (a) evidence of informed consent; (b) the statement of your topic and explanation for your choice; (c) your kinship chart with legend and notes; and (d) a short essay in which you outline what you learned about your topic and reflections upon your research experience. As part of the latter, you should discuss any problems you had with using the genealogical method, and any observations you made about its strengths and weaknesses.

A FEW SELECTED READINGS FOR FURTHER INFORMATION

deRoche, Constance P. 1985. *The Village, the Vertex: Adaptation to Regionalism and Development in a Complex Society.* Occasional Papers in Anthropology 12. Halifax, NS: St. Mary's University, Department of Anthropology.

Keesing, Roger. 1971. *Kin Groups and Social Structure.* New York: Holt, Rinehart and Winston.

Murdock, George Peter. 1949. *Social Structure.* New York: Macmillan.

Pasternak, Burton. 1976. *Introduction to Kinship and Social Organization.* Englewood Cliffs, NJ: Prentice Hall.

Rivers, W. H. R. 1910. The Genealogical Method of Anthropological Inquiry. *Sociological Review* 3:1–12.

Schusky, Ernest. 1972. *Manual for Kinship Analysis.* New York: Holt, Rinehart and Winston.

Society for Applied Anthropology. 2003. Statement on Professional and Ethical Responsibilities. *Human Organization* 62(1):86.

Stacey, Judith. 1990. *Brave New Families: Stories of Domestic Upheaval in Late Twentieth Century America.* New York: Basic Books.

Stack, Carol. 1974. *All Our Kin: Strategies for Survival in a Black Community.* New York: Harper and Row.

Valentine, Charles A. 1969. *Culture and Poverty: Critique and Counterproposals.* Chicago: University of Chicago Press.

WEB SITES FOR FURTHER INFORMATION

http://www.ceifo.su.se/eng/ (CEIFO, The Center for Research in International Migration and Ethnic Relations)

http://www.anthro.palomar.edu/kinship/default.htm (an interactive kinship tutorial by Professor Dennis O'Neil of Palomar College)

http://www.umanitoba.ca/anthropology/kintitle.html (an interactive kinship tutorial by Professor Brian Schwimmer of the University of Manitoba)

http://www.aaanet.org/committees/ethics/ethics.htm (American Anthropological Association on ethics)

3

Conducting a
Life History Interview

Michael V. Angrosino

A RESEARCH PROJECT

In 1980 I received a postdoctoral fellowship from the National Institutes of Mental Health, which wanted to help social scientists learn more about how public policy in the United States is formulated, implemented, and evaluated. During the fellowship year, I was affiliated with the Institute for Public Policy Studies at Vanderbilt University. Because Vanderbilt was home to a major research unit devoted to mental retardation, I turned my attention to that aspect of the larger mental health realm. At the time of the fellowship, mental health policy had just taken a new and exciting turn away from treatment based in large institutions and toward care based in community agencies. The "deinstitutionalization movement," as it was called, reflected a philosophy drawn from the civil-rights and other liberation movements of the 1960s and 1970s—all people, including those with various conditions considered disabling, had a fundamental right to live their lives in the least restrictive possible environment and to gain access to all necessary public services with a minimum of obstacles. This philosophy was made possible in the lives of people with chronic mental illness and mental retardation by advances in pharmacology—new medications that alleviate behavioral symptoms so that it is possible to live without constant, institutional supervision. An economic factor also played a part in the deinstitutionalization movement: allowing people with disabilities to live in their own homes was thought to be considerably less costly than maintaining them full time (often for their entire lives) in large, high-maintenance institutions.

In order for deinstitutionalization to work, it was important for necessary services actually to be available in local communities. In addition to their medications, people with mental retardation needed housing, transportation, employment, and education. We all know how complex modern society is and we recognize how difficult it can be to make contact with providers of all the many services we may need to help us get through life. It is therefore not surprising that people who begin with mental deficits—and who have lived much of their lives in protective shelters where they never learned the skills needed to fend for themselves—were not entirely successful in making the transition from institution to community. A few years into the great deinstitutionalization experiment, there were numerous reports in the popular press linking the policy to an increase in the number of homeless, haphazardly medicated people with mental problems wandering the streets.

It was clear that there had been a lack of connection between the policymakers and the intended beneficiaries of the policy. As an anthropologist, I wondered what the clients themselves thought about what they needed and what would help them make a more successful transition. My question was treated with some skepticism by the policy experts: people with mental retardation, I was told, could not organize their thoughts or develop a coherent perspective on their problems—and even if they could do so, they were so limited in their ability to communicate that they could not meaningfully articulate their point of view.

At first, I lacked the firsthand experience that would have allowed me to challenge the received wisdom. Therefore, when at the end of the fellowship year I returned to my own department at the University of South Florida, I decided to work with a local agency that served deinstitutionalized people in order to get to know them and understand how they viewed their circumstances. Seeing things from the insiders' perspective is, of course, one of the hallmarks of the ethnographic method. So I came to be affiliated with an agency that I have called "Opportunity House" (OH) in various publications. It served a clientele composed of deinstitutionalized adults, all of them males in the age range 20–42, when I first began working with the program. They were all dually diagnosed: mentally ill as well as mentally retarded. All had been convicted of some felony since their deinstitutionalization and had been remanded by the courts to OH in lieu of a prison sentence. OH was established to help people who had thus far failed to achieve the goals of the deinstitutionalization movement, and its educational and psychotherapeutic programs were designed to give these men another chance to succeed in the community. The OH staff taught basic classroom skills (reading, writing, arithmetic), life skills (telling time, making change), and social skills. Job training was offered in a greenhouse, a landscaping service, and a thrift store operated by OH, which also helped its clients find apartments of their own when they had successfully completed the program.

I began my affiliation with OH as a classroom volunteer, assisting the teacher by working one-on-one with the students as they learned their basic skills. I also helped out at the store, provided occasional transportation services, assisted clients who were ready to leave the OH group home and move into independent housing, consulted with a community "buddy" program that paired up young adults with mental retardation with people of similar age at the university, and worked on various fund-raising projects. I was eventually asked to join the OH Board of Directors. I also conducted a number of research projects designed to evaluate client progress and to track former clients who had graduated from the program. These projects included both graduate and undergraduate students as research assistants. By working closely with the clients, I came to the conclusion that the stereotype I had instinctively rejected was indeed false. The OH clients certainly had a great many problems organizing their lives, and a number of them were not readily able to communicate their plight except in the highly formal context of therapy sessions. But many of them were quite cognizant of what was happening to them. They also had some pretty definite ideas about what was wrong and about how they wanted their lives to turn out.

THE LIFE HISTORY INTERVIEW AS A TOOL OF ETHNOGRAPHIC RESEARCH

In order to document these feelings more carefully, I turned to a traditional ethnographic data-collection technique: the life history interview. This technique will be described in greater detail below, but for the moment, let us consider a few basic points. First, when I work with those who share the stories of their lives, I get a sense of how they understand their own identities and place in the world. The process is not designed to be therapeutic in the clinical sense, although it can certainly have secondary therapeutic benefits. The opportunity to rethink one's life, discern patterns, and consider what it all means can be deeply satisfying (even if occasionally scary), even for someone who has some difficulty organizing his thoughts.

Moreover, conducting a life history interview allows me to see how people conceive of their relationships to the wider society, since, unlike a clin-

is not focused on the details of one's "condition," but on all
ces that have affected one's life. We may have come up with
institutionalization policy in the first place because we concen-
e disability as if it were a thing in isolation. But people experience
oilities as part of a continuous flow of life and they interpret their
against a backdrop of everything else they have ever experienced. A
story interview yields an extraordinarily rich body of information that
ws us to view social problems as part of a normal flow of life and not as
lated events amenable to single, quick-fix solutions.

For example, as I recorded the life stories recounted by the OH men, I
noticed that almost all of them were simultaneously preoccupied with and
deeply confused about their status as adults. They all knew that chronologi-
cally speaking they were adults and yet they had never been allowed to act or
express themselves as adults. Some of the men had been suppressed out of
misplaced kindness (their caretakers believed that if they acted too independently they would do inadvertent harm to themselves); others were thwarted
by people reacting out of ignorance or fear as a result of common stereotypes
about people with retardation. In any case, the men understood that even a
benevolent agency like OH was complicit in keeping them childlike unless it
granted them the possibility of experiencing adult life on its own terms. The
theoretical literature on mental retardation sometimes speaks of allowing clients the "dignity of risk"—the opportunity that everyone else has for making
mistakes and learning from them. To deny any adult the possibility of learning from mistakes, even with the best of motives, is to deny him or her the
possibility of truly being an adult.

The OH men were particularly concerned about sexuality as a component
of adulthood. It is virtually impossible to live in our society without absorbing
numerous, often contradictory, images and messages about sex. It is equally
impossible to escape the conclusion that, whatever else may be said about it, sex
is really, really important in politics, advertising, music, and so many other
aspects of our culture. Even people with mental retardation take in these lessons. Although some people with mental retardation are physically incapable of
sexual expression, the vast majority are biologically normal. But unlike other
biologically normal young adults, they have never been allowed to explore their
own sexuality. They have been the victims of two opposite, but equally stifling,
stereotypes: it is widely believed that people with mental retardation are either
helpless innocents who need to be protected from the difficulties of sexuality, or
ravenous monsters whose sexual appetites, once unleashed, cannot be contained except by force. Both extremes undoubtedly exist—as they do in the general population. But most adults with retardation are—like many adolescents—
simply confused about sex. The life histories I elicited from the OH clients were
full of unrealistic expectations and inappropriate role models—not because the
men were mentally disordered, but because they had never been given a chance
to sort out their ideas about sexuality. No one had ever bothered to talk to them
about it except as part of a checklist of "don'ts" in various institutional settings.

A focus on the disability of mental retardation per se is limiting, insofar as it is seen primarily in cognitive terms, the remedy for which is "skills" based instruction. Important as such training undoubtedly is, it is not the whole story. By contrast, when we place the disability in the context of an entire life as the person retrospectively reconstructs it, we can see that more general concerns about being an adult often take precedence over the learning of specific skills. Using this insight, I was able to convince the OH staff to institute sexuality education as part of the curriculum. The program emphasized forming, sustaining, and making decisions about interpersonal relationships, rather than the mechanics of sex or details of anatomy.

THE LIFE HISTORY INTERVIEW: A BRIEF HISTORY

The life history interview was pioneered by cultural anthropologists—but readily taken up by sociologists, social psychologists, and oral historians—early in the twentieth century. In many cases it was used to provide data when no other ethnographic technique would suffice. For example, by the time anthropologists turned their attention to documenting the cultures of Native Americans, it was no longer possible to find many fully intact communities in which traditional practices and beliefs could be observed. Therefore, researchers turned to the surviving elders of decimated tribal societies. In telling about their own lives, the culture of which they were once members could be illustrated. In a similar manner, sociologists working in large urban settings would have been hard-pressed to meet or interview all the members of a community (of recently arrived immigrants, for example). So a few "typical" or "representative" individuals were chosen for intensive interviewing insofar as their life experiences could be illustrative of those of the entire group. In still other cases, individuals who were clearly *not* typical (e.g., chiefs, shamans, great artists) were interviewed because their achievements were said to represent the highest values and aspirations of the common folk in their communities.

Two general traditions eventually emerged when it came to conducting life history-based ethnography. One, usually (although certainly not exclusively) associated with North American scholars, featured the biography of the single individual, either a representative or an exemplary member of his or her culture. The other, usually the product of European scholars, featured collective portraits—portions of the life experiences of a number of linked individuals that were put together to form a kind of mosaic of the community as a whole.

In our own time, a certain philosophical skepticism has come over life history researchers. It is now no longer so easily taken for granted that the individual biography represents the culture in microcosm, or, conversely, that the group ethnography is the individual personality writ large. There is now a concentrate on the ways in which narratives are constructed, the specific content of the stories; indeed, it is often held that far from representing documentable fact, is actually the product influences (such as gender, race/ethnicity, or socioeconomic can disguise more than it reveals. Nevertheless, it seems reasonable conclude that most people who are asked to tell their stories do so without rate intention to deceive. We do, however, need to be cautious—material presented in a life history interview should never be taken at face value as the sole source of evidence, as the human memory is an imperfect thing. It should be cross-checked whenever possible by other kinds of archival or documentary evidence.

Despite these ambiguities, contemporary ethnographers have given new emphasis to the old life history method because it has proven to be an effective way to get the voices of previously silent people on to the historical record. Official history has, until recently, been a record of the activity and accomplishment of elites. Women, poor people, members of minority groups, and those considered "deviant" for any reason were all around and active while those elites were engaged in their business. But we rarely hear about them, except through secondhand reports. Since such people have not until our own time left much of a paper trail, the only way to recapture their experiences, and to add their viewpoint to the larger historical record, has been through *oral* history, of which the life history interview is an important component. As a result, ethnographers interested in the history and development of roles of women, racial and ethnic minorities, members of different socioeconomic strata, people with disabilities, or those of nonstandard sexual orientation have made extensive use of life history interviewing.

THE LIFE HISTORY INTERVIEW: THE PROCESS

People are usually very eager to cooperate with someone who actually wants them to tell their life stories. As noted above, reflecting on one's life can be personally very satisfying, particularly when it can be shared with a sympathetic audience. It might therefore seem that there is nothing more to the life history data-collection technique than turning on a tape recorder and sitting back to relax while the storyteller spins the tale. But even leaving aside the particular problems inherent with working with people with mental deficits, the process is by no means so carefree. Being a good interviewer in any context requires being a good listener, which means being an active participant in the storytelling process, not simply an extension of the tape recorder. The following considerations all factor into the development of one's skills as a good listener.

First, you must choose a person to interview who has valuable information and who is able to convey that information in a reasonable manner.

(Allowances can be made for people with mental retardation who have trouble expressing themselves, or older people who may suffer memory lapses. But such problems should not rule such people out of consideration if their life experiences can help illuminate some issue you are interested in learning more about.) The chosen narrator should be someone who doesn't mind talking and who is reliable (that is, someone who will show up for the interview and be prepared to address the topic at hand). Although it is sometimes necessary to approach a potential narrator through intermediaries (for example, if the person is in frail health or is a celebrity), it should always be that person with whom you make the final agreement to conduct an interview. Never depend on others to set things up for you all the way through.

Before the interview even begins, learn as much as you can about your narrator. The intention is not to trap the person in little inconsistencies, but simply to make you better able to put his or her comments into context, and to allow you to ask the most intelligent questions about his or her experiences. Phone or write the narrator in advance, spelling out your goals in a way that is clear to that person. (Remember that the academic jargon that we use in describing a research project is a foreign language to most people, even highly intelligent ones.) It is usually wise to avoid generalities. For example, don't say that you want to interview the person so as to produce his or her life history; most people do not consider themselves qualified to speak as historians, and in any case do not typically see their own lives as part of history— the very term can be intimidating. Say instead that you want to talk about "your experiences and the people you've known."

In addition to background research on your narrator him/herself, do some prior research on those topics that you expect will figure most prominently in his or her story. You need not become a great expert—indeed, it will be helpful if you can honestly seem to be in need of enlightening information from your narrator. But neither should you seem as if you are totally in the dark, since then the narrator will wonder why you are going to all the trouble of doing an interview on a topic that seems to mean nothing to you. Background research can help the interviewer ask informed questions, know what details to probe for, and be aware of both what is and is not generally known about the topic. It can help the interviewer avoid vagueness by uncovering new information. It also helps establish rapport by demonstrating some familiarity with material close to the narrator's heart. Sources of information for such background research might include: college libraries (particularly if they have special collections devoted to local history); government documents; county and church records; back files of newspapers; local historical societies; or personal collections of old magazines, photos, architectural plans, and other mementos. The Internet is an increasingly valuable source of information as well.

As you prepare for the interview, be sure to familiarize yourself with any equipment you may be using. Make sure that it is in good operating condition and that you know how to work it without making a big fuss during the interview. Most life history interviewers now work with inexpensive, small, battery-powered cassette tape recorders with built-in microphones. Using battery power rather than plugging into a wall outlet gives you greater mobility and flexibility. For example, if a wall outlet happens to be near a noisy air conditioner duct, your sound quality will suffer if you don't have the option of going somewhere else. (If your interview involves material that requires better sound quality—for example, if you are interviewing a musician and are recording his or her performance—you may need to invest in a better machine. Some projects also call for video, as well as sound recording. My remarks here, however, will be confined to basic tape recording.) See if you can get a machine with a "pause" button, which can turn the tape off and on during the interview without turning the machine off completely; repeatedly turning the machine off and on can damage the tape. Do not use "voice-activated" systems since they have a tendency to lag in pick-up and thus lose parts of sentences, particularly if the person is speaking in a relatively soft voice. Do use a machine with a digital counter and a battery-power indicator. Bring an ample supply of fresh batteries to the interview. Opinions vary on this point, but I recommend using 60-minute tapes. Tapes with longer playing times tend to be thin and subject to breakage. Choose a cassette in a plastic case that is bolted, not glued, together. (If the tape gets tangled, it is easier to open a bolted case to straighten it out.) The case should be clear, not dark or opaque, so that you can more easily see how much tape is left. Technology is changing rapidly. Please do not rely on this general advice as the final word on the topic.

Arrange a time and place for the interview that is mutually convenient and comfortable. Although priority should be given to the preferences of your narrator, keep in mind that you are an active participant in this interview and you should not feel inconvenienced or uncomfortable, lest your frustration spoil the atmosphere.

Before the interview begins, have the narrator sign a legal release form that spells out the aims and conditions of the interview, including expectations of what will happen with the taped record, transcripts (if any), and the results of the research (e.g., "a paper for my course that only my instructor will see," or "a book that will be published by a major international press"). Such "informed consent" is absolutely required when a research project involving human subjects is conducted under the auspices of an institution that receives federal funding, although classroom projects may be exempt. Even if the form is not mandated at your school, you should get into the habit of using one, to protect both you and your narrator. Your instructor will show you examples of release forms that are in use at your own school.

Tape a "lead" before starting the interview. It should consist of the date, name of both narrator and interviewer, location of interview, and a brief description of the expected content. The lead is useful when the tape is archived; it serves the secondary purpose of giving you something to play when you get to the interview to make sure that everything is operating properly.

Unless the person you are interviewing is very pressed for time, do not feel that you need to get to the point all at once. Allow yourself time to break the ice with ordinary conversation. Remember that good interviewing technique is essentially a matter of paying attention. Look at the person you are talking to. Meeting the narrator's gaze easily and frequently (but not constantly—no one feels comfortable when being stared at) and not allowing yourself to be distracted will indicate a sincere interest. Sit in a relaxed, yet alert position and try to control fidgeting or unnecessary fiddling with the tape recorder. It is important to be responsive, which can be indicated either verbally ("Yes," "I see," "Uh-huh" all indicate that you are paying attention), through gestures, or by facial expression.

It is a good idea to keep notes during the interview. You may want to jot down words or names whose meaning or spelling are not clear to you and that you want to check out later on. There may be dates or chronologies that you want to verify. You may also want to note details of the setting that might help place the narrator's words in some context. But do not become so immersed in taking notes that you fail to maintain your conversational tone. You are an interviewer, not a stenographer.

Try not to interrupt your narrator, even if he or she seems to be wandering off the topic. If you have chosen a topic of real interest to the narrator, then he or she will get back to it eventually, in his or her own way. And if your topic really is the person's whole life, don't be too quick to judge what is and is not relevant to the person's recollections. Some oral history guidebooks insist that the interviewer should never interject personal opinion. I do not agree. I believe that the interview is a kind of conversation, and while you certainly want to be careful not to hijack the narrative and turn it into *your* story, I believe that sharing some of your own experiences (whether they complement or contrast with those of the narrator) indicates your real interest in the topic and also gives the narrator some further food for thought, which could spark a response that might not otherwise have been forthcoming. And certainly if the narrator says something that is personally offensive, you need not feel obliged to let it go by without comment.

Don't be afraid of silences. A brief lag in the conversation is perfectly normal, and you should not feel compelled to fill every second with idle chatter. Sometimes people pause because they are trying to remember a specific detail, or because they have been overcome with emotion at the recollection of a particular person or event. The interviewer should respect such pauses and learn to distinguish them from an actual stop that indicates that the narrator does not care to continue.

Use open-ended questions whenever possible, because they call for descriptive answers rather than for brief bits of data. Try to practice framing your questions in a two-part format: in the first part, you explain why you are asking something, and in the second part you go ahead and ask it. (For example: "I've noticed that everyone in the group home has his own radio in his room. What kind of music do you like to play?") Doing so indicates that you are observant and putting the narrator's experience into context and not simply conducting a witness-stand grilling. Questions should not, however, be so open-ended that they become impossibly general. A question like, "What was your life like when you were at the hospital?" is simply too vague for most people to respond to meaningfully. But try not to get *too* specific—at least until you know the person better—lest you come off as overly nosy, prying into personal matters that the narrator feels are none of your business.

Ask only one question at a time. It is sometimes tempting, when you are truly interested and excited about a topic, to bombard the person with inquiries. But hold back: if you are afraid you will forget a question, jot it down for future reference—don't blurt out everything all at once. Avoid questions that seem to make an assumption about what the answer is going to be. For example, ask, "How were you treated in the foster home?" not, "How often were you beaten in the foster home?" There is a tendency for narrators to tell interviewers what they think they want to hear; in some cases, a narrator may deliberately do the opposite just to be ornery. By phrasing the question in as neutral as possible a manner, you are more likely to get an honest response. For the same reason, avoid questions that only require verification of information. (Ask, "How do you get to work?" not, "You get to work from the group home on the Number 4 bus that runs past the mall, don't you?") There is, of course, a tendency to be "helpful" when working with people with mental disabilities, or frail elders, and so forth, but even in such cases, don't be so "helpful" that you end up telling the story yourself.

Don't interpret your narrator's responses, particularly when it comes to emotional expression. For example, don't say, "You must have been very relieved when they sent you to OH and not to jail," but rather, "How did you feel when you were sent to OH?" Don't use emotionally charged words or turns of phrase (e.g., "How did you feel when the cops nabbed you?" seems to call for a negative response. It is better to ask, "How did you feel when you were arrested?"). Don't supply your own adjectives ("What did you think when you first saw this nice, clean group home?").

Above all, let your interview flow naturally. Avoid making it seem like a survey questionnaire. It is perfectly all right for you to have a checklist of questions that you want to deal with, but don't structure the interview so rigidly that your agenda becomes obvious. Sometimes the narrator's digressions will provide the most interesting and important material. Let your narrator's body language or actual verbal cues tell you when he or she has finished with a particular topic.

When the narrator indicates that he or she has nothing further to say, do not simply turn off the tape recorder and leave abruptly. Stay for a while to chat (if the narrator's circumstances—and your own schedule—permit). Sometimes the casual chat reminds the narrator of something he or she forgot, and the interview starts again. If your own schedule is such that you cannot stay longer at that point, make an appointment for a follow-up interview. Before leaving, take a photo of the person and the surroundings (if the narrator permits it and if doing so has been spelled out in the informed consent form). Check your notes regarding unfamiliar words or spellings that you need to verify.

Once you are back home, immediately label all tapes (both sides) with your name, the narrator's name, the date, time, and place of the interview. Number each side of each tape in consecutive order. File all signed release forms so that you can easily retrieve them. Remove the plastic tabs from the backs of the cassettes to prevent accidental erasure. After a day or two, write a letter (or e-mail, if appropriate) or make a phone call thanking the narrator for the meeting and confirming the follow-up interview, if there is to be one.

Although some people like to see full transcriptions of their interviews (and they may so stipulate on the informed consent form), it is rarely necessary to make and keep full transcripts unless you are publishing a complete autobiography. If your narrator does want to see a transcript, establish in the informed consent form whether or not he or she will have the option of editing the material before you use it in your report. Instead, most oral historians rely on indexing as a way to retrieve specific information from the tapes. Indexing by minute (using a stopwatch if possible) is best, since the meter/counter number may vary from one machine to another. Divide the tape into approximately five-minute segments, or by obvious breaks in the subject matter. Make the index as detailed as possible, and do it as soon as possible after the interview so that the material is still fresh in your mind.

YOUR PROJECT

In order to practice your skills as a life history interviewer, select *one* person whose life story you want to record. That person should be part of some larger group or community whose overall ethnography you are interested in studying. That group should be one that has historically been left out of the public record. My project with deinstitutionalized adults with mental retardation is only an example. You might be interested in learning more about the historical roles of women, or members of particular racial or ethnic minorities, or native people, or members of particular occupational groups. In any case you should select someone to whom you have easy access. Be careful, though, if you select a member of your family or a close friend—you are likely to take too many parts of the story for granted and will not be as attentive as you might be to filling in the gaps.

Write out a brief justification for your selection. This paragraph should indicate some larger topic and theme that you are interested in exploring. (For example, "I want to find out more about how refugees from Southeast Asia first came to our town because I studied the Vietnam War in an American history course. We learned a lot about the political and military perspective of the United States, but I want to understand how the war affected the people who actually lived there.") This initial interview is your way of entering that community or deepening your understanding of that issue. If you know the *category* of person you would like to interview, but don't know how to contact a specific individual in that category, consult with your instructor, who should be able to guide you to campus or other local links who can make an introduction for you. When you make your initial contact with the selected narrator, share your justification statement with him/her so that he/she understands why you think it is important to conduct this interview. For this reason, the justification statement should be written in plain language, not academic jargon.

Conduct the appropriate background research and develop a question guide. Set up and conduct the interview (in as many sessions as seem necessary) according to the principles suggested in the previous section. Take care of the housekeeping chores suggested for the period immediately following the interview and then proceed as soon as possible to the indexing of your tapes. Your final report to your instructor should include the index, accompanied by any photos or documentation that your narrator has given you permission to use. A copy of the signed informed consent form should be appended to your report. You should also write a brief essay in which you explain what you have learned about the narrator, about the group that he/she represents (or the historical event in which s/he participated), and about yourself as an interviewer.

A Few Selected Readings for Further Information

Angrosino, Michael V. 1998. *Opportunity House: Ethnographic Stories of Mental Retardation.* Walnut Creek, CA: AltaMira.

Denzin, Norman K. 1989. *Interpretive Biography.* Newbury Park, CA: Sage.

Hoopes, James. 1979. *Oral History: An Introduction for Students.* Chapel Hill: University of North Carolina Press.

Ives, Edward D. 1974. *The Tape-Recorded Interview.* Knoxville: University of Tennessee Press.

Langness, L. L., and Gelya Frank. 1981. *Lives: An Anthropological Approach to Biography.* Novato, CA: Chandler and Sharp.

Thompson, Paul. 1992. *The Voice of the Past.* New York: Oxford University Press.

Yow, Valerie R. 2005. *Recording Oral History: A Practical Guide for Social Scientists*, 2nd ed. Thousand Oaks, CA: Sage.

4

Analyzing Narrative Data

Nancy Redfern-Vance

A RESEARCH PROJECT

I worked in the field of women's health as a nurse-midwife before I became an anthropologist. Numerous women have shared intimate details of their personal stories and life experiences, both joyful and tragic, with me over the years. I listened to women as they described their feelings about their bodies, their place in the world, their critical life junctures, their transformative journeys, and their processes of aging. Women's accounts of violence and rape were especially difficult for me to process and absorb. When it came time to choose a dissertation topic, I applied for and was awarded a Veterans Administration (VA) predoctoral fellowship, funded through the VA Office of Academic Affairs, and elected to study sexual abuse of women veterans. Violence toward women had surfaced as a major problem in the field of women's health and was a key issue for the VA. Sexual abuse is costly to the military and VA in terms of decreased productivity, unused talent, health care treatment, and litigation. The predoctoral fellowship enabled me to complete this research project and provided me with office space, materials, and a stipend, as well as a whole network of research mentoring support at the James A. Haley VA Hospital in Tampa, Florida.

The percentage of women in the military has steadily risen, especially since the armed services became voluntary in 1973. The number of women entering the armed services and subsequently transitioning out as veterans continues to increase in proportion to men. More women veterans are served by Florida VA hospitals and clinics as a result. Florida was an ideal location for this study since it is second only to California in population of women veterans.

In 1992, the armed services introduced a "zero tolerance" policy with regard to sexual assault and harassment; nevertheless, highly publicized incidents like Tailhook and Aberdeen continue to surface. Research demonstrates the prevalence of sexual abuse of military women. For example, we have learned that a woman in the military has more chance of being sexually assaulted in her average four to six years of enlistment than a civilian woman does in her entire lifetime. The VA health care facilities are left to deal with the aftermath.

There are still a number of questions left to be addressed. For example, definitions of the term "sexual abuse" remain ambiguous and contested. Even contemporary feminist scholars cannot agree on a definition. To some, only overt forms of violent sexual abuse or clear abuses of power should be addressed as a political issue, with the rest kept on a personal level. Others extend the definition to include any sexual infraction, however minor it may appear, as a form of rape that should be fought publicly. Researchers and women's health advocates do agree, however, that the damage caused by sexual abuse can be costly, both personally and financially.

A missing link was a definition of sexual abuse that was meaningful to the women who have experienced it. I felt that examination of the problem from the standpoint of women veterans within a historical, cultural context would be critical to achieving positive changes in the approach to sexual abuse and other targeted issues facing women in the VA today. I set out to discover how military women themselves define sexual abuse as it occurs within the context of their lives and how their individual biographies intersected with the organizational culture of the military. In anthropology we explore issues as they occur in a particular historical, political-economic, and personal context. We are in an era in which "sexual harassment" is a household word and "sexual abuse" has leaped from closets onto family-room television screens.

My goal was to contribute to policy and programs for dealing with this complex problem. I experimented to see if narrative analysis was a method that could be used to make policy recommendations and design better programs for women who experienced sexual abuse in the military. I thought life histories were well suited for studying a topic as sensitive as sexual abuse. I was confident that with this personalized, unhurried, interactive, relatively informal style of data gathering, I could capture more illustrative data than I could with survey research. Indeed, the narratives elicited from nineteen women veterans taught me about the significant role culture plays in defining sexual abuse.

In order to identify participants, I sent letters of invitation that described my project to women veterans residing in the area. I was uneasy at first, knowing that the harm a woman suffers from sexual abuse is often compounded by the legal, economic, and medical systems of society. I did not want to add to any woman's distress, and so I arranged for VA mental health counselors to be available for the women if the interviews brought feelings to the surface they found difficult to handle. The women contacted me by phone or e-mail. Two who initially agreed to participate later changed their minds, saying that they feared the retelling of the incidents would be too difficult for them to deal with.

I conducted interviews with others at the VA who were professionally interested in this issue. I also attended VA research conferences and special programs for women veterans, and tagged along with military recruiters to observe their process. I toured the VA Benefits Office and veterans' outreach centers. All these activities helped me become more sensitized to the issue of sexual abuse in the military. I helped revise and analyze a women's violence screening questionnaire for the VA Women's Center. Doing so reinforced what I had read about the scope of the problem. Out of 686 new women veteran patients surveyed at the Women's Center between 1996 and 1999, 24.8% said someone had used force or the threat of force to have sex with them against their will. An additional 33.5% said they received uninvited and unwanted sexual attention, such as touching, cornering, pressure for sexual favors, and verbal remarks.

I usually began the interview by saying something like, "Everyone has a life story, and I'm interested in yours," or "Please tell me how you got from where you were when you were a little girl, to where you are now in your life, and include in your story your experiences in the military." The interviews were conducted in various settings. I asked the women where they would be most comfortable talking. Sometimes it was in their homes or offices, other times at my VA office or in a reserved library room. One interview took place in my home and another in an outdoor setting. The women selected their own pseudonyms. The interviews ranged from two to six hours in length. Every interview was audiotaped and transcribed verbatim. At times I felt I had entered a foreign culture, complete with its own language. I found it helpful to construct a dictionary of military terms to define unfamiliar words or phrases I encountered in the interviews.

The veterans defined rape in terms consistent with the common legal definition, focusing on physical sexual assault; they saw it as clearly different from sexual harassment. Their definitions, however, became ambiguous when they tried to identify where tolerable flirting ends and harassment begins. A number of women were particularly bothered by what has been called "gender harassment" in the research literature. Such harassment may not be overtly sexual; it may entail the women being stereotyped and treated differently just because they are women. Defining a "hostile work environment" narrowly, by including only explicit sexual overtures, excludes some of the most debilitating harassment faced by the women. Their wounds were not limited to sexual assault and harassment. The veterans' definitions were broader and included harassment resulting from a double standard of treatment. There were also women veterans suffering from discrimination because they are gay or of a certain ethnicity. They encountered abuse that, while not necessarily sexual, they felt was damaging to them as women.

NARRATIVE ANALYSIS AS A TOOL OF ETHNOGRAPHIC RESEARCH

I confirmed to my own satisfaction that narrative methods could indeed be useful with policy research. Narrative research frees us from oversimplification and stereotypical assumptions when designing programs and policies. It has the potential to attract wider audiences and political attention because narratives grasp the human dimension and are more readable, interesting, and compelling than charts and statistical tables.

Applied anthropology is about finding answers that translate into problem solving. Where better to start than with those who are at the point of the struggle? People closest to the problem are often the first to think of workable solutions. We can develop better intervention programs and policies by understanding the individual meanings humans attach to particular life events. I was able to offer a number of program and policy suggestions for the VA health care system, the VA benefits division, and the Department of Defense human-resources planning offices.

An earlier chapter in this book has already described the process of collecting narrative data (in the form of life histories) and has explained the rationale for using such data in ethnographic research. This chapter focuses on the ways we can deal with those data. Narrative research (particularly a project like mine at the VA that involved interviews with multiple participants) yields a mass of information; in this case, the verbatim transcripts alone amounted to several hundred pages. Data from survey research come from even larger population samples, but they are relatively easy to handle because they are numerical in nature and fall into predetermined categories. Narrative data, by contrast, often flow in a stream of consciousness, cover many different topics and themes (especially if they are *life* stories and not simply focused interviews on highly selected topics), and do not necessarily fall into easily perceived patterns for analysis. I therefore want to explore the ways in which we can make sense of this extremely rich, but potentially confusing, source of cultural information.

ANALYZING NARRATIVE DATA: THE PROCESS

After completing my interviews, I found myself surrounded by stacks of pages of transcribed life histories, memos, and field notes. There is no standard method for analyzing such material, so I tried a variety of approaches that have been suggested in the research literature. Some scholars have compared narrative research to a choreographed production. I agree, and so gravitated toward those analytic approaches that allowed me to treat the narrative like an interpretive dance with a distinct form, signature moves, a connection with the audience, and an underlying rhythm.

After some particularly exhausting interviews, I recorded some notes in my car on the way home but could not face typing up those notes until my sadness over the tragic events narrated had subsided a bit. It became standard procedure for me to carry a small tape recorder at all times so that I could keep a running diary of thoughts and insights that occurred to me even before I had gotten around to a formal analysis of the material. I found it helpful to share some of these memos to myself with my dissertation advisor, just to get an objective outsider's reaction to something I had been told and to my interpretation of that comment.

My main concern in analysis was not to fracture the narratives, but to preserve and study them within the holistic context in which they were told. I examined them as they were organized and performed by the narrators themselves. The women veterans tied together components of their life stories in their own individual fashions. They selected the way the narrative would unfold to get at the points they wanted to emphasize (e.g., some liked to get right to the point and begin with critical incidents; others preferred a more circuitous route, circling around important milestones and surrounding them with preparatory detail). They selected themes and the ways in which those themes were connected (e.g., some followed linear chronology, linking life events in a this-happened-and-then-as-a-result-that-happened format, while others leaped around, allowing something that had happened recently to trigger a memory of something in childhood that seemed in their minds to be related). They set the stage, selected the props, introduced the major characters, and narrated the script from their personal repertoire of cultural resources.

I looked first at classic structural approaches used in literary theory and was amazed to discover the diverse ways the women arranged their narratives into coherent forms. I was curious about what the women placed in the forefront and what they relegated to the background, so I created interpretive diagrams to help me visualize the diverse ways story plots were organized into global coherence. The organization of the women's narratives seemed to fall into one of five basic formats: spiral, time line, geographical map, series of dramatic scenes (not obviously related to one another), and chapters in a novel (dramatic scenes all of which revolve around a common theme or point). An example of the latter is Flora's narrative; her style is to introduce an overall theme, often in the form of a question she seeks to resolve for herself, followed by a set of linked stories that illustrate aspects of that issue, all of which build to a resolution—an answer to her question. For example, she begins one segment by asking "Why don't I tell stories about my childhood to my kids?" She then tells several stories: she loved stories as a child, especially because her dad changed the endings so she wouldn't be scared; she worked very hard to distance herself from childhood sexual abuse; she attended a conference at which she felt personally affirmed and got up the courage to work on her recovery by leaving home; she tried to protect herself against her stepfather, but her mother was not protective; her own son was sexually abused by one of her brothers; family events were essentially drunken brawls where the police would be called. And so she realizes that the reason she doesn't tell stories to her kids is because "there are no good stories to tell!"

The narrative form is a literary performance with dramatic expression in its presentation. I listened to the narratives carefully several times and parsed them based on auditory clues. I attempted to segment phrases the way the women did in the telling, and added pauses, intonation contours, changes in pace, word emphasis, gestures, sound effects, and other embellishments. I noted their vocabulary choices, syntax, rhetorical style, and connectors used for entrances and exits to their narrative segments. I found the women's narratives often fit into stanzas, sometimes accompanied by rhyme, repetition, and poetic rhythm.

Andi's utterances sound poetic in the way she repeats both words and phrases. In the following example, she describes a commander who was anti-female and self-absorbed. She repeats the thought three times, each time adding more words to the phrase until she ends with a complete sentence: "He was out for himself and not [pause] anybody else and didn't care about anybody else, okay? He really didn't care about anybody else [pause] in the unit."

Metaphors are basic linguistic tools that provide us with a semantic container to express abstract meanings in an imaginative, yet concrete, manner. Metaphoric expressions are a key to deeper cultural conceptions. I examined the narratives for prevailing metaphors and themes, particularly those of self-identity. Who the woman "really" was became less important than the symbolic image she created for herself. The idea was not simply to take the narrative at face value, but to search for the intersections between personal biographies and the collective culture. I coded interviews using the computer software program QSR Nud*ist 4 (Non-numerical Unstructured Data Indexing Searching and Theory-building—see Exercise Four). An example of a prevailing metaphor of self-identity comes from Betty. Her narrative was organized by geographic, tourist, and map metaphors. Betty told me, "There's no moss growing under my feet. I bounce with the wind." It seemed wherever Betty landed on her narrative map, a travel metaphor would creep in: "Because I'm the oldest, it's just a natural ride." "It just trips me out!"

"I'm strictly a suitcase student." "I was able to get from point A to point B." "It's been a long time since I've been to Vegas [referring to whether or not she should gamble on orthopedic surgery]."

I also studied the interactive components of the interviews because the narrative is not simply a text divorced from the situation in which it was generated. The veterans and I negotiated the sea of cultural performance and meanings until we found a wave that would carry us to a shore of understanding. An example that was prevalent in the narratives was the phrase, "you know?" This apparently meaningless filler actually expresses the thought that the narrator and the interviewer share some culture; using it is a way to bring the two together—either by reinforcing what the narrator assumes the interviewer should already know or by instructing her so that she is now an initiate into the narrator's world.

YOUR PROJECT

You may use the life history you produced in the course of completing the assignment for an earlier chapter or, if you prefer, you may use Lynn's narrative from my own research, excerpts of which are reproduced below. Complete Exercise One (see below) and as many of the other suggested exercises as you have time for or as your instructor chooses to assign. Please note my code system, which you may want to use in working with your own narrative, although you should feel free to devise one of your own:

[p] pause of 2–3 seconds
[P] pause of 4–5 seconds
[LP] long pause of 6–7 seconds
[VLP] very long pause or silence for more than 7 seconds
. . . indicates voice trails off
items in italics are words that were emphasized in speech
items underlined are words that were very strongly emphasized in speech
\\ indicates a slowing of pace or a lowering pitch of voice
// indicates a louder pitch or more animated voice tone
(I:) refers to the Interviewer
[ ] indicates side comments, usually indicating emotional overtones or activities, such as [laughs] or [cries]; also used to indicate tone of voice, such as [angrily] or [in a monotone].

Note that the transcription is set out in separate phrases, which reflects the way Lynn, like most people, actually talks. Few people reel off complete, grammatically correct sentences in informal dialogue. In this transcription, periods mark points at which Lynn's voice drops, indicating that she has reached a conclusion, and a question mark indicates that her voice rises (even if what she is saying isn't strictly speaking a question); otherwise punctuation is kept to a minimum, as it would impose an order that is lacking in an informal verbal exchange.

LYNN'S NARRATIVE

(From my field notes: Lynn was vivacious, attractive, and extroverted. She laughed frequently with a carefree toss of her hair. Used gestures liberally, eye contact nearly continual. Interview conducted in a private room at her workplace. Lynn puzzles me because the cheerfulness and resilience she projects is unusual compared with others I've talked with.)

See, after being in [p] uh [P] the military...

This environment here [p] at the university is uh [p] is like...

I [p] call it a safe haven.

Because people are so protected here, you know? (I: uh huh)

In the military they want the *image* [p] that everyone is the same [p] you know? (I: oh, okay)

That's why [switches from animated to monotone] they make you cut your hair [p] the same

That's the way they make the uniforms all l-look alike

It's to help p-promote [p] uh [p] espirit de corps—teamwork, you know? (I: Ahh)

You're just one piece of a working *machine*, you know? (I: uh huh)

Your individuality doesn't count [P] um [P] as much as [VLP] your presence to make a *whole*, you know?

I mean it's not like... (I: And they let you know that real *clearly*)

[animated] Oh! That's their *whole*—that's a [p] *basic* part of their *philosophy.*

Quality management won't *work* in certain aspects of the military

You can't have [p] you can't have [p] somebody [p] in the *army*

Be told to go out there on the front line

And say, "Wait, you know! I think we should *talk* about this—I might have a *better* idea!" [chuckles]

It doesn't *work*! (I: Right!)

You know, the person has to go out there [p] they've signed an agreement

They've given *up* their constitutional rights

They have their rights under the Uniformed Code of Military Justice (I: justice)

It's not the same.

You don't have freedom of speech

You don't have freedom of the press

You don't have... [P] because you have to keep some things confidential

You have to... [p] you're not allowed to say certain things

You're not allowed to *write* certain things . . .

And that can't *happen* in the civilian world

(Continues to describe differences between civilian and military life, and contrasts the latter with her present work environment, which she says is like "dying and going to Heaven," but hastens to add:)

I *loved* the military [P] I loved every minute of it!

I retired from the military, so [p]

(I: You *did!* [surprised because Lynn is so young]. So you got a whole career. Oh, I gotta hear everything!)

[monotone, like a recitation] You know, I was one of the first girls [p] in my career field

I was the first girl [p] that ever [P] did my job at the first base I went to

And . . . you know, it wasn't really welcome there

(Describes her opinion of sexual harassment, giving examples of how some of her colleagues handled certain situations. Thinks sexual harassment is based on childlike curiosity or resistance to change, and is a contest that you learn how to handle at a young age as a social skill.)

But I've had a great life!

(I: Yes, *tell* me about [p] your life—usually I just say [p] ask you to explain how you got from when you were tiny to where you are *now* in your life)

[monotone] \\ Okay—um [P] wonderful childhood [p] magical [p] (I: In what way?)

Nothing bad [P] uh [p] Mom and Dad [P] loving, good [p] no bad stuff

Uh [p] no abuse in the family. . . (I: No dysfunction?)

// [laughs] No! (I: Wow! The one in a million?) [both laugh]

I was the dysfunctional one [p] if there was *any*, you know? [both laugh again]

Um [p] I had a brother who was really, really smart [p]

Never got into trouble unless maybe staying up too late [p] *reading* [laughs] That would be *it!*

[monotone] \\ Then there was me [P] I was always a tomboy growing up

I was always, you know [p] into something

I was always causing [P] always coming up with something [p] Mom and Dad weren't prepared for . . .

(Describes a childhood incident where she was sexually abused by a babysitter, though she did not recognize it as abuse until later. Thinks the boy was only curious, but admits she found it "scary" when he threatened if she told on him, something "bad" would happen, since Lynn had never had any "bad's gonna happen" in her life before.)

I [p] in my life [p] I've been // *raped* before

And I've been [p] um [P] \\ date-raped type thing before

Um [P] one was totally innocent on my part

Um, just jogging in my neighborhood

Before I joined the Air Force

Somebody came up from behind me [p] asked me for directions

// It was <u>midnight</u> [p] I probably had no *reason* [p] but I never had a reason <u>not</u> to jog at midnight

I was getting ready to go to basic training, you know

And I—I couldn't sleep, I was excited

\\ I'd go out and practice running

And somebody came up to me and put a knife to my throat

And pulled my tee-shirt up over my head

And said they were gonna kill me [p] and the whole nine yards

And it was really scary (I: Yeah!)

And I was living by myself at the time . . .

// But [p] um [P] I *lived through* it (I: um hum)

[small laugh] I don't have any [P] <u>scars</u>, you know

Nothing—he didn't—he *didn't* hurt me

I [p] for somehow [P] remembered a bunch of <u>scripture</u>!

And started [laughs] reciting it [laughs] (I: Wow! How interesting!)

And yeah, and *yeah* [laughs]

And he was like, "*This* is too *much!*"

And let me go (I: That's too much! Like I thought you were talking in tongues!)

I couldn't *believe* it! (I: *Really!* What a strategy!)

I guess it's like [p] good thing he believed in <u>God</u>, you know? [both laugh]

You know, I was *lucky*, I was <u>lucky</u> (I: Strange, huh?)

Yeah, I got away after—and [p] I mean, he <u>did</u> what he was gonna *do*

[spoken rapidly] But he didn't cut me up in little pieces and leave me in the *bushes* like he said

So *hey!* I felt like I was a <u>winner</u>!

Now some people might have felt like a <u>victim</u> after that

But I felt like a *survivor* after that (I: What's the difference, do you think? I'm always so curious about the difference in that perception.)

[P] I don't know [LP] I was [P]

I <u>think</u> [p] it's because I felt more [p] <u>clever</u> than he was

Like I convinced him not to *hurt* me any more [p] and to let me go and leave!

And maybe that was his intention all the time [P] and maybe he never *meant* to hurt me [p] or kill me

But I felt like I <u>won</u> that battle . . .

(Lynn discusses mild residual effects. If someone comes up behind her, her heart will race, for example.)

Ummm [p] let's see [p] when I was in the military though

After basic training [P] I was in a \\ coed flight [P] and drum and bugle

Had [p] uh [p] 10 girls and 42 guys [p] in our flight

And [p] uh [p] // let me tell you what

That was about as *easy* of a basic training as you could have [chuckles]

We had two guys [p] um [p] training instructors

And they couldn't come into the barracks [P] because we were girls

Until a certain time (I: So they couldn't inspect?)

Well [p] not during the *night*—you know, they couldn't come in at night,

And we would have like [p] little [p] *slumber* parties [p] and stuff [laughs]

And like, it wasn't like other people have in the military (I: Sounds like camp!)

I <u>mean</u>, so all my time [P] I've had *good* parts, you know [p] I've had bad things happen to me,

But I've had [slows pace for emphasis] // a really *good, lucky, lucky* life,

You know what I mean? (I: uh huh)

I've always had it extra easy [p] than most people

So maybe when bad things happen [p] maybe I can handle it a little better, I don't know.

Um, now [p] I [p] I have been irresponsible at times

And drank too much?

And in one situation when I was in technical school?

When I was in technical school?

And we were doing one of these drinking games, you know (I: Yeah? Oh no!)

It was called Cardinal Puff [p] is what it was called

And you'd have to recite this long [p] um [P] verb [P] verbiage thing,

This whole long big [p] like recited thing

And if you didn't say it right and [p] tap your knee three times [p] or something

Then every time you messed up [p] you had to take a drink.

// And I got plowed [p] *Plowed!* <u>Plowed!</u> (I: Aw!)

And it was a bunch of *really* dear friends of mine that I'd made

And [P] the guys carried me [p] to my room [P]

And they put me to bed [P] and they locked me in there

And they laid me on my stomach [p] in case I got sick, you know?

So I wouldn't kill myself in my sleep (I: uh huh)

And [p] um [P] there was this *guy* [p] who'd been threatening the girl next door

Saying, [p] "*I've* got a master key [p] I'm gonna come in your room and *get* ya one night"

Well he saw them carrying me into my room

\\ And [p] um [P] when I woke up [P] I woke up and there was somebody in my room

And he was on top of me [p] the whole nine yards

// And I was *sick* [P] I was <u>so</u> sick [p] I was like throwing up

I woke up, I [p] I'd thrown up in my *hair!*

I mean, I *wasn't* gonna go to the hospital without taking a <u>shower</u>!

You know, *no!* [laughs]

So I went to the hospital after I'd taken a shower and made the report

The guys in the [p] in the dorm and the girl next door

They all [P] gave [p] statements, saying that,

You know, this guy said that I'd asked him in and opened the door for him [chuckle]

[laughing] And they were like, "There's *no way!*

She was passed out *cold* [laughs] you know, this and that"

And they said that [p] he had held up the key [p] and flashed it

And threatened this other girl [p] and that's how he got in the room

And you know, the bad part about the military

I was at this point [p] *ashamed*

Because it was my fault this time [P] because I'd let myself get so [p] drunk [P] that (I: but . . .)

Well, it's *still* wrong what he *did*, but I felt ashamed [p] that time,

'Cause I had some control over it [p] had I been more [p] alert. (I: So you felt had you not let yourself be vulnerable by getting drunk . . .)

Right. So um [P] but they said

In the military—then it was [p] 1978

And he told [P] and I was told it would be handled

That this guy would be taken care of and it would be handled . . .

(Lynn explains that she assumed the guy would be in big trouble but instead, she and all those who made statements on her behalf were kicked out of the privileged drum and bugle corps and sent back to their regular squadrons for technical training.)

We got punished [P] *we* got punished [p] for it. (I: And him?)

Uh [p] I don't know [p] all I know is that he got stationed somewhere else

And later on [P] before I left that base [P] in a Commander's Call? (I: uh hum)

They were making jokes about some girl [p] who'd claimed that some guy'd come into her room [embarrassed laugh]

And I was just *appalled!* [p] I was just appalled (I: [murmur of sympathy])

I was never invited [p] or privileged to any information as to what *happened to him*, where he *went*—anything.

So it was just that good ole boys' network, you know (I: protecting him)

So it wasn't just *my* word against his [p] you know?

It was a whole group of people's word [p] against his

And it was just [p] brushed under the table [p] and we were all punished [p] and [P]

And this other guy was just sent off somewhere else to another base— and another job

He was sent off that base (I: uh huh)

But that was all [P] that ever happened to him [P] you know?

And he'd *hurt* one girl—me [P] and he'd *threatened* another

And that's all that ever happened to him [P] to my knowledge. (I: That's not right. But I've heard that . . .

Yeah, so that's my bad story [P] that's my bad story.

But on the other hand, there was a real nice chaplain?

That talked to me [p] he made me hot chocolate [slight laugh] and he talked to me that next whole day

And he made things really, really easy for me . . .

I was never given a report [P] never given any follow-up action, you know?

And it was a *crime* I reported. (I: That's right!)

But I never even got, "Ahh, you're crazy"

I never even got [p] even if you report a crime and [P] you lose

Somebody *still* lets you know [P] and they didn't ever let me know

And that was my [P] biggest disappointment the whole time I was in the military

They let me down there

The *rest* of the time [P] I was as *proud* as could be [P] to be [laughs] to be in the Air Force!

And that was in the very beginning [P] and I just blew that off

I figured, well [P] I'll probably mess up myself once or twice every now and then.

I'll give you a mistake in the beginning [chuckles] if you'll give me a mistake later on, you know?

That was my internal way of dealing with it, you know? (I: Nice that you're gentle with yourself)

I just, um—I'm [p] really <u>proud</u> to be an [p] American? (I: uh hum)

I'm really *proud* [p] to be a Floridian? (I: uh hum)

And I'm not gonna let something like *that*

Take away a lifetime of belief [p] in a system, or a culture or [p] anything like that.

You know, I know that even though it might have been [P] institutional type of [p] um, um

What do you call that? Discrimination? (I: uh huh) You know, the systematic—the way it was set up?

It was still [P] <u>applied</u> by individuals [p] you know what I mean?

That decided among themselves individually [P] that it might not be important enough to pursue

It wasn't like the Secretary of the Air Force or anybody else

So I don't hold it against the Air Force . . .

(Lynn then talks about how she gave up a golf scholarship to join the Air Force and kept re-enlisting because she was enjoying herself.)

When you're in the military [P] you're all transplanted [p] and moved around from one place to another

And that [p] in <u>itself</u> [p] besides your basic training that you all become familiar with

And have that under your belt [p] your training in your specialty [p] you have *that* in common

But you also have that common bond of being transplanted and displaced. (I: Ah, that's right.)

So that helps build com [p] camaraderie

Well [p] with people you never probably would have made *friends* with any other way

You *know?* (I: 'Cause you're thrown together and there's no one else?)

// Yeah, you know [P] you're hanging out with somebody and they're from Nebraska,

Not because they wanted to move to *Florida*

But because they got stationed here [p] whether they *like* it or <u>not</u> [both laugh]

You know? Those are the only people I think [p] are allowed to complain about the *weather!*

For the most part [p] they were all like big brothers [p] they were *nice!*

You know, they helped me *move* [P] they helped me [P] *shop,*

They helped me fix my *car* [P] they helped me *buy* my car,

I mean, it was like a *family!*

And I miss it [P] today, but [p] // don't think I wasn't ready to get out when I was able to get a *pension* for the rest of my life!

But, you know, I loved it . . .

(Discusses her opinion of Clinton affair and ole boys' club in the military. Describes her work on flight simulators, then talks about foot accident and how military surgeons were able to save her foot from an amputation. Tells next of being dumped three weeks before her wedding. Then describes her home that her uncle financed, her car that was a gift from her parents, her pension, and her great health benefits.)

See, we're talking storybook life!

(She describes her childhood and how her parents and grandparents were always there for her.)

They never had those roles—those traditional roles where the mom stayed home? (I: yeah)

The men in my family always cooked and did the dishes. (I: So [p] no traditional expectations for you to like go into nursing or be a schoolteacher!)

No [p] nope [P] my dad was Marine in World War II (I: Oh wow)

So I didn't have any exposure to that!

You know, but, ah, he was saying [P] you know [P] you could be a Marine *Yes* you can [p] *girls* can be Marines too.

I'd go, "*Harumph!*" [p] you know, that kind of thing . . . they never . . .

(Talks lovingly and describes more about her family and her feeling of security.)

I always had security [P] I never felt insecure

I never felt insecure in the military [p] and now that I'm retired [p] I still have that security

And now [p] I have the security of another [p] government job (I: oh yeah)

I'm *big* on security! [laughs] I'm big on security . . .

I don't like the ability of anyone to be able [P] to take anything away from me

So I don't [p] give anybody that ability [p] or that power [p] to take anything away from me

And I think now that's why I'm single, you know? (I: uh huh)

Because I don't think I'd want anybody to . . .

The way I look at it, I've had people die to get me what I have

And that was very devastating and it was [P] that shook me up.

If I've ever had a loss in my entire life

That would have been the death of my uncle [p] he was very close to me

(Describes her close relationship with her uncle and how she was with him and held him when he died.)

I had [P] I have a dreamy life when it comes to that!

Yeah [P] I might have been abused or harassed by outside [p] entities

By people that aren't really [p] of my world, but

They didn't—they didn't hurt my world.

They might have caused me some disappointment [p] in a system

Or disappointment [p] in some people

Or [p] even disappointment [p] in myself here or there

But nothing that couldn't have been improved or remedied or [P]

You haven't met very many people as lucky as me, have you? (I: No)

I don't mind to claim it either

You know, I know people [P] I know people [P] I know women [p] that have been raped [p] not *even* as bad or as scarily as I was, okay?

That [p] to this day [P] are haunted by it [P] they let it consume their *whole* life.

Now do you *really* [p] want to give that situation *that* much power?

Do you want to give that guy that did that to you that much power? That much credit?

Now [P] I let my uncle's *death* devastate me

And I say I let it devastate me [P] because that's the only way it could [p] devastate me

You know, I was glad [p] I was there for him

But you see, I *loved* him [P] and he was a very big part of my world

So he's allowed to devastate me!

A stranger [p] or somebody who doesn't like [p] who I don't like

Or who I don't know [p] I don't let devastate me [laugh]

They don't get that far [P] that's the way I look at it

I don't let them devastate me . . .

(Tells a long story about a friend who lost a leg and who was an inspiration to her. Describes how she gets her philosophy from the way her mother and father have dealt with cancer and Parkinson's respectively.)

You can feel [p] anyway you want to about something

Just like vanilla and chocolate [P] everybody loves [p] *both* of 'em [laughs], you know?

You know, you just gotta look at how you like it, you know?

Like what's right for you [P] so that's the way I look at that

You can't let things get to you [P] there's always a brighter day
You can let yourself laugh
You get through it—you get well. (I: I hear a lot of gratitude—I've heard that since I sat down! And looking on the good side. Definitely a glass-half-full person, huh? Or ¾?)
Yeah, yeah, I'm not [P] I've got plenty!
Yeah, I don't need it full [p] but as long as I don't get thirsty! [both laugh]
My glass is full enough [P] I never really never wanted to be [p] rich
I've got everything I need [p] I have a good life
I'm very happy [P] I'm very content.

EXERCISE ONE: FIELD NOTES AND MEMOS

Write a "field note" highlighting your initial impressions. Narratives are interpretations and are not meant to mirror some reality that is "out there." Narrative analysis is about searching for meanings that are constructed out of the interaction of the interviewer and the narrator. Value your own interpretations as a starting point. You may be surprised to discover some of your own cultural preconceptions in the process. Some questions you might ask yourself: How do this narrator's conceptions differ from my own? Does this narrator reflect what can be called "culturally prescribed" behaviors? What beliefs of the narrator can I identify from the narrative? What did I learn about the person's cultural setting? Does the narrator fit my idea of a stereotypical member of the group to which s/he belongs? Which setting, stage props, major characters, and script or storyline have been selected by the narrator? Does the personal narrative correspond with any collective cultural values? What questions would I ask this narrator now if I had the opportunity?

EXERCISE TWO: STRUCTURE AND FUNCTION

Take a large sheet of drawing paper and some colored pencils and enlist your creative imagination. Draw the narrator's plot in any shape or form you think fits. Try to depict patterns within the narrator's personal story. How does s/he treat the disruptions that occur in life and explain them so that they form a coherent pattern? How does s/he glue the discordant pieces of life together into a concordant whole? Can you identify an overarching theme in the narrator's account? What title would you give the narrative?

EXERCISE THREE: DRAMATIC PRESENTATION

Examine the narrative for literary performance. Try to find examples of the following: repetition, pauses, poetic stanzas, pace changes, voice pitch changes, word emphasis, vocabulary choices. Does the speaker use rapid, staccato-like speech, a conversational style, or a prepared recitation? Does s/he speak in short phrases or long, convoluted sentences? How frequently does the narrator use conversational fillers like "um" and "uh"? Address dramatic expression in the narrative: does the narrator take time to set up the story or plunge right in? Where does the narrator enhance details? Is the narrative organized or scrambled in terms of time, location, and theme? What verb tense does the narrator use? Do you sense that the person is exhibiting restraint or purposely avoiding certain topics? Does the narrator present the story from an abstract or a concrete orientation?

EXERCISE FOUR: METAPHORS AND THEMES

For this exercise you may try using QSR Nud*ist or another qualitative research software tool. Programs like Nud*ist are ideal for detailed dissection of content because they assist in indexing and coding large amounts of data. But even if you use such software, go over the data with the old-fashioned "ear and eyeball" method so as to identify the larger elements of trajectory, shape, and literary performance. With Nud*ist you can set up cross-referencing networks and jump back to the original document within seconds, or print out a coding summary report that includes the links and excerpts from your original documents. There are "find and display" capabilities for text searching; you may, for example, want to count the number of times a certain word is used. In Nud*ist you create your own custom coding system by assigning your data to what the program calls "nodes." These nodes are flexible and can also be layered as an outline.

If you do not have access to such software, you may use Microsoft Word and split the screen using the document-map icon. Doing so brings up a separate pane, and each category you identify can be set as a first-, second-, or third-level outline heading, which allows you to rapidly navigate through the document to code without losing your place. Don't forget to include your own memos, diary, or field notes in your textual analysis.

In this exercise, you will categorize symbols and metaphors you find in the narrative. What do you see that reflects the narrator's conceptual system? What original imagery can you find? Can you identify recurring themes or symbols? Look for a pattern of personal myth (a consistent way in which the narrator symbolizes him/herself), which may be stated outright or merely implied. Some themes might include betrayal, life-death contrasts, freedom, romance, adventure, and so forth.

EXERCISE FIVE: ANALYSIS OF INTERACTIONS

Examine the narrative as an interactive document. Write a paragraph about the exchanges between the narrator and the interviewer. What insight does their exchange give you about the larger cultural context? Note how the script can change depending on the audience. For example, how might the narrator tell the story differently to an aunt or uncle, as opposed to a close friend or to a researcher from the university? What factors influence which version a person selects to suit different types of situations? Can you find instances where the interaction itself changes the momentum in the narrative encounter?

A FEW SELECTED READINGS FOR FURTHER INFORMATION

Angrosino, Michael V. 1989. *Documents of Interaction: Biography, Autobiography, and Life History in Social Science Perspective.* Gainesville: University of Florida Press.

Becker, Gay. 1997. *Disrupted Lives: How People Create Meaning in a Chaotic World.* Berkeley: University of California Press.

Gee, James P. Units in the Production of Narrative Discourse. *Discourse Processes* 9:391–422.

Janesick, Valerie J. 1994. The Dance of Qualitative Research Design. In *Handbook of Qualitative Research*, ed. Norman K. Denzin and Yvonna S. Lincoln, 209–219. Thousand Oaks, CA: Sage.

Lakoff, George, and Mark Johnson. 1980. *Metaphors We Live By.* Chicago: University of Chicago Press.

Riessman, Catherine K. 1993. *Narrative Analysis.* Newbury Park, CA: Sage.

5

Reconstructing a Community through Archival Research

Cheryl Rodriguez & Yvette Baber

A RESEARCH PROJECT

Urban renewal has impacted African-American business enclaves in some typical and predictable ways. In the 1930s and 1940s such communities served as the hubs of commercial, political, and cultural activity, but by the mid-1950s they were experiencing a rapid decline. Various forces, including neglect by city government, dramatic social changes resulting from the civil-rights movement, and construction of interstate highways, all contributed to the despair that eroded the economic and cultural foundations of such communities, which came to be identified as pockets of poverty, crime, and ongoing racial unrest. By the 1960s the planned destruction and demolition of the communities were well underway despite protests from loosely organized groups of concerned citizens. By the late 1970s formerly thriving and vibrant communities were leveled and gone, often with no marker or sign to acknowledge their former importance and no formal or organized documentation of the beliefs, achievements, and histories of those who lived and worked there. Virtually every major American city has seen a variant of this basic scenario, which must be pieced together from oral narratives, scattered magazine or newspaper articles, dusty photographs, and public records.

It is true that the stories of most of the demolished African-American communities have a basic similarity. Nevertheless, the distinctive history of each community has value for those who once frequented the place, whose heritage is all too often misrepresented, or ignored altogether, in historical accounts of the city. Negative images of the community's declining years loom large in the minds of those who choose to remember only the trouble brought on by dispirited residents. Other members of the larger community are too young to recollect images of the lost community as a thriving refuge for black people from all walks of life. Public anthropology, in the form of community heritage projects, can illuminate, revive, and reconstruct these lost histories. As members of communities, urban anthropologists can make significant and substantive contributions to local knowledge by recapturing images of hope, self-determination, agency, and strength. Such was our goal in the early 1990s when we became involved with the Central Avenue project, a commemoration and celebration of African-American history in Tampa, Florida. Several ethnographic data-collection techniques were used to reconstruct this lost history, but the collection and analysis of archival data played a key role in the project. The official title of the project was "Central Avenue Legacies: Commerce and Community in Tampa's African American History," and it was initiated by faculty and students in the departments of Anthropology and Africana Studies at the University of South Florida (USF). The researchers were supported by an advisory committee composed of local residents and city employees.

ARCHIVAL RESEARCH AS A TOOL OF ETHNOGRAPHIC RESEARCH

Archival data are qualitative and quantitative materials stored for research, service, and other official and unofficial purposes by researchers, service organizations, and other groups. The data are stored in the formats in which they were collected, although sometimes they have been transformed into computer-readable formats.

Archival data properly speaking are materials originally collected for bureaucratic or administrative purposes that are transformed into data for research purposes. Examples include: maps that can identify physical features and structures in communities and neighborhoods; municipal records of births, marriages, real-estate transactions, and property ownership; census, tax, and voting lists; specialized surveys; service system records from human service organizations; court proceedings; minutes of meetings of local groups. Also useful are "secondary data," raw data that other researchers collected for their own purposes but that can be analyzed for other purposes; it is sometimes possible, for example, to access the personal field notes of prior researchers, or to use formal ethnographic databases such as the *Atlas of World Cultures* or the Human Relations Area Files. Local secondary data, material collected in the community under study, are particularly valuable, although secondary data obtained from related research conducted elsewhere on related topics or similar populations are also important sources.

Archival research has a number of advantages that enhance qualitative research. It is nonreactive (i.e., the researcher does not influence people's responses, since he/she is not interacting directly with those providing the information). It is relatively inexpensive. It supports the study of cultural processes through time. And it is possible to study topics that might be too politically or socially controversial to study firsthand. Moreover, the use of data from archival and secondary sources can also enhance the comprehensiveness of data collection by allowing for cross-cultural and cross-national comparability and generalizability. On the other hand, archival data cannot always be considered "clean" or unbiased, nor can they be used without due consideration for the ways in which the information was stored and coded. The standards of documentation that we expect today were not always observed in the past. Even modern statistical databases, which may seem ideally bias-free (especially if they come from data banks and are already packaged on computer tape, coded and ready to be analyzed) can still be riddled with errors. It is important to consider carefully all the possible sources of bias that can be at work in the setting down of the data. Archival data are not always stored in ways that support ease of retrieval. They may be in filing cabinets or folders, and the researcher may have to organize and code the material manually. Since doing so can be very time-consuming, it is a good idea to make an early decision about which data are most important to your study.

ARCHIVAL RESEARCH: THE PROCESS

In the 1890s the largest segment of the black[1] population in Tampa was located in an area called the Scrub. This community, which had been settled by freed slaves, was neglected, undeveloped, and poverty-ridden. Clapboard shacks and makeshift dwellings leaned precariously and haphazardly along unpaved neighborhood streets. Despite its squalor, however, the Scrub had the advantage of being located close to the shipping docks and railroads, important sources of employment, particularly for African-American men. As Tampa's citrus, cigar, and phosphate industries flourished, African-Americans migrated to the area in large numbers.

In the 1880s and 1890s, black barbers, seamstresses, and bootmakers had shops in downtown Tampa, where they served a predominantly white clientele. As Tampa's African-American population grew in the Scrub and surrounding neighborhoods, the passage of Jim Crow laws dictated segregation of public facilities, schools, and businesses. The black business owners were strongly encouraged to leave downtown and operate in specially designated areas of the city. Central Avenue, which bordered the Scrub, was very close to downtown and it became a prime location for the development of black businesses. In 1893 there were five black-owned businesses on Central, including a barber shop, a restaurant, and two grocery stores. In 1899 there were more than twenty-eight businesses, and by 1918 more than eighty shops, stores, and professional offices had been developed to serve Tampa's black residents. Central Avenue became more than just buildings and services. In the 1920s the election of a "mayor" of Central Avenue became an annual fund-raising event. A tradition of parades began in response to the exclusion of blacks from major civic festivities elsewhere in Tampa. One such parade, the "Tilt of the Maroon and Gold," was held during an annual football rivalry between two historically black colleges—Florida A&M University and Bethune-Cookman College.

During its heyday in the 1940s and 1950s, Central Avenue thrived as the "main drag," the functional equivalent to downtown for the city's black population. It was a site of black entertainment known throughout Florida, and nationally renowned artists such as Cab Calloway, B. B. King, and Ray Charles all performed in Central Avenue night clubs early in their careers. Black entertainers, however, like all other black travelers, had limited access to public accommodations in Tampa. The Central Hotel provided shelter and community for these entertainers as well as for other black visitors. Aside from entertainment venues, there were social clubs, fraternal organizations, burial societies, church groups, and literary clubs. These groups worked together to create libraries, day-care centers, scholarship funds, and other responses to community emergencies. The black community's first newspaper, which still thrives, was published and delivered on Central. These events and activities fostered solidarity among African-Americans and defined the Central Avenue community as one that could create and sustain itself.

There was a strong tradition of activism in the community as well, and it was a center for the continuing fight for civil rights. Tampa's Urban League, the National Association for the Advancement of Colored People (NAACP), and the Longshoremen's Union were all located in the Central Avenue community. Tampa's first black law firm began on Central, and its lead attorney became the chief legal counsel for the NAACP. Many of the major discrimination lawsuits filed in Tampa and in the state of Florida were initiated by this firm. Civil-rights leaders from all over the US met at the St. Paul AME Church (which continues to have an active congregation) to plan sit-ins and demonstrations that eventually facilitated the dismantling of Jim Crow laws in Tampa.

Despite this rich history of self-determination and entrepreneurship, the Central Avenue business district began to falter in the 1960s. Some people blame desegregation for its loss, while some attribute the decline to a riot or civil disturbance on Central Avenue in 1967. Others argue that racial discrimination blocked black business owners' access to loans that would have supported the revitalization of the area. In any case, by 1974 Central Avenue's demise was finalized with wrecking balls and bulldozers. The 387 multi-storied structures of the community were reduced to rubble in a matter of days, although the plans to demolish the businesses had been in the works for years. In 1973 the mayor of Tampa announced a $4.7 million HUD grant to level the buildings and replace them with a park named in honor of a local African-American community leader. Today there are no physical reminders of a bustling economic enclave. The street itself became Orange Avenue, a nondescript, half-mile thoroughfare leading to Interstates 4 and 75. Beyond the sidewalk that borders Orange Avenue is Perry Harvey, Sr. Park, where children from the Central Park Village public-housing complex play. The only structures remaining from the days of Central Avenue are the Longshoremen's Hall and Kid Mason Center, a recreational facility operated by the city of Tampa. These buildings, along with two churches in the immediate area, are historic, but even today their survival remains uncertain as redevelopment continues to threaten the area.

The final products of the USF researchers' efforts and the planning of the community advisory committee were a photo exhibit, a panel discussion, and a walking tour of the area that once had been Central Avenue. The photo exhibit and discussion were based at Kid Mason Center, and the walking tour was facilitated through a series of exhibits erected in the park and standing on the sites of bygone businesses. The exhibits were doors collected from junkyards, and each one represented an address of a former business. Photographs and other memorabilia associated with the businesses were displayed on the doors. The walking tours were led by a police officer who had once walked the Central Avenue beat and by an older resident who had worked on Central Avenue.

Despite the overwhelming success of the day-long community program, our tasks in developing this public heritage project were many and complex. Some of the challenges faced in the course of research were the result of the mere fact that the businesses and residences had been destroyed. Moreover, many potential informants were either deceased or elderly with failing memories. The research team also had to organize and catalogue materials and artifacts including personal photos (with questionable dates), unannotated newspaper clippings, and interview transcripts (with accompanying tapes) from a study of Tampa's African-American community conducted in the 1970s. The transcripts and tapes represented the only remaining evidence of the early lives of seventy of Tampa's African-American residents. While photographs from the *Florida Sentinel-Bulletin*, the local African-American newspaper, were critical to the project, they were not filed in a way that made for ease of access. We often had to go through the storage boxes one picture at a time.

Our research was designed to document the impact of federal, state, and local urban renewal policy on the Central Avenue neighborhood. We were interested in the ways in which community members responded to the impending destruction of their neighborhood. We were particularly concerned about confirming or refuting the widespread story that "riots" had precipitated the demise of the neighborhood. It was also important for us to understand which individuals or entities benefited most from the demise of Central Avenue and to learn about the impact of the destruction on the African-American community in Tampa. In order to achieve these research aims, we attempted to construct a longitudinal review of property ownership in the area using a combination of archival resources, ethnographic interviews, personal materials from key informants, and content analysis of local newspapers.

An important first step in archival research is to identify the data you will be retrieving. You will need support in this process from the offices, institutions, or individuals who are in possession of the information. You must therefore learn who controls access to the data and then identify and carry out formal and informal procedures for gaining access to the data. The formal procedures may include paperwork, and it is important to understand the informal relationships and "chain-of-command" issues that could facilitate (or slow down) your research. It is almost always necessary to obtain informed consent if the data describe individual cases. If you are borrowing valuable personal items (e.g., photos or other mementos), be sure to work out a plan to protect them while they are in your custody and to return them safely to their owners at the conclusion of the project. Even before accessing the data, you should develop a means for recording and/or copying them. Technological advances have simplified this process, but it is important to consider the costs of copying materials that you cannot take away with you.

Researchers need to make decisions about how much time to spend collecting the data based on availability and storage methods. Do not forget to factor in the time it takes to secure necessary permission to access the information. You should also consider the amount of staff cooperation you will need—such people are likely to be very busy and will not be enthusiastic about helping with your project if they think they will end up spending lots of time on your agenda. If it seems that you will be able to access a large quantity of information, you may want to think about whether all of it needs to be collected, or if only a sample will suffice.

Before collecting data, create a way to record it. Your recording system should identify the source of information, the dates, and the location of the files (or other sources). Always allow space for comments. A database file (e.g., Microsoft Access or FileMaker Pro) may serve this purpose, as might a conventional spreadsheet. You will then be able to sort information by date, location, and other pertinent indices.

YOUR PROJECT

In most localities, both urban and rural, there are areas that have a long history of settlement, often by people of a common ethnic, racial, or family background. Over the years, however, such areas may undergo changes in occupancy, in socioeconomic status, or in land use as a result of governmental policies related to development.

Your assignment is to trace the history of such a neighborhood in your locality, documenting its founding and any significant changes it has undergone over time. Using archival resources such as residential directories, newspapers, maps, and minutes of meetings of public bodies such as city councils or county commissions, you will identify the historical trajectory that led to the neighborhood's change; analyze the impact of federal, state, and local policies on neighborhood change; describe changes in the neighborhood's economic base, the ethnic/racial make-up of the residents over time, and the social institutions of the neighborhood; become familiar with the process of accessing and interpreting data at the city, county, state, and federal levels; and understand the importance of paper, microform, and electronic media resources in providing contextual descriptions of neighborhood change.

This project is best conducted as a team. Break up the tasks among members of the team, assigning one source per person. It is important, however, to share the fruits of individual research so that everyone on the team has at least a basic familiarity with all the sources and the kinds of data to be used. Everyone should agree on a recording/coding system and use it consistently.

Your final report should include a historical time line or table that highlights key events that shaped the area under study. It may be that each member of the team comes up with his/her own time line based on the particular data source he/she worked with. But all the team members should pool their tables into one common time line.

The report should describe the origins, history, and current status of the community under study. What is its heritage? How was it founded? What have been the major influences for change over time (e.g., economic factors, race, social class)? What has happened to the original residents? What does the area look like now? Are there plans (or policies) in place that may bring about further change in the area? Be sure to include your own personal observations about the process and about the neighborhood you are learning about.

NOTE

[1] In this chapter we use the terms "African-American" and "black" interchangeably. Please note, however, that in other contexts, the former term is often restricted to people of African heritage whose family history has been in the United States, while the latter refers to others of the "African diaspora" whose family histories are in Cuba, the Bahamas, Jamaica, and other parts of the Caribbean. Even if they later came to the US, they often maintained their own distinctive cultural and national identities.

A FEW SELECTED READINGS FOR FURTHER INFORMATION

Bernard, H. Russell. 1988. *Research Methods in Cultural Anthropology.* Newbury Park, CA: Sage.

Butler, John Sibley. 1991. *Entrepreneurship and Self-Help among Black Americans.* Albany: State University of New York Press.

Greenbaum, Susan, and Cheryl Rodriguez. 1998. Central Avenue Legacies. *Practicing Anthropology* 20(1):2–30.

Lewis, Earl. 1996. Connecting Memory, Self, and the Power of Place in African American Urban History. In *The New African American Urban History,* ed. Kenneth W. Goings and Raymond A. Mohl, 1–15. Thousand Oaks, CA: Sage.

Schensul, Stephen L., Jean J. Schensul, and Margaret LeCompte. 1999. *Essential Ethnographic Methods: Observations, Interviews, and Questionnaires.* Walnut Creek, CA: AltaMira.

6

Using a Museum as a Resource for Ethnographic Research *

Serena Nanda

As human beings we transform the world around us to create objects through which we adapt to our environments. As the cultural animal, par excellence, humans also assign meaning and value to the objects they create. The universal human capacity to imagine ideal types—how things *should* be—means that in addition to practical function, objects are also produced with imagination, a spirit of workmanship, and aesthetic standards. In creating this material culture, humans not only make things, but attempt to make them well.

Museums are the repositories of material culture: they were created to collect, preserve, and publicly interpret the wide range of artifacts that represents the best in the past and the present in human societies. The high aesthetic standards that underlie museum collections and exhibits mean that

---

* Unless specifically noted, museums mentioned here are in New York City. I would like to thank Stanley Freed, Beth Pacheco, and Paisley Gregg for sharing their ideas about museums with me.

71

museums provide thrilling encounters with the richness of human culture through its material expression.

The grand and culturally meaningful structures in which many museum collections are displayed add to the unique learning environment that museums afford. In Staten Island, New York City, for example, the permanent collection of the Jacques Marchais Center of Tibetan Art is housed in a building that closely resembles a Tibetan Buddhist mountain temple. The terraced gardens, lily ponds and view of the bay of lower New York add to the reflective mood that viewing Asian art requires.

In addition to the intrinsic aesthetic rewards of museums, the innovative organization of contemporary museum exhibitions, the meticulous scholarship that underlies and explains the exhibits, and the presentation of objects that are rare treasures mean that museums have become a truly essential source of ethnographic understanding of our own and of other cultures.

In addition to the inspiration provided by reflecting on the richness of human culture—and human cultures—offered by museums, museums provide an environment for learning largely free of the distractions of modern life. Generally, museums and museum exhibits encourage one to linger and to look at an individual pace, allowing for emotional response and reflection that are poles apart from the "sound bites," "voice-overs," Muzak, and canned laughter that structure the world of popular culture.

While the museum can be an individual experience, museums also lend themselves to exploration with family, friends, and classmates, providing an interactive intellectual experience.

The scholarly, collecting, interpretive, and display functions of museums make them useful adjuncts to ethnographic research, the subject of the first section of this chapter. Next, I offer some ways of thinking about museums and museum exhibits themselves as subjects for ethnographic research.

MUSEUMS AS RESOURCES IN ETHNOGRAPHIC RESEARCH

Using museum exhibits for ethnographic research draws on and reinforces many ethnographic skills. Because of their visual focus, museums utilize and improve observational skills, forcing us to pay attention to detail and the relationship of details to the whole, which is at the heart of good ethnographic research. Absorbing ethnographic data from museum exhibits also improves note-taking skills: not only from object labels, but more significantly, in constructing and noting our own sense of what is important about an object in relation to our particular research interests. In requiring analysis of both individual objects and objects in relation to each other, museum exhibits also foster critical thinking and ethnographic theory building.

The display of accurately labeled material culture is only the tip of the information iceberg available in museums. Most museums today have libraries, Web sites, CDs, catalogues, brochures, photographic and audio archives, educational centers (for teachers, families, and children), film libraries, lectures, seminar series, cultural performances, demonstrations, and photographs to accompany exhibits, as well as tours by extremely competent guides (docents), all of which are useful in constructing ethnographies.

If you are undecided about your ethnographic subject, wandering around a museum may inspire ideas and help focus your ethnographic interests. Individuals respond differently to different objects: without knowing much about any of the objects displayed in a museum, you may nevertheless find yourself attracted by certain objects, styles, or cultures. Some of my own favorites are wooden hats from the Northwest Coast of North America; gold weights from Asante, in Ghana; feathered mantles from South American Amazonian societies; Hopi kachina dolls; Islamic calligraphy; and photographs of African-American life in Harlem in the 1920s.

As museums branch out from their once early focus on the eclectic and unorganized display of objects from "exotic" cultures to incorporate broader cultural and historical themes, there is literally no end to the beauty and interest to be found in museum collections, which range from the Rock and Roll Hall of Fame and Museum in Cleveland, to the Museum of Apartheid in South Africa, to the many museums of local history in almost all small cities in the United States, to museums which feature the arts of particular ethnic groups within any one nation. Your "gut" response to an item of material culture or a special subject museum is a good basis on which to choose the subject of your ethnographic research, as a compelling interest is the mainstay of any extended ethnographic project.

This kind of "aimless" wandering around the ethnographic collections in the African Room in the American Museum of Natural History led to one of my current ethnographic research projects. I was intrigued by a carving of a slave ship with an Englishman in the bow, and began to look in other museum exhibits and collections for objects from non-European cultures that represented Europeans. As often happens, once you get an idea and know what you are looking for, information begins to pile up. I scoured museum collections with a more focused eye, and found many objects that were relevant to my project, often in unexpected places.

While the richness of museums can be awesome and inspiring, museums can also be overwhelming, and "wandering around" a great museum may make you dizzy from sensory overload. Generally, a museum collection or exhibit will be most useful for your ethnographic research if you already have at least some idea of a subject in mind, even if it is only vaguely formulated. You can then begin by searching out exhibits in your local museum that have some relevance to that subject (or look up museum collections or exhibits on their Web sites).

Because contemporary museum exhibits often tell a story, or arrange objects according to a few underlying principles, you should familiarize yourself with the organization of the exhibits you view. Different principles under-lie the exhibition of objects in different kinds of museums. A fine arts museum, a private collection, a natural history or science museum, an ethno-graphic museum, a local history or ethnic museum, a university museum, or a children's museum, all select and arrange their objects differently. In addi-tion, special exhibits are also arranged to tell a particular story. The meaning of an object in the culture that created it may be different than the meaning of an object in a museum display, and you should be alert to this when you think about objects in terms of your particular ethnographic project.

Very often the beginning of an exhibit will include a written introduc-tion, on the wall or in a brochure, which you should read before you begin your viewing. In ethnographic and historical museums (and increasingly, in art museums), wall panels often contain a map or a history of the culture that is the subject of the exhibit, as well as explaining the theme of the exhibit and the relations of the objects to the main theme and to each other. Exhibitions often include background information on important cultural beliefs and prac-tices related to the material objects displayed, so in one sense, a lot of the eth-nographic work in contemporary museums and exhibits is done for you.

Where museum exhibits are organized to tell a story or reflect an ethno-graphic theme, they may suggest approaches in your ethnographic research that you have not thought about before. Using a museum for ethnographic research is an interactive process: visiting a museum with some ethnographic focus and questions helps shape a more constructive visit, but the very pro-cess of looking at and thinking about objects and exhibits in a museum gener-ates new questions and perspectives on an ethnographic research project. Many museums have ongoing videotapes running in conjunction with their exhibits that put the exhibited objects in a rich, cultural context. For example, a recent exhibit of the ritual art of the Luba in the Congo, at the Museum of African Art, was accompanied by a videotape of the ceremonies in which the objects are used. This was extremely helpful ethnographically and made an immediate impact that would have taken hundreds of pages of print to dupli-cate. Many museum exhibits also include CDs that are accessible from com-puters in the exhibit itself, extending the ethnographic understanding of a culture beyond what is possible by an exhibition.

In large ethnographic or natural history museums, a geographically related group of cultures may be represented in one room. The South Ameri-can Room at the American Museum of Natural History, for example, con-tains culturally accurate and detailed dioramas, including life-sized human figures, using many of the objects displayed in the exhibits so that an object's function is immediately understandable. This exhibit room, which includes a continuous video on various aspects of Amazonian culture, is organized around the main aspects of life in these cultures, with the display cases conve-niently divided into the familiar anthropological textbook categories of eco-nomics, rituals, social structure, life-cycle ceremonies, etc., which are widely shared among South American horticulturalists. It is truly a textbook come alive. This type of regional exhibit may contribute useful information for any ethnographic project, even if the exact society you are studying is not represented in its full dimensions. At the same time, regional displays, like "African art," for example, are usually careful to label the exact cultural origin of an object since geographic overgeneralizations also can be misleading. So you need to tread carefully here.

Even when a museum exhibit is not organized in terms of your own ethnographic interests, the exhibit can still be mined for ethnographic information. The Barry Goldwater collection of Hopi kachina dolls at the Heard Museum (Phoenix), for example, reflects one individual's tastes with no real ethnographic organization, but the wide range of the collection and high aesthetic quality of the objects make them ethnographically significant. You can make your own detailed observations of individual pieces in such an exhibition and follow this up in museum (and other) publications. Because museum exhibits by their nature are selective, and therefore always limited in their themes, learning from museum exhibits is an active, not a passive, experience. This means that in addition to grasping the theme of museum exhibits, you must also interrogate them, asking questions generated by your own interests and from your own point of view.

This is particularly necessary in art museums. While ethnographic, local historical, or ethnic museums are the most obviously relevant for ethnographic research, art museums also have a great deal to offer an ethnographic project. The material cultures of Africa and Native Americans, for example, are frequently found in both ethnographic and art museums (see the following section). Although art museums tend to exhibit objects with much less cultural or historical information or context than ethnographic museums, you can mine these exhibits for ethnographic data by asking anthropological questions about them. For example, the masterpieces of sculpture in the African Room in the Metropolitan Museum of Art provide ethnographic data in the details of dress, adornment, body decoration, and hairstyles of the figures, and also suggest, by the frequent mother/child and male/female grouping, the significant cultural theme of fertility.

Descriptive labels are an essential source of ethnographic information, even the minimalist labels typical of art museums, which generally give the approximate date of an object, the society in which it is made, the material it is made of, and sometimes how it is used. As a result of some of the issues to be discussed subsequently, art museums are now expanding the cultural information on their labels, making them even more useful for ethnographic research, and indeed, indicate some contemporary blurring of lines between ethnographic and art museum exhibits.

Ethnographic museum labels tend to give much more cultural information, but even here you can ask additional questions relevant to your ethnography project: Who made the object? For whom was it made? How and how much was the artist paid for producing it? How does the object function in the culture's gender system? Is the object still being used? With what modifications? What does the object suggest about the prestige or wealth system of the culture? How were the skills needed to make the object passed on to others? Was the object used in other than economic exchanges? Who could use the object? Was its use restricted in some way, to certain persons or certain contexts? If the object is no longer in use, what objects have taken its place? What are the external influences that can be detected in the object? Is it similar in style to an object in another culture? Why was the object made in that particular way? In this way we move outward from an object to ethnographic research. Like Bronislaw Malinowski, who "began with a canoe" in his study of the Trobriand Islands, you may be led from studying one object in all its cultural ramifications to a deep ethnographic understanding of a whole culture.

A museum exhibit might even inspire you to focus your ethnographic research on material culture itself. One advantage in this approach is that people are very often more willing, and able, to discuss material culture than to talk about other aspects of their culture, such as social relationships, which engender more ambivalence, are more abstract, and may be more out of their conscious awareness. The questions listed above might be a beginning for this kind of ethnographic research focus.

As cultural anthropology and ethnography have developed new concepts, so have ethnographic and art museums. Compared to the simpler chronological and technological emphases of earlier museum exhibits, contemporary museums (like contemporary anthropology) represent "culture" in much more complex and dynamic ways, highlighting, for example, the complex interactions among society, culture and environments, and cultural variations within geographical regions.

This is illustrated in a recent costume exhibit on Morocco in the Jewish Museum in New York. The exhibit theme was the ethnic interrelationships between Jews and Muslims in Morocco, manifested in similarities of dress and adornment. By its very nature, a costume exhibit tells us a great deal ethnographically about gender roles, prestige and power, and cultural values, but the "ethnic interaction" theme also included important information on occupational specialization. Because Muslims were forbidden to handle certain kinds of materials, many Jews in Morocco became tailors, and the two communities thus became economically and culturally interdependent. This kind of cultural interaction has become a more common theme in museums in recognition of globalization and the complex interactions between cultures. The older idea of culture as a bounded, isolated world no longer holds true in anthropology and museums have followed suit. An exhibit of Vietnamese culture in the American Museum of Natural History, for example, included exhibits on the culture of various Vietnamese tribal and religious groups, and also on Vietnamese culture as influenced by the Vietnam (or in Vietnam, called the American) War and tourism.

These dynamic, more culturally complex exhibit themes are also reflected in other ways in contemporary museums. Formerly, museum exhibits mainly represented and legitimated the dominant and elite culture of the nation-state. Museums today are moving toward much more inclusive histories, incorporating ethnic diversity and looking at history from "the bottom up." As with a recent exhibit on Haitian voodun religion at the American Museum of Natural History, these kinds of exhibits not only display aesthetically exciting objects, largely unknown to most Americans, but the very act of placing voodun material culture in such a prestigious institution helped inform people about the religion and to rethink the negative stereotypes many Americans hold toward these religious practices.

The comparative, historical, aesthetic, or cultural perspectives of contemporary museum exhibits provide new ways of looking at both familiar and unfamiliar items of material culture.

THE POLITICS OF CULTURE: MUSEUMS AND THE REPRESENTATION OF CULTURE

During the past thirty years, many of the ethical, substantive, and political issues raised in relation to ethnography by postmodernism and postcolonialism have also affected museums. There is now a general consensus in anthropology that the representation of cultures—whether in written ethnographies or in museums—is a political act: it emerges from particular positions of power and it has political effects. The politics of culture, with regard to ethnography and museums, is about how we choose to represent ourselves and others in the world. The cultural representations offered by art, ethnographic, and historical museum exhibits are now frequently subjects of controversy, the dimensions of which reveal new thinking about the roles of museums in society and conflicts over important cultural values. Museum collections, and particularly museum exhibits, are now critically examined for what they say about the cultures they aim to represent. From this perspective, museum collections, conservation practices, financing policies, scholarly research, hiring practices, and particularly exhibitions and catalogues themselves, all become interesting subjects for ethnographic research.

Museums, like other cultural institutions, have particular histories. They originated as national treasure houses, scientific institutions, cabinets of curiosities, preservers of "disappearing" cultures, and individual or family art or ethnographic collections; today museums operate within still other cultural contexts, including fluctuating art markets, politically charged funding policies, competition with commercial ventures such as theme parks, anthropological theorizing, and more recently, in the reconstruction of national histories and identities, or what has been called "collective memory making."

The role of museums in building new national identities is richly illustrated in the current efforts of South Africa. Unlike many museums in new nations, which create national identity by emphasizing more glorious portions of the past, South Africa's museums focus on representing the histories and cultures suppressed under apartheid, exposing the history and processes of apartheid itself. Through their exhibits, associated programs, and publications, these museums aim explicitly at contributing to social and political change, both at home and internationally by illustrating the consequences of inhuman social systems like apartheid. Like the Jewish Holocaust museums in the United States and Europe, these South African museums, such as the Robben Island Prison Museum (Capetown) and the Apartheid Museum in Johannesburg, bear witness to peoples' inhumanity to others so that it will never be forgotten and never be repeated (Nanda 2004).

Contemporary cultural history museums, like those of South Africa, or the New York Historical Society, with its 2005 exhibit on slavery in New York, explicitly articulate the stories that underlie their exhibits. In contrast, earlier natural history and ethnography museum exhibits were also based on stories, but they were implicit, framed by the unquestioned theories and assumptions of their time. One of these "stories" was that of cultural evolution, in which some cultures, mainly those of indigenous peoples, were viewed as culturally inferior to those of Europe or the United States. In US ethnographic museums, for example, exhibits about American Indians were often framed by a master narrative of "cultural disappearance." Other narratives were contested by native peoples as either irrelevant or misleading.

Native Americans also contest exhibits of their material culture in traditional art museums, claiming they: represent their societies as timeless, rather than changing; do not include Native American voices, consultation, or collaboration; neglect contemporary Native American artists; display objects collected under suspicious circumstances; display sacred/religious objects that should not be seen by the public; and ignore any representation of contemporary political issues. These traditional approaches are now being replaced by more empowering stories of Native American cultural revitalization, remembrance, and struggle, and in spite of some curatorial protests, consultation and collaboration with Native Americans is now generally standard practice in ethnographic, and even some art, museums in which these cultures are exhibited. This collaboration is now legally demanded with the passage of NAGPRA, a federal law that requires the repatriation of human remains and other cultural objects to relevant Native American groups. The changes in representing Native American cultures are dramatically displayed in the new Smithsonian National Museum of the American Indian in Washington, DC.

An outstanding example of what can be achieved in museum exhibits that include collaboration with indigenous communities was the American Museum of Natural History's exhibit, The Enduring Potlatch (1991). This exhibit included not only masterworks of Northwest Coast art and a great deal of important scholarly information, but also dioramas of contemporary potlatches, which included plastic objects and mass produced blankets, bringing the potlatch right into the late twentieth century. It also included a properly contextualized exhibit of the Canadian government's repression of the potlatch and the confiscation of potlatch items, which have subsequently been returned to Northwest Coast groups. None of this additional historical context in any way detracted from the artistic quality of the exhibition, which was superb, and it added a much more accurate historical picture. This exhibit, and others like it (for example, Aztec: The World of Moctezuma at the Denver Museum of Natural History [1991–1992], held in the contentious year of the Columbian quincentenary), indicate that museums can hold to their traditional mandates of collecting and displaying the best of human artistic creations as well as present historically and ethnographically accurate representations of cultures. This radically changing nature of how museums exhibit Native American art reveals a great deal about the ethnohistory of the United States and is a good subject for ethnographic research.

In addition to the changing politics of culture discussed previously, new anthropological approaches in studying material culture have also influenced museums. These include examining the shifts in context and meaning of objects over time (for example, when an object becomes part of a museum display); the role of ceremonial objects as part of the symbolic process through which nation-states establish their cultural and historical identities; the display of material objects as emblems of class and ethnic and national identity; and the ways in which European and American ethnographic and art museum exhibits have manifested colonial views of non-Western peoples, particularly through the notion of "the primitive" (Price 1989).

In keeping with this discussion, one of the most controversial museum exhibits to date was the Museum of Modern Art exhibit, Primitivism in 20th Century Art: Affinity of the Tribal and the Modern (1984). Although the exhibit curators claimed that putting "tribal" art in a prestigious art museum context (and showing how it influenced some of the West's greatest artists, like Picasso) was a tribute to the "primitive," the show generated much controversy. Critics claimed that exhibiting the objects without identifying their cultural contexts, their functions, the symbolic meanings to those who made and used them, or the names of the individual artists, was both a distortion and a denigration of "tribal" culture. For example, the absence of cultural context reinforces a separation between art and other aspects of culture, which is characteristic of Western cultures, but not tribal cultures. The Western museum's preoccupation with the antique, the pure, and the authentic in tribal art also grows out of a Western capitalist system of values that ignores the values and voices of those it claims to celebrate by displaying their art.

Museums both reflect and influence cultural values. They are important cultural institutions, and as such are rewarding subjects of ethnography and sources of ethnographic information.

YOUR PROJECT

The exercises below are just two examples of how museum exhibits can add to your ethnographic research.

1. Select any object in a museum exhibit that strikes your interest. Describe, in writing, its appearance, its form and material, its style, its function, and its cultural context (the meaning and value attached to it, among other things). Raise questions about the object that you would need answered if you were doing ethnographic research on the culture the object was used in.

2. Outline in written form how you would organize an ethnography of your own culture as a museum exhibition. What would be the theme of your exhibit? What objects would you use in the exhibit to carry through the theme and why would you choose these objects (keep in mind both the aesthetic and cultural aspects of museum displays)? What kind of space would you design for your project? What media would you choose to accompany the exhibit (video, seminars, children's educational programs, photographs, etc.). Who might you ask to collaborate or consult with on this project? (When you have completed this exercise for your own culture, you may find it applicable to your ethnographic research project on a culture other than your own.)

REFERENCES

Nanda, Serena. 2004. South African Museums and the Creation of a New National Identity. *American Anthropologist* 106(2):379–384.
Price, Sally. 1989. *Primitive Art in Civilized Places.* Chicago: University of Chicago Press.

A FEW SELECTED READINGS FOR FURTHER INFORMATION

Center for Arts and Culture. 2000. *The Politics of Culture: Policy Perspectives for Individuals, Institutions, and Communities.* Washington, DC and New York: The New Press.
Clifford, James. 1997. *Routes: Travel and Translation in the Late Twentieth Century.* Cambridge, MA: Harvard University.

Dubin, Steven C. 1999. *Displays of Power: Memory and Amnesia in the American Museum.* New York: New York University Press.

Jones, Anna Laura. 1993. Exploding Canons: The Anthropology of Museums. *Annual Review of Anthropology* 22:201–220.

Marcus, George E., and Fred R. Myers, eds. 1995. *The Traffic in Culture: Refiguring Art and Anthropology.* Berkeley: University of California Press.

Stocking, George W., ed. 1985. *Objects and Others: Essays on Museums and Material Culture.* Madison: University of Wisconsin Press.

WEB SITES FOR FURTHER INFORMATION

http://www.aam-us.org (American Association of Museums)

http://www.conexus.si.edu (National Museum of the American Indian)

http://www.amnh.org (American Museum of Natural History)

http://www.nmnh.si.edu/anthro/cma/index.html (Council for Museum Anthropology)

http://www.nmnh.si.edu/departments/anthro.html (Anthronotes—an excellent newsletter from the Smithsonian, National Museum of Natural History, Washington, DC)

7

Observing a Workplace

Kathryn Borman, Ellen Puccia,
Amy Fox McNulty, & Bill Goddard

A RESEARCH PROJECT

During the 1990s the National Science Foundation (NSF) responded to a general concern among employers about the shortage of highly skilled workers for the nation's expanding high-tech workplace. Whereas prior research had focused on the transition from high school directly into the workplace, the new NSF initiative concentrated on building the curriculum at the level of the community college in order to provide employers with problem-solving technicians who could work well in teams and adapt their skills to challenges in rapidly changing technical workplace settings.

In 1996, the NSF awarded funds to a three-year project, "Addressing National Needs for Skilled Technical Graduates," led by Kathryn Borman at the University of South Florida (USF) and Jeanne Diesen, an independent contractor working with the Indian River Community College (IRCC). The research team was made up of graduate students in applied anthropology at USF, and faculty members and other staff at IRCC. The overarching aim of the research was to determine the core of skills and knowledge that all Associate of Science (AS) degree students must possess in order to function in the workplace. We were particularly interested in the so-called "SMET skills" (science, math, engineering, and technology). This common core would then be used to improve the education sought by AS students at the community college, allowing for a more efficient and meaningful acquisition of workplace skills. Our study was undertaken as a sort of hybrid, in that it was both a study of high-tech workplaces and workers and also a project designed to inform policy considerations. The location of the study was the central east coast of Florida. Our sample included workers and supervisors in this region in work sites from five industries chosen on the basis of local and national job-growth projections: computer programming and applications; drafting and design; electronics engineering technology; radiography; and respiratory care.

One primary tool for data collection was the workplace observation, a method that has been used in a wide variety of studies in ethnographic research both descriptive and evaluative. Our research design combined the ethnographic methods of workplace observation and interviews with workers and supervisors at key sites with structured surveys administered to the supervisors. We also employed the Experience Sampling Method (ESM), an innovative new methodology that allows for an immediate response to surveys at random times of day. Each data-collection strategy provided important information, although for the purposes of this chapter, we will concentrate on data collection by means of workplace observation.

WORKPLACE OBSERVATION AS A TOOL OF ETHNOGRAPHIC RESEARCH

Although we used multiple data-collection methods to address the research questions and identify the common core of SMET skills needed for the workplace, we recognized the importance of broadening the research to include a study of the culture of contemporary technical work. In designing the research tool kit, we therefore determined that observations would provide valuable firsthand knowledge of the workers' jobs, responsibilities, skills, and competencies. Moreover, workplace observations allowed us to understand the work setting and the context of technical work. We were interested in such issues as gender status in the workplace, the structure of management, the transmission of new knowledge, and the role of informal learning in the new technological workplace.

Site-based or contextual skills are essential in the acquisition of new technical knowledge. Contextual knowledge is knowledge that is used in the workplace, and access to such information is very important for workers who want to solve problems efficiently so as to perform their jobs well. Knowledge and skills learned outside the classroom are often imparted through "communities of practice"; in other words, workers learn from others on the job. In addition to the training and preparation AS-degree graduates receive at the community college, they continue to learn through informal instruction on the job. Such informal learning is an important part of the ongoing training of technical workers. Because of the wide variety of tasks performed by technical workers and evolving technology, technical workers must constantly update their knowledge and skills.

Observations were essential to the gathering of data about such matters in the workplace. We observed fourteen AS-degree graduates in the five selected occupations (three in computer programming and applications, three in drafting and design, two in electronics engineering technology, three in radiography, and three in respiratory care). Because our study involved five researchers in multiple and diverse settings, we had to make sure that everyone followed an observation protocol that was reliable and valid, yet flexible. We wanted to capture both the details of the people's work and the environments in which they worked. We examined the relevant literature, reviewed the research questions, refined the interview protocol and survey, and created our own observation protocol. Our team of researchers needed to make sure that we collected similar data despite the diversity of fields being observed. Our observation protocol contained a list of variables that would be identified at each workplace. These variables included: a map of the work area; census information about coworkers and clients (if applicable); detailed descriptions of the workers' activities; conversations (when possible); approaches to problem solving and decision making; and descriptions of the workplace environment (e.g., gender status, the workplace hierarchy). Observers agreed on a notation system for recording different types of information, distinguishing among observations, conversations, and the observer's own reflections.

The researchers conducted interviews and observations in the same technical field. For example, the researcher who interviewed graduates in drafting and design also conducted the observations of a sample of workers in that field. Each observation lasted between ten and twenty hours and occurred over a two- to four-day period. Observations took place over four months in the summer of 1997. It is important to note that there were several limitations on the observations. For example, some employers in the electronics industry expressed concerns about security, while those in the health fields were mainly concerned about patient confidentiality.

Our observations made it possible for us to identify the skills used by technical workers in carrying out their daily routines. They also allowed us to understand the great importance of informal learning in all five fields. Because the community college was interested in identifying a common core of skills and competencies, it was important to observe the routines of workers and compare their skills across the industries. For example, observations highlighted the importance of social skills, such as negotiating and problem solving with the cooperation of coworkers, and the ability to juggle multiple tasks and responsibilities without losing track of the larger context of the job.

One of our key findings—the result mainly of our ethnographic observations—was that women frequently cooperate and work as team members, especially with female coworkers in fields such as radiography and respiratory care, which have a high percentage of female workers. But in fields with a higher percentage of male workers, women may be excluded from acquiring workplace skills, and they may even lose confidence in their abilities to perform even basic tasks.

With regard to the common core of skills, we discovered that thirty-one competencies were identified in all five industries. In addition to the SMET skills, we identified such skills as thinking, employability, interpersonal, and writing/reading skills. Supervisors agreed that their workers needed to possess problem-solving abilities and common sense as well as good work habits, time-management skills, flexibility, and initiative. Workers also need to be able to communicate with people both within and outside of the company. In fact, seventeen of the common core skills are not SMET skills, and of the fourteen SMET skills, seven were mathematical, two were scientific, and five were technological.

Our ethnographic work also allowed both supervisors and workers to make recommendations about how to improve community college education. The most common recommendation was to increase computer training, especially as related to up-to-date software packages relevant to each field of interest. Supervisors and workers also agreed that there is not at present a sufficiently clear emphasis on interpersonal and communications skills in the community college curricula and that students should be trained in the customer orientation of their chosen occupations. As a result of these recommendations, the community college is taking steps to form permanent relationships with the local industries as it makes changes in the AS curriculum.

WORKPLACE OBSERVATION: A BRIEF HISTORY

Ethnographies of workplaces based on observational methods go back at least to the 1920s, when a noted study at a Westinghouse plant revealed the potentially reactive nature of conducting such research. In that much-analyzed study, it became clear that the mere presence of the researchers affected the responses of the workers under observation, hence the need, discussed earlier, for using carefully constructed protocols to guide the research.

The liveliest and richest workplace ethnographies are those that focus on the workplace as a community of practice and that emphasize both the importance of interpersonal relations with coworkers and the kinds of tasks undertaken in those contexts. Borman's earlier research on young workers in their first jobs after high school demonstrated the importance of social skills (the capacity to solve problems in and learn through small work groups), just as she found in the later community college study. One influential model of community of practice is that of Jean Lave and her colleagues, who borrow from the traditional relationship between craft apprentices and craft masters and journey workers, who impart the skills of their trade to novices. In such communities, the transmission of skill is dependent on the strength of the social relationships between novice and expert. In its most customary sense, most of this knowledge is transferred verbally and is dependent on interpersonal relations. Like many a traditional society, the workplace community of practice is a kind of oral culture.

Communities of practice serve as the transmission mechanism for workplace knowledge; they are also the repositories of work skills. Within these communities of coworkers, methods of strategizing and problem solving are forged, communicated, negotiated, and learned. It would be misleading, however, to assume that the entire compliment of respiratory workers on a given work shift, for example, automatically constitute a community of practice. Some workers may function outside the community, continually at the periphery. In our observations, temporary or per diem workers were likely to hold such a position, but in a few cases, a committed "temp" might enjoy the benefits of membership in a community of practice.

WORKPLACE OBSERVATION: THE PROCESS

Carrying out a series of workplace observations can contribute to an understanding of not only the skills and competencies required to do a particular job; such activities can also provide a deep understanding of the task structure of jobs—what people do on a daily basis and how what they do is organized and accomplished. With additional effort, the ethnographer can also learn about power relationships—for example, how gender figures in workplace dynamics, an aspect of our project that became increasingly important in understanding high-tech workplaces as settings for the young workers we observed. In carrying out a set of weekly observations over a period of several weeks in multiple workplaces, we followed ten steps, working first individually and then gradually more as a collectivity, pooling information, talking informally about our research experiences, and developing coding rubrics and analytic processes. The ten steps are not discrete items that follow one after the other—many of them must be undertaken simultaneously, and some follow through the entire research process.

The first step is to focus the observation, which enables the observers to capture similar types of information in a systematic manner. At first, we approached our work settings in a manner that allowed us to make general observations of the context and setting for our more focused observations of the technicians, who were our main concern. We gradually centered our observations on the individual worker who was the participant in our research at each of the settings.

It is necessary to create an observation protocol to provide a framework for data collection. An observation protocol should clearly delineate the types of information to be noted (e.g., number of people in the room, interactions, relevant conversations). Our protocol was for the most part an effort to standardize our workplace observations by noting the activities underway at intervals of approximately five to ten minutes throughout the work day. Our observations lasted the full duration of the worker's work day.

As in all research involving human subjects, it is vital to obtain informed consent. Before even beginning the study, researchers should clearly explain the purpose(s) of their project and obtain written permission to observe individuals. Our informed consent form stipulated that any information gathered during the course of study would be maintained in secured files and that pseudonyms would be used to protect workers' identities. As in all the projects in this book, your instructor will help you access your own school's particular informed consent guidelines.

Once a protocol has been developed it must be pilot tested and, if necessary, revised. Our protocol consisted mainly of carrying out a running record of our observations, although other workplace studies have used protocols that took the form of a checklist of the occurrence of particular events and/or behaviors. In either case, it is important to ascertain the validity and reliability of both the tools and your own capacities to capture whatever might be occurring in the setting. A pilot test enables researchers to try out their data-collection instruments with a representative sample of people similar to those who will be involved in the actual study. Following a pilot test, researchers should discuss any complications, problems, or questions that arose and revise the protocol accordingly. Working as a pair or in a team facilitates this process, as a lone individual might take too much for granted and not see all the potential problems.

With the revised protocol in place, it is possible to go ahead and conduct the observations and to do so in a systematic manner. Each observation should be of a specified duration, and the number of such observations should be determined beforehand.

Observers must begin to build rapport with those they will observe as soon as they begin interacting with those workers. Establishing rapport is a process of building a relationship that carries through the duration of the research. Researchers who come off as impersonal observers or mechanical interviewers are unlikely to build much rapport; they may obtain a certain amount of information, but they will miss the full richness that can come from a true ethnographic immersion in the culture under study.

Observers can play a variety of roles in the research process, with more or less active participation in the setting and with the people depending on the nature of the setting and the constraints of time and other resources on the research. Particularly in a team project, it is important that all members of the team establish and maintain the same role in all the settings under observation. In our project, although we attempted to personalize our presence, we did not become active participants in the work-related activities of the settings.

Type notes immediately following observations while the material is still fresh in mind. Include both objective descriptions as well as subjective reflections on the process in as much detail and with as many nuances as possible.

A codebook should be developed to help researchers examine their notes and classify the information into categories or codes that relate to research questions. By coding data, researchers can look for themes and examine relevant sections of the data. Our codebook was based on several variables, including science skills, math skills, technical skills, and engineering skills. Within each category we further refined the codes to reflect the specific types of skills employed.

Finally, the research team should hold one or more "coding parties" to establish reliability. After completing a codebook, researchers should independently code the same sample of data and then come together to compare their classifications. A "coding party" allows researchers to compare their analyses of data and increase reliability from one rater to another.

YOUR PROJECT

You are to select a workplace to observe, first obtaining permission from the relevant authorities to conduct research there. In your first contact, you should explain that your project is for a class assignment; tell your contact why you chose this place to study and what you hope to learn. Speaking with people or observing in a place that is not public requires informed consent, and you must complete your school's informed-consent form and append it to the report you submit for this project. Your observations should take a minimum of six hours. You may conduct this project either on your own or in pairs.

Your final paper should address the following questions: What workplace did you observe? What did you hope to discover through your observations? (Note that this question requires a very specific answer, not "I want to learn about working in this company.") Describe the physical setting. Report on a census (How many people are there? To what demographic categories— gender, age, ethnicity, etc.—do they seem to belong [that is, you may not have the opportunity to ask each of them individually to verify your hunch]?). Describe the people you see and what they are doing. What do people generally do in this place? Are people interacting with others? Who? How? If they are mostly alone, what are they doing? What is the "tone" of the setting (tense? serene? exciting?)? How do you know? Do you think that this tone is deliberately set, or did it arise on its own?

Your paper should also provide some information about you as a researcher. Explain why you chose this place. Did you bring any preconceived notions about this place (or others like it) to the observation? If so, were they modified? How? Explain how you went about structuring your observations: What protocol did you use, and how did you develop and pilot test it? What role did you adopt? Why? How did you record notes? How did you code your data for analysis?

Finally, what in general did you learn about the workplace from your observation? Do you have any suggestions to make to the workers or the employers for improving the situation?

A FEW SELECTED READINGS FOR FURTHER INFORMATION

Barley, Stephen R., and Julian Orr. 1997. *Between Craft and Science: Technical Work in U.S. Settings*. Ithaca, NY: Cornell University Press.

Borman, Kathryn M. 1991. *The First "Real" Job: A Study of Young Workers*. Albany: State University of New York Press.

Darrah, Charles. 1994. Skill Requirements at Work. *Work and Occupations* 31(1):68–84.

Lave, Jean, and Etienne Wenger. 1991. *Situated Learning: Legitimate Peripheral Participation*. Cambridge, UK: Cambridge University Press.

Orr, Julian. 1996. *Talking about Machines: An Ethnography of a Modern Job*. Ithaca, NY: ILR Press.

8

Carrying Out a Structured Observation

Laurie J. Price

A RESEARCH PROJECT

Although it may seem that ethnographers observe people and behavior just in the act of hanging around, it is sometimes necessary for them to carry out more structured observations in order to answer specific questions. For example, I was involved in a needle hygiene study that sought to gather information about the transmission of HIV/AIDS among injection-drug users. We required very systematic observations of personal risk behaviors. The virus spreads in part when users of illegal drugs use each others' injection syringes, and public health programs needed to know the extent and varieties of needle sharing in order to understand clients' risks and the impact that education and counseling can have on risk-taking behavior.

Ethnographic methods have long been an important part of research on drug-use behavior, perhaps because the activity is covert and researchers are not granted access unless they are around long enough to develop rapport and trust. Ethnographic observation is particularly important when the subject is one about which participants might not be entirely forthcoming when asked questions about their behavior. Structured observations allow the researcher to develop some reasonably objective data to confirm (or perhaps to modify) what people tell us.

I became involved with research on injection behaviors as a member of a research and HIV-prevention program for drug users in northern Arizona: the Flagstaff Multicultural AIDS Prevention Project (FMAPP), which was funded by the National Institute on Drug Abuse. FMAPP collaborated with about twenty other such programs around the country as part of a collaborative agreement. I designed the needle-hygiene study with two other anthropologists within this collaborative arrangement, Stephen Koester and Michael Clatts. We developed the protocol (the formal guidelines for conducting the research) that was used to collect data in seven study sites around the United States. Structured observation was chosen as our primary method partly to ensure that the data from these different sites could be readily compared.

Most of the sites were in large urban areas. Flagstaff, by contrast, is a small town. Even so, over 800 people were clients of FMAPP during the 1990s. These clients took part in a two-session standard education program or a four-session enhanced education/counseling program. They also were offered free HIV testing and counseling. Our research observations were conducted almost entirely with people who had either been or were about to become FMAPP clients. We observed six injection episodes involving a total of twenty-seven individuals.

Our approach had two major aims. First, we needed to observe and record a variety of injection-drug behaviors in groups of people in natural settings and to do so in a systematic way. Second, we needed to take notes on what people said during these episodes, the better to understand how they interact with one another and how they interpret their own risks with regard to HIV. We developed the protocol in order to record: material culture at the scene; background pertinent to the group and its drug use on that occasion; about twenty different specific behaviors; and a small number of direct (verbatim) quotes of what people said.

Needle-related risks include direct re-use of another's syringe, drug management practices (e.g., syringe mixing and syringe-based measurement), and ineffective syringe cleaning practices. Most drug users in northern Arizona fit into one of four types of social patterns, differentiated by their level of openness to new members and the closeness and duration of relationships among group members. To gain a more complete picture of needle use in our community, the study design called for observation in each type of group. Such an approach illustrates an important general principle in structured observation: the researcher often needs to make considered choices about who and where to observe; in other words, it is necessary to devise deliberate sampling strategies.

We learned several important things about needle hygiene as a result of our structured observations. First, we noted that there are two kinds of direct needle sharing: intended and unintended. Direct intended sharing of syringes involves one person deliberately loaning his or her syringe to another and occurred in only two of the six groups we observed. Four people (15% of the total study population) were potentially exposed to the virus in this way. Our observations indicate that unintended direct sharing is the more common method. It would be necessary to confirm these observations by following syringe trajectories over time (i.e., through more than one episode). But based on our single observations, we ascertained that 30–40% of the syringes were "status unknown" (i.e., previously used and not properly cleaned). Most of the participants believed that they were using syringes they themselves had used before, but there was no way to prove this contention since the equipment was not always carefully marked when stored.

All the groups included at least a few FMAPP clients who were known by the researchers to be aware of the risks associated with direct sharing. These people also knew about the observations ahead of time. They therefore had the opportunity to locate their own syringes and thus avoid obvious direct sharing during the observed episode. But over the long run, they could not be assumed to be using similar care in the storage and subsequent usage of the equipment. Unintended direct sharing therefore becomes an important potential source of infection, one that needs to be studied at greater length.

We were also able to observe indirect sharing, which involves the use of common rinse water or cookers. It may also involve the use of one person's syringe as a measuring device for the whole group. A group of people will frequently pool their resources to buy a quantity of heroin, as it is usually cheaper to buy in bulk. It is easier to measure each person's share after the drug is mixed with water and cooked. We observed one episode when a common cooker was used; the first person took up some of the drug in his syringe, but since he was deemed to have taken more than his share, he had to empty some of it back into the cooker. Any blood residue in his syringe from previous injections was therefore mixed with the remaining solution in the cooker. If he had HIV, the other five people in the group would then be exposed to the virus.

Ethnographers recorded other kinds of indirect sharing. For example, one syringe was used to measure water for the group's common cooker. Three syringes were later left floating in one glass of water. The first person to inject returned his syringe to this glass, thus potentially contaminating the other two. Moreover, one group member stored cottons for future use that had been used during injection by another group member; they may have contained blood residue.

One of the most precise parts of our observation protocol involved syringe-cleaning behavior. Bleach is the only substance that really deactivates the HIV virus, so we noted whether people cleaned their syringes and whether they used water, alcohol, bleach, or something else. Even bleach must be left standing for at least sixty seconds to kill the virus. So when people did use bleach, we timed the number of seconds they left it in the syringes.

We found that more often than not, the bleach was left in for only twenty to forty seconds, not long enough for effective decontamination. This finding has clear implications for HIV-prevention programs: clients needed to be taught the sixty-second bleach rule more effectively.

In sum, we documented both intended and unintended direct sharing, as well as the prevalence of indirect sharing, especially when drugs are bought in common. We also documented the inadequacy of syringe-cleaning practices, noting cleaning substances and the frequent time deficits even when people did use bleach. All of these behaviors are associated with potential transmission of HIV (as well as hepatitis). These behaviors need to be specifically addressed in AIDS prevention education and counseling programs for injection-drug users. Structured observations are most useful for documenting behaviors of which people are only partially conscious or about which they have reason to be evasive.

THE STRUCTURED OBSERVATION AS A TOOL OF ETHNOGRAPHIC RESEARCH

Structured observation has been used in ethnographic studies for a variety of purposes, including: characterizing physical locations; understanding the "proxemic spacing" typical of a culture (i.e., how people use spatial arrangements in order to communicate nonverbally); determining the meanings of other forms of nonverbal communication (e.g., eye contact, body language); describing purchasing behaviors; analyzing the components of large and complex natural behavioral settings; describing shifts in group size and composition. Perhaps the most famous and ambitious research project to use structured observations was the Six Cultures Study directed by John and Beatrice Whiting beginning in the 1950s. Twenty-four children were selected in each of six locales (East Africa, Okinawa, Mexico, North India, the Philippines, New England), which were subdivided into behavioral settings (e.g., home, school, playground) where children would typically be found. The activities of the children were observed in each setting during a minimum of fourteen five-minute observation periods. The observers were to record the time and place of the activity, note the persons present, and describe all the stimuli that may have resulted in the observed behavior of the children. The Whitings' aim was to collect structured, systematic data in order to draw reliable conclusions about cultural differences in how children assert dominance, seek attention, initiate play, and reprimand other children.

I also used structured observations in a project I conducted in Ecuador. My focus was on purchasing behaviors of customers in two urban pharmacies. I wanted to document the kinds of prescription drugs bought without a prescription (which turned out to include the antibiotics tetracycline and chloramphenicol, as well as steroids, barbiturates, and clioquinol and dipyrone, drugs banned in most of the industrialized world because they are unsafe). Fifty-one percent of 619 observed sales transactions were for prescription drugs bought without prescriptions. Often as few as two or three capsules of antibiotic were bought in such transactions. I was also interested in describing the ways in which customers sought out drugstore clerks for medical advice.

Richard Lee used a structured-observation protocol in his widely read ethnographic study of the !Kung (Ju'/hoansi) San of southern Africa. His focus was on sources of food and composition of diet, and so he measured such things as: the distance people walked from camp to the gathering or hunting sites; the weight of nuts collected or animals killed per hour of labor; camp members' average caloric intake from both plant and animal sources; the number of different foods consumed; and social relationships of those who shared food of different types.

THE STRUCTURED OBSERVATION: THE PROCESS

The first step in designing a structured-observation study is to decide what specific questions you want to answer. It is usually a good idea to use this data-collection technique with a topic that you are already somewhat familiar, so that you will have a reasonably good idea of which variables are important and which measures of those variables will be most pertinent to the group under observation. When we drafted the protocol for the needle-hygiene study, for example, all three of us had prior experience in qualitative research with drug users. We selected the following items for observation based on those prior exposures:

- Date/time in/time out
- Name(s) of observer(s)
- Setting and context (e.g., house; car; shooting gallery)
- Participants (using ID numbers or pseudonyms)
- Descriptions of participants (age, ethnicity, sexual orientation, social relationships with each other)
- Chronology of events
- Description of injection equipment participants come in with: Are the syringes new, used, rented, or bought from someone at the site? Are cookers individual or common? Is rinse water individual or common? Are cottons individual or common?
- Drugs injected: Which ones? How were they procured?

- Description of sequential order of participants' needle-sharing; from whom do they borrow (i.e., social relationship)?; statements (if any) regarding their reasons for sharing
- Is there a pile of syringes at any point?
- Cleaning of syringes: With what? How long (carefully timed)?
- Record of other verbal interactions among participants (get verbatim quotes whenever possible)

Many of these items are standard for ethnographic observation, but note that we made sure to use ID numbers to preserve confidentiality. The observation of social relations among members of the group was particularly important for our purposes, as were the questions focused on the material culture (i.e., the injection equipment, its preparation and treatment) and the social relations that revolved around those items. Questions about cleaning the syringes were necessary in order to make recommendations about public health: water, alcohol, and bleach are commonly used to clean equipment, although only bleach will actually kill the HIV virus, and then only if it sits in the syringe for at least sixty seconds. We therefore used our watches to time exactly how many seconds the syringes were cleaned.

Verbal behaviors can be an important part of what you decide to include in a structured observation protocol. Because you are writing notes on so many different aspects of the situation, however, you probably will need to make a decision about what kinds of statements are most worthy of being recorded. After all, it takes some time to write down even a few sentences verbatim. A few pithy quotes are often worth as much as half a page of general notes on topics people talked about. In our protocol, we decided to try to record what people said about the drugs, about the drug equipment and how to handle it, and about HIV/AIDS.

The biggest problem in conducting structured observations is often information overload. In our project, the groups could be fairly large (five to seven people) and the action unfolded at a rapid pace (especially during the injection phase); it was a challenge to observe and record all the variables we had identified on our protocol. One solution to this problem was to have each observation conducted by a team of ethnographers; the researchers were positioned in different parts of the room. We undoubtedly missed some things, although certainly not as many as would have been the case with a solitary researcher.

Another potential problem in a project such as ours is cross-site consistency. Although all the ethnographers in all the seven sites were using the same protocol, it was not always possible for them to interpret the variables in the same way. Observers, in fact, varied in how much detail they recorded and in how much background information they collected.

A third issue has to do with the need to conduct some interviewing, as observation alone does not always provide all the information needed for a correct interpretation of the behaviors in question. We tried to ask questions that elicited contextual information, the better to understand what was going on at this particular time in this particular setting. Some background information can be collected at the beginning of the observation, and some questions designed to clarify what just happened are most appropriately left to the end. But the main part of the behavior should be allowed to flow without the researchers' intervention.

YOUR PROJECT

Food is loaded with cultural meanings, and people have a lot to say about what they prefer to eat and what it means to them. But food consumption also calls for observational methods. While not covert in the same way that drug use is, food consumption is often the result of unconscious cues, and our ways of talking about it may be colored, and hence obscured, by our notions of what is socially acceptable. Therefore, your assignment is to observe multiple people eating at a fast-food restaurant. Your main research questions will be: a) What are the food choices that people are actually making? b) How much of their daily caloric and fat consumption do these choices entail? c) Although we call it "fast food," how fast do people actually eat in such places? d) Do customers use these outlets to socialize with others (as opposed to just eating)? e) Do they seem to be enjoying themselves?

To carry out this research, you must first devise an observation protocol. It will probably include many of the same variables noted on our needle-hygiene study protocol (e.g., date, location, time in/out, ethnographic observer(s), setting and context, chronology of events). Each person observed should be assigned either a letter or a pseudonym to preserve confidentiality and should be described in terms of gender, estimated age, ethnicity, probable social relationships with others at the table, and body shape/weight. A small sketch of how the people are arranged at the table will be useful in understanding your notes on group interaction.

If you are working alone, your protocol should be made up primarily of the starred items below; if you are working as a team, you may include other items as time permits. Suggested points to observe:

*• What items are bought? Who did the purchasing? Did everyone stand in line together, or did one person buy everything to bring back to the table?

*• What are the food choices of each person in the group?

*• How much time does a group spend, from the moment they come in the door (include both standing in line waiting for their order and then at the table)? Note that this process should be timed with a watch, at least in minutes, if not in seconds.

- Is food choice a focus of discussion between adults and children, or among adults themselves? (Note that it may or may not be possible to hear such verbal interaction; observation in a public place is taken for granted, but it is just common courtesy to avoid obvious eavesdropping.) Are toys or other promotional items part of the choices being made?

*• What is the caloric and fat content of the items? (Many fast food restaurants now post these measures. Try to choose a restaurant that does so.)

- Are people sharing their food? If so, who is sharing with whom?

*• What is the nature of the social interaction of groups eating together?

- How much eye contact is there? (This variable could also be timed, if it seems important to you to do so.)

- How would you characterize the tone of voice (pleasant, excited, angry, etc.)? Is anyone eating in silence? (This variable should be sampled at least three or four times during each group's meal, at regularly spaced intervals of, say, five minutes.)

- Who is doing most of the talking, and who is less talkative? (Remember to use the ID or pseudonym.)

*• Does anyone go back for more food? What items do they get? (Add any such additions to your calorie/fat inventory.)

- What reaction, if any, is there to someone going back for more?

- What kind of mood does the group appear to be in when they exit the restaurant?

- Do they take any food with them? If so, what?

- Do they clear their places? Who in the group does so?

Once you have selected your variables, type them up as a formal protocol. A notebook is useful for recording notes and maps of the observation site. As in the needle-hygiene study, your analysis will include both qualitative characterizations and quantitative data. When you have finished your analysis, you should be able to draw some conclusions about fast-food chains and how they relate to both food consumption and the social interactions centered on food.

A FEW SELECTED READINGS FOR FURTHER INFORMATION

Lee, Richard B. 1993. *The Dobe !Kung*. New York: Holt, Rinehart and Winston.

Price, Laurie J. 1989. In the Shadow of Biomedicine: Self-medication in Two Ecuadorian Pharmacies. *Social Science and Medicine* 28(9):905–915.

Whiting, John W. M., Irvin L. Child, and William W. Lambert. 1966. *Field Guide for the Study of Socialization*. New York: Wiley.

9

Designing a Questionnaire for Cross-Cultural Research

Roberta D. Baer & Susan C. Weller

A RESEARCH PROJECT

In 1989, Roberta Baer, Susan Weller, Lee Pachter, and Robert Trotter were attending the annual meetings of the Society for Applied Anthropology, where they discovered that they had all done separate studies of the folk illness *empacho*. *Empacho* is an illness characterized by gastrointestinal symptoms and is common in Latino populations. Pachter and associates carried out research on Puerto Ricans in the northeastern United States; Trotter studied *empacho* and other folk illnesses among Mexican-Americans in the southwestern United States; Baer investigated *empacho* in Mexico; and Weller and associates worked in Guatemala. The four anthropologists realized, however, that since they had used different data-collection techniques in their separate studies, it

was difficult to compare their findings. They could not even determine defini-
tively whether *empacho* was the same illness in all these populations. They
therefore decided to construct and administer a single questionnaire that
could be used at all four research sites. They were ultimately able to conclude
that there was indeed a shared set of beliefs about susceptibility, causes, symptoms, and treatments that characterized *empacho* across these four regions.

That experience led to a series of cross-cultural studies of illnesses, both
those recognized by the biomedical establishment and those defined mainly
in the experiences of everyday, nonprofessional people ("folk" illnesses).
Their research dealt with AIDS, diabetes, colds, asthma, *nervios, caida de mol-
lera, susto,* and *mal de ojo.* These illnesses were selected because they represented a range of conditions among Latin American populations. Studies
initially concentrated on the four regions mentioned above. In the United
States, interviews were conducted with Puerto Ricans in Hartford, Connecticut, a medium-sized city in the northeastern United States with a population
that is approximately one-third Hispanic. Also in the United States, interviews were conducted with Mexican-Americans in Edinburg, Texas, a largely
Hispanic town in an agricultural region of the lower Rio Grande Valley along
the US-Mexico border. Outside the United States, interviews were conducted
in Guadalajara, a large industrialized city in central Mexico. Residents of
Guadalajara are from both rural and urban backgrounds and are predominantly *mestizo* (Spanish speakers who do not identify with an indigenous
group). Another international site was in Guatemala, among Spanish-speaking *ladinos* (a local term equivalent to *mestizo* in Mexico) in four rural villages
on the agricultural Pacific coastal plain in the department of Esquintla.

Although slight differences were expected in these various Hispanic
populations, the researchers decided to do some additional interviews among
middle-class Americans of predominantly northern European origin, mainly
to add another cross-cultural dimension to the study. These interviews (dealing only with AIDS and the common cold) were conducted in Tampa, a
medium-sized city in west central Florida.

The first concern in designing these linked studies was to create interview materials that were truly comparable, even though they were to be
administered in communities with different demographic and cultural characteristics. The interview locations were selected for their socioeconomic,
historical, and ethnic differences. Interviewing and informant selection took
place in two stages. First, a "convenience sample" of 20 women was selected
at each of the four Latino sites for open-ended, descriptive interviewing. A
"convenience" sample, as the name implies, is simply a sample of people who
are members of the population of interest and who are available and amenable to being interviewed. The purpose at this initial point in the study was
simply to gather themes, topics, and descriptions, not to form conclusions or
make generalizations, which would require a representative sample.

Responses from the open-ended, descriptive interviews were used to
develop questionnaires. Data were gathered on the perceived causes, symp-

toms, and treatments of each of the illness. We used a "free-listing" technique (i.e., we asked the respondents to list as many causes, symptoms, and treatments as they knew about, rather than restricting them to a list of choices preset by the research team). Listing-type questions collect more information per respondent than simple short-answer questions. We made sure to record and use verbatim responses in the informants' language, so that preparing the questionnaires would be more straightforward (paraphrasing, especially in another language, could introduce unwarranted interpretation or bias into the process). Items that were listed by at least 10% of each sample were included in the structured questionnaires. We also incorporated items and themes obtained from the Cornell Medical Index and some concepts that had been reported in the literature by ethnographic researchers working on other illnesses.

A true-false questionnaire was developed for each of the illnesses in the study. Each instrument had an average of 130 questions about possible causes, symptoms, and treatments. Each questionnaire also included basic demographic data on the respondents, as well as questions about personal experiences with the illness. Each questionnaire was translated into the form of Spanish or English spoken at each site. Since free-listing interviews had preceded the creation of a formal questionnaire, we had the most salient items for each site, and since most items were obtained verbatim from each site in Spanish, most of those items were modified only minimally for use at all four sites. In general, the adequacy of the translation (Spanish to Spanish) was verified by reviewing all the questions, one by one, with two local interviewers.

After the structured interview materials were developed, we sought representative samples for interviewing at each site. Because of the differences between the sites, different strategies were used to select the samples. For both of the US sites, a two-stage random sampling design was used. First, a sampling unit (e.g., a census tract or a neighborhood) was selected. Then, an actual city block was selected, and households on the block were approached for interviewing. In Edinburg, the entire city was sampled from the census tracts. In Hartford, interviews were conducted in the census tracts with the highest concentration of Puerto Ricans. For the international sites, a different strategy was used. In Guadalajara, sampling focused on three neighborhoods, representing the social and economic variation in the city: middle class, working class, and poor. Each type of neighborhood was sampled in proportion to the percentage it represented in the total population of the city. The appropriate number of blocks was randomly selected, and then houses. In Guatemala, the communities were small enough so that a simple strategy could be used: households were selected, moving from the center to the periphery (to capture the range of social-class variation) in each of the four villages. For the fifth site a strategy was used similar to that in Mexico. In Tampa, interviews were conducted in two middle-income neighborhoods, with blocks and houses determined by random sampling.

Our main interest was in beliefs among Latinos. In both Edinburg and Hartford, we relied on people's self-identification as either Mexican-American or Puerto Rican, respectively. We preferred to interview adults (who would have more experience with the selected illnesses), and usually focused on women, who are typically the household members with the most responsibility for heath care. Interviews were conducted by local interviewers fluent in the local dialect. In Texas and Connecticut, Spanish or a combination of Spanish and English was used, according to the preference of the respondent. In Tampa, interviews were conducted by graduate students as part of a class project.

THE QUESTIONNAIRE AS A TOOL OF CROSS-CULTURAL ETHNOGRAPHIC RESEARCH: A BRIEF OVERVIEW

Anthropology has always been interested in cross-cultural comparisons, but for the most part researchers have had to rely on data collected by different scholars, using different methods, at different points in time. A more modern approach to cross-cultural research involves the attempt to standardize the process, making sure that a group of researchers will be using the same instrument in the same way in order to elicit truly comparable information from informants in various research sites. A questionnaire is often the most efficient tool for data collection in this context, since it minimizes (although it cannot eliminate completely) the subjective variation that might be introduced in other forms of ethnographic research. A good questionnaire from an anthropological perspective is one that grows directly out of a more broadly based ethnographic understanding of the community in which it is to be administered. The anthropological purpose would be defeated were the questionnaire to be devised by the researchers in their offices, and then taken out to the field. Rather, the questionnaire should be designed only after considerable ethnographic exposure to the people and the settings to be surveyed.

In creating our cross-cultural questionnaires, we followed the basic rules of questionnaire construction. As anthropologists, we believe that a structured questionnaire is only useful if it captures the reality of the people being studied. As such, the initial part of any investigation should focus on the collection of qualitative data on the topic under investigation. The goal is to identify issues of interest to the population being studied that are also relevant to the topic under investigation. It is of great importance to discover if the topic you are concerned with is relevant to the people you are studying and to find out the appropriate questions to ask. This initial stage of qualitative investigation can use any ethnographic technique, such as participant observation, key informant interviews, as well as more structured techniques such as free listing (Weller 1998) or focus groups. The key is to find out enough background information on how the population you are studying conceptualizes the topic under consideration. An excellent resource for this stage of the investigation is Spradley's (1979) book on *Ethnographic Interviewing*.

The next stage of the process is to analyze the qualitative data and use them to develop a structured questionnaire. Such questionnaires also generally include basic demographic data, as well as inclusion and exclusion criteria. If you only want a certain type of person in your sample (e.g., Latino), it is important to determine immediately if the person you are approaching meets your criteria for interviewing.

Using questionnaires as the basis of cross-cultural research requires that the questionnaire be designed so that the same question is asked in a meaningful way in each population under study. The questions may have to be rephrased so that they are understandable to people of different ethnic and linguistic backgrounds, even though they are tapping into the same basic body of knowledge. An important issue in adapting standardized questionnaires, such as those used in general health or mental health research, is whether the topic itself is even understood by the population being studied. Martha Ward (2005), in her book *Nest in the Wind*, discusses the problems of trying to do a study on high blood pressure and possible cardiovascular disease as a response to social stress and cultural change in a population that has no concept of or words for "heart disease" and "blood pressure." In such situations, it may be necessary to add items to the standardized questionnaire.

THE ETHNOGRAPHIC QUESTIONNAIRE: THE PROCESS

Our research project encountered a number of important issues during the process of designing an effective set of questions suitable for cross-cultural research; although the details are, of course, specific to our particular research settings, they illustrate problems that are of concern to any researchers who use this data-collection technique.

Perhaps the most basic issue is one of translation. In our case, even though virtually all our Latino respondents spoke Spanish, there were discernible regional variations in the vocabulary. The problem, to be sure, is magnified in cross-cultural research in which completely different languages may be used. For example, our questionnaire relating to the illness known as mal de ojo ("evil eye") included (in English) a somewhat puzzling question: "Does sweeping a person with a big pepper help treat mal de ojo?" In Spanish, it was no less odd: "Para tratar mal de ojo, se le pasa la enfermo con un chile." The item was included because in the original free-list interviews from Guatemala, *pimienta gorda* had been a frequent response. The person who created the draft questionnaire, however, was not Guatemalan, and translated the term *pimienta* (from the original *pimienta gorda* [literally fat pepper in English]) as the familiar Mexican-American *chile*. The whole term then became *chile gorda* ("fat chile"). And when chile gorda was translated back to English, the result was "big pepper." When Baer tried to use the questionnaire at her site in Guadalajara, she quickly realized that it made no sense in either Mexican Spanish or in English. From prior experience conducting fieldwork in Guatemala, she knew that what had been intended was not a chile at all, but a cooking spice—allspice (known as *pimienta gorda* in Guatemala). She was unsure of how to translate allspice into Mexican Spanish until she searched a local supermarket and found a jar labeled *pimienta dulce* ("sweet pepper").

Another issue was the preferred language for the interviews. We initially assumed that the preferred language in south Texas would be Spanish, and had prepared a locally acceptable Spanish version of each question. However, some respondents used Tex-Mex, which is a combination of Spanish and English for their interview. A problem, however, emerged on the *mal de ojo* questionnaire regarding the use of *barridas* as a treatment. The word is commonly translated into English as "sweeping," because in healing rituals the healer may literally sweep a branch of herbs or other material over the body of the affected person; but the south Texas respondents did not recognize the English word in this context. So although some questionnaires were administered in English, the Spanish word *barrida* needed to be retained to describe this particular treatment.

One item used on a number of the questionnaires dealt with the role of drinking unboiled water as a cause of illness. The Spanish version of this question administered in Guatemala and Mexico made complete sense; in those areas, most tap water is not safe to drink unless it is boiled. The English version of this question administered in south Texas also made sense, as that population was familiar with the problem of unsafe tap water through contact with family members on the Mexican sides of the border. When, however, the question was pretested in Tampa, where most people drink the municipally processed tap water, it proved confusing. We reworded it to read, "Can drinking unboiled or impure water cause this illness?"

Slang usage of certain terms was a factor in the revision of the one of the questions on the English version of the AIDS questionnaire administered in Tampa. The original English question was, "With AIDS, does a person want to eat sweet things?" In some gay populations, this question would have had a sexual connotation, and so we reworded it as, "With AIDS, does a person want to eat or crave sweet things or sweet foods?"

Moving interview materials through different languages—or even different dialects of the same language—can be difficult. Cross-cultural psychologists have probably written the most about these issues, as they are central to cross-cultural testing. A key issue in any interviewing process is that the questions must be interpreted in the same way by all respondents. The best way to begin to create comparable interview materials is to begin with open-ended or free-listed interviews to collect salient, verbatim responses. Incorporation of those responses or themes into more structured interview materials ensures that locally relevant themes are used and are couched in the local language. The free-listing interviews with probes should be used to elicit clear, understandable items that, when repeated to others, are interpreted in the same way. Incorporation of these verbatim responses simply avoids many problems inherent in working with multiple groups.

Once questions are written, their "interpretability" can be tested. During a set of pilot interviews (done with individuals or in groups), respondents may be asked to respond to questions and to "think out loud" about what the question means, what possible answers might be, and how they arrive at a response. The goal is to modify questions so that each and every one is interpreted in the same way by each and every informant.

Cross-cultural psychologists recommend that translation adequacy be achieved through the use of two full translation loops. In other words, the material is translated from the original language to the second and then back again. Two pairs of translators (four people) should go through this process, and the results should be compared. The double translation in and out of the source language at each loop helps ensure that concepts can, in fact, move between the two languages.

During the course of developing four (or five) separate versions of nine illness questionnaires of 125–130 questions, we were able to correct most problems with questions during initial pilot testing, although a few slipped by and were not corrected until the final version of the structured questionnaire was prepared. In a few instances, the problems were not even evident until data analysis had begun. Nevertheless, we do not believe that these problems are so numerous as to discourage others from undertaking questionnaire-based cross-cultural research.

YOUR PROJECT

You (working independently or as part of a team) are to select a topic that is appropriate to study in populations of different cultural backgrounds. For example, you might want to learn more about family, diet, work, or other aspects of life that are found in every culture. Make up at least ten questions in English that address your chosen topic. Using a "convenience sample," ask key informants to list all the things they can on the topic (free-listing technique). You might perhaps ask someone to list all the foods that might be eaten at a morning meal. Be careful to phrase questions so that they request information and are not answerable with a simple "yes" or "no." Be sure to get clarification on all responses, so that another respondent would know exactly what was meant by the reply.

You can use the responses to these interviews to then design a structured interview. The advantage of a structured interview is that all respondents must answer the same questions. When all respondents answer the same questions, answers can be compared across people and across sites. When different questions are asked of different people, answers cannot be compared across the groups. A structured questionnaire might be a set of true/false questions to estimate cultural values and beliefs, or it might contain questions that involve ratings like attitudinal scales or some other kind of task. For now, all the questions should be on a single topic and all in the same format.

Find at least two different cultural groups in which to administer the questionnaire. (Depending on the size of your project team, you can expand the numbers of groups to be surveyed.) Try to work with groups that contrast in terms of their ethnicity, social class, educational level, age, gender, or some other recognizable demographic factor. Unless you are fluent in other languages, it might be more efficient if you can find contrasting groups composed of speakers of English. Identify at least ten people from each group to whom you will administer your questionnaire. With such a very small sample, you can come up with suggestive trends in need of more comprehensive research; you cannot establish general patterns in any conclusive way.

Alternatively, take an interview that has already been standardized and administered in some population, and check to see whether it is meaningful in a local population that may not have been part of the original administration. For example, Baer took a survey widely used by mental-health professionals to assess the level of psychological problems among populations in the United States and administered it to Mexican and Mexican-American farmworkers in Florida. She found that their responses regarding symptoms would have been interpreted by clinical psychologists as signs of depression, although the people themselves understood their condition as resulting from exhaustion due to hard physical work. You can do a similar exercise by taking a standard survey and administering it to several representatives of a local population. When you do so, make sure that you get, in addition to the answers to the questions themselves, explanations of what the respondents thought the questions meant, and why they answered the way they did.

In either case, your report should include a brief summary of your findings (i.e., what did you learn from the responses to the questionnaire?), although the focus should be on the process: write about how you developed the survey instrument, and discuss the ways in which it was understood (or not) by everyone to whom it was administered. Which questions would need to be reworded, and how? To what extent did you encounter any of the translation problems discussed above?

REFERENCES

Spradley, James P. 1979. *The Ethnographic Interview.* Fort Worth: Harcourt Brace Jovanovich.

Ward, Martha. 2005. *Nest in the Wind*, 2nd ed. Long Grove, IL: Waveland Press.

Weller, Susan C. 1998 Structured Interviewing and Questionnaire Construction. In *Handbook of Methods in Cultural Anthropology*, ed. H. Russell Bernard, 365–409, Walnut Creek, CA: Sage.

A FEW SELECTED READINGS FOR FURTHER INFORMATION

Baer, Roberta D. 1989. Lead Based Remedies for *Empacho*: Patterns and Consequences. *Social Science and Medicine* 29(12):1373–1379.

———. 1996. Health and Mental Health among Mexican-American Migrant Workers: Implications for Survey Research. *Human Organization* 55:58–66.

Baer, Roberta D., and Susan C. Weller. 1999. Beliefs about AIDS in Five Latin and Anglo-American Populations. *Anthropology and Medicine* 6(1):13–29.

———. 1999. Cross-Cultural Perspectives on the Common Cold. *Human Organization* 58(3):251–260.

Brislin, Richard. 1986. The Wording and Translation of Research Instruments. In *Field Methods in Cross-Cultural Research*, ed. Walter J. Looner and John W. Berry, 137–164. Beverly Hills, CA: Sage.

Pachter, Lee, B. Bernstein, and A. Osorio. 1992. *Empacho* in a Mainland Puerto Rican Population. *Medical Anthropology* 13(4):285–299.

Trotter, Robert. 1985. Greta and Azarcon. *Human Organization* 44(1):64–72.

Trotter, Robert, Susan C. Weller, and Roberta D. Baer. Consensus Theory Model of AIDS/SIDA in Four Latino Populations. *AIDS Education and Prevention* 11(5):414–426.

Weller, Susan C., and Roberta D. Baer. 1999. Latino Beliefs about Diabetes. *Diabetes Care* 22(5):722–728.

Weller, Susan C., Lee Pachter, Robert Trotter, and Roberta D. Baer. 1993. *Empacho* in Four Latino Groups. *Medical Anthropology* 15:109–136.

Weller, Susan C., T. K. Ruebush, and R. Klein. 1990. An Epidemiological Description of a Folk Illness. *Medical Anthropology* 13:19–31.

10

Working with Numerical Data

Martha W. Rees

A RESEARCH PROJECT

Introductory courses in the social sciences sometimes leave students with the impression that there is a sharp and permanent divide between ethnographic data (which are presumed to be subjective, impressionistic, and somehow "soft") and numerical data (which are thought to be objective, scientific, and "hard"). But in fact most social scientists need to learn how to work comfortably with both kinds of data, and certain kinds of research questions actually call for a creative combination of the two. For example, I have been involved in a study of the growing Latino presence in Atlanta, and at one point a question arose as to the number of immigrant Mexican women in the population. Since there were no published census figures that could supply an easy answer, our research team used a combination of ethnographic means in order to come up with some workable estimated numbers.

We know that the number of Latino women in the US labor market is on the rise, but the category "Latino" includes non-Mexicans and non-immigrants, but does refer to people of Latin American origin. Definitions of ethnic categories are political in nature. Decisions about who is Latino influence: school budgets; the availability of English-as-a-Second-Language (ESL) training; the allocation of resources for bilingual education and translation services; and the languages in which ballots and driver's license exams are printed. In the United States, native-born citizens (some of whom have roots in the region that go back to before there even was a United States) who speak Spanish or have Spanish surnames are typically lumped together with more recent migrants from the Americas and other parts of the Spanish-speaking world. Given the broadness of the category, we have to take published figures with a grain of salt. So when we read that the participation of "Latino women" in the labor force increased 14% between 1960 and 1980, we must ask whether this increase is due to immigration or to the presence of more US citizens of Latino descent entering the workforce.

Within the larger category of "Latino," there is a demographically important subcategory of people of Mexican heritage. We know that the number of Mexican migrants to the US has been increasing, but information about the characteristics of that migrant population is sketchy. And information about women within that migrant population is still harder to obtain. Most of the research on Mexican migration has focused on males who leave their homeland to work and then send remittances back to their families. Scholars working with this "push" theory of migration assume that male migration is an individual income-maximizing strategy. The real situation, however, is almost certainly more complex. For one thing, women who stay at home are not simply idly waiting for remittance payments; most women work for pay, and their incomes actually make it possible for the men to migrate. Moreover, remittances do form the third largest source of foreign exchange in Mexico and cannot be underestimated as an important factor in people's decisions about earning a living; but it is clear that there is increasing female migration as well—women are entering the US either as individuals or to join husbands, and most of them become part of the workforce as they do so.

The pace of Mexican migration to the US increased in the 1980s, and this new wave of migrants seems to have included more families and more single women. Conditions in Mexico contributed to this upsurge in migration: in 1986 the price of petroleum fell and Mexico, for the first time in three decades, suffered negative economic growth and triple-digit inflation. One result of this economic crisis was lower wages; indeed, wages in Mexico fell to their lowest point in 1987. Recovery of international confidence came at the cost of salary increases and social subsidies. Economic conditions worsened for the working and middle classes and the potential for social unrest increased. The crisis encouraged both males and females to move from Mexico to the United States, where wages were higher.

At the same time, the US economy was undergoing changes of its own. US companies were moving production to lower-wage areas, including Mexico, and the labor market in the US itself became increasingly service-oriented. But there was still a need for cheap, low-skilled labor, and many employers seemed to prefer undocumented migrants for such tasks, since undocumented laborers tend to be more compliant, living as they do in constant fear of deportation.

In sum, Mexican migration to the United States can only be explained in terms of multiple local, national, and global factors. Female migration also requires a multi-dimensional explanation; it must also take into account household characteristics and women's activities in Mexico. Entire households may be more likely to migrate if there is work for both spouses, which seems to be the case in Atlanta, which has a high demand for workers in meatpacking and domestic services.

Atlanta is the largest urban center in the southeastern United States, and since the 1980s the region has undergone profound social, cultural, and demographic change. Historically the region had been home to two main ethnic groups: African-Americans and European-Americans. In the 1970s and 1980s, however, more than 10,000 migrants and refugees from Vietnam arrived, changing not only the ethnic make-up, but also the political, economic, and social relations of the region. The Latino population of Georgia has also grown, especially in the metropolitan area of Atlanta, made up of Fulton, DeKalb, Gwinnett, Cobb, and Cherokee counties. Latinos now form the largest nontraditional minority group, growing in numbers from 30,000 in 1982 to over 110,000 in 1992, a 260% increase in ten years. Between 1992 and 1996, the Latino population of the Atlanta metro area grew to over 231,619, an increase of 100% in just six years. Four percent of this population (9,571 individuals) are children in school whose first language is Spanish.

The increase in the number of Latinos in the southeastern US indicates that there is a specific demand for their labor, due in part to construction associated with the 1996 Olympic Games, but also to the growth of industries such as meatpacking, carpet and textile manufacture, and services in homes, gardens, and restaurants.

This Latino population is, by common agreement, undercounted in census figures. In order to find out about Mexican women (a subset of a subcategory within that larger population), it is necessary to estimate. Our research team therefore used whatever census figures were available, but supplemented them with survey data and ethnographic data. The survey data were collected during the course of interviews with both male and female Mexican migrants in Atlanta in 1998 (T. Danyael Miller and Mariposa Arillo, research scholars at Agnes Scott College, helped collect the data), and the ethnographic information resulted from interviews extending from 1993 to 2000.

WORKING WITH NUMERICAL DATA: THE PROCESS

I interviewed intake personnel at health, religious, and social service agencies about the percentage of Latinos who are Mexican. Ethnographic data from social service centers that deal with Latinos indicate that about 90% of Latinos are Mexican. Thinking it best to err on the side of caution, I used the figure of 80% as a working estimate. So if there are, by official count, 231,619 Latinos in the Atlanta metropolitan area, there should be 185,295 Mexicans. Of these, how many are women? The answer is not so easily ascertained. Although historically the majority of Mexican immigrants have been male, the situation is certainly changing, and so historical estimates may no longer be useful. Many Mexicans are undocumented, and women in particular seem to enter the US without papers, a situation that makes them all the more difficult to count. Since our research team lacked the resources to carry out a large-scale survey of all women in the metropolitan area to determine how many were Mexican, we designed a survey questionnaire that asked for basic demographic and household information and applied it to an opportunity sample of Mexican women in the metropolitan area. We interviewed forty-nine women in the spring of 1998 at the Mexican consulate, at a social service center, at a local Catholic mission, and elsewhere as the opportunity arose. We found many more women than expected—at a Catholic mass, more than half were women (compared, however, to 90% in Mexico). There are lots of Mexican women (*mexicanas*) working in restaurants, in domestic service, in meatpacking companies, in carpet factories, and in hotels. How could we get at a reasonably accurate number?

We started with some data that we actually did have. We knew, for example, that in 1996 there were at least 9,571 children in public schools whose first language was Spanish. If the proportion of Mexicans in the larger Latino population is the same for children as for adults (80%, as noted above), then there were 7,656 Mexican children in school. Women are obviously linked to their children, and we thought we could calculate the number of women on the basis of the average number of children that each woman has. The forty-nine women represented in our survey had a total of twenty-six children of school age (i.e., between the ages of six and eighteen). Each woman therefore had an average of .53 children. So if one child represents two women, the 7,656 Mexican children represent 14,445 Mexican women. I concluded that there were therefore about 14,000 Mexican women in Atlanta in early 1999. (The continued rapid growth in the number of Mexicans in the metropolitan area means that this figure must be revised upward.)

This estimate must be used with some caution. First, it is based on an opportunity sample, not a random sample. We do not know the size (or even the location) of the entire population of Mexican women, so we cannot draw a statistically accurate sample. By sampling different venues, we tried to cover different types of Mexican women (those who come to clinics with their children, to the consulate for official documents, and so forth), but again we do not know the characteristics of the population as a whole, so we can only guess as to the degree to which the women we interviewed were representative. Since our survey was carried out in social service agencies, it may be biased toward working-class migrants, although all kinds of Mexicans come to the consulate. It may well be that the results of an opportunity sample are as accurate as those of a truly random sample, but we cannot count on such a convergence. Another problem with the survey is that it may overestimate the number of children in school. Many Mexican children drop out between tenth and eleventh grade. Moreover, some of the women may have children (especially older ones) back in Mexico.

Despite these problems, it was necessary to work with our estimate. More and more mexicanas are migrating to the US in general, and to Atlanta in particular. Atlanta seems to be a destination of choice for younger women who follow their husbands within a few years of their marriage and his initial migration. If the 1999 estimate of 14,000 Mexican women in Atlanta is even roughly correct, then they were still a small portion of the Mexican population of 185,000, which itself was 80% of the total Latino population. But we have every reason to believe that women are systematically undercounted, a problem that has only increased since 1996 when schools were no longer required to collect and report data about Spanish-speaking students—a main source of the inferences in our estimate. The presence of Mexican women in Atlanta obviously affects the Mexican community, social services, employment, and culture—factors that will become ever more important as the numbers continue to grow. It is to our advantage to develop more accurate ways of counting their numbers. Until then, estimates based on ethnographic data collection will have to do.

YOUR PROJECT

In addition to undocumented immigrants, there are many undercounted, almost hidden populations in our midst. For example, how would you count the homeless, HIV-positive people, gays and lesbians, or drug users? Getting at least some estimates for any of these groups would have a real impact on the nature and delivery of social and health services. Select one such population in your local area. It is probably best to work as a team, whose assignment is to predict changes in demand for health or other social services as a result of changes in an undercounted, underserved population. Using a combination of published census or other official figures and ethnographic surveys and/or interviews, as we did in the Atlanta study, come up with a working estimate of the number of people in your selected population. Your report should also include a discussion of the pros and cons of the process, particularly with regard to the reliability and validity of the selected measures.

A FEW SELECTED READINGS FOR FURTHER INFORMATION

Babbie, Earl. 1994. *The Practice of Social Research.* Belmont, CA: Wadsworth.

Bustamante, Jorge, Clark W. Reynolds, and Raúl A. Hinojosa Ojeda. 1992. *U.S.–Mexico Relations: Labor Market Interdependences.* Stanford, CA: Stanford University Press.

Castells, Manuel. 1980. *The Economic Crisis and American Society.* Princeton, NJ: Princeton University Press.

Collins, Jane. 1988. *Unseasonal Migrations: The Effects of Rural Labor Scarcity in Peru.* Princeton, NJ: Princeton University Press.

Cornelius, Wayne A. 1991. Los Migrantes de la Crisis: The Changing Profile of Mexican Migration to the U.S. In *Social Responses to Mexico's Economic Crisis of the 1980s,* ed. Mercedes González de la Rocha and Agustín Escobar Latapí, 155–192. San Diego: University of California, San Diego, Center for U.S.–Mexican Studies.

Donato, Katherine. 1992. Current Trends and Patterns of Female Migration: Evidence from Mexico. *International Migration Review* 27(4):748–771.

Hondagneu-Sotelo, Pierrette. 1994. *Gendered Transitions: Mexican Experiences of Immigration.* Berkeley: University of California Press.

Jenkins, J. Craig. 1977. Push/Pull in Recent Mexican Migration to the U.S. *International Migration Review* 11:178–189.

Massey, Douglas S., Joaquín Arango, Graeme Hugo, Ali Kouaouci, Adela Pellerino, and J. Edward Taylor. 1994. An Evaluation of International Migration Theory: The North American Case. *Population and Development Review* 20(4):899–951.

Stier, Haya, and Marta Tienda. 1992. Family, Work, and Women: The Labor Supply of Hispanic Immigrant Wives. *International Migration Review* 26(4):1291–1313.

11

Planning and Moderating Focus Group Research

Carol Bryant

A RESEARCH PROJECT

In 1993, I directed a social marketing research project for the Texas Department of Health to increase participation in the Special Supplemental Nutrition Program for Women, Infants and Children (WIC) (Bryant et al. 2001). WIC offers nutrition information, supplemental food packages, health screenings and referrals, and immunizations to pregnant women, infants, and children living in households that fall below 250% of the poverty guidelines. Numerous studies have documented the program's positive impact on the nutritional status of pregnant women, nursing mothers, and young children as well as reductions in low birth weight, preterm delivery, and fetal death. Yet, despite these benefits, many families who were eligible for the program were not participating; therefore the Texas Department of Health had to return millions of dollars of unused funds to the federal government. For help in developing a strategic plan to boost enrollment, the Texas Department of

115

Health turned to Best Start Social Marketing Inc. I was hired to direct the consumer research needed to understand why families in need of WIC services did not enroll in the program or why they quit after signing up.

Although some studies rely exclusively on focus groups, in this project I used a variety of qualitative and quantitative methods (Bryant et al. 2001). Focus groups were used in the earliest phases of the project to identify the issues or concerns of greatest importance to consumers and the appropriate vocabulary to use in questionnaires for surveying large, random samples of program users, eligible nonusers, and staff members. Group interviews also were used to gain a more in-depth understanding of survey results, especially some families' reluctance to accept governmental assistance. The focus group research provided important insights that supplemented those gained from other sources and played an essential role in designing strategies to solve the problem.

FOCUS GROUP RESEARCH AS A TOOL OF ETHNOGRAPHIC RESEARCH

I selected focus groups as a technique for collecting data in Texas because I wanted to hear what people had to say about the WIC program when talking with their peers as well as observe how the information they learned from each other influenced their decisions about program participation. Group interaction is a central feature of focus groups—the researcher carefully moderates the group's discussion to uncover individual members' opinions and observe how participants influence each other's ideas. Because of this interaction, focus groups enable researchers to explore group norms and attitudes, making them valuable in many cross-cultural situations (Kitzinger 1995).

As participants share ideas during the interview, they may reach consensus on some topics; but it is equally valuable when they do not. Dissent allows the moderator to hear the reasoning behind differing viewpoints and observe the strength of participants' convictions as they defend their positions. Because the Texas Health Department wanted to convince eligible families to enroll in WIC, it was especially useful to learn how some discussants persuaded others in the group to join the program.

Focus groups are an ideal methodology for an exploratory study like the Texas WIC project because they generate a breadth of new information rapidly. In contrast to individual interviews, in which one person's ideas are explored in-depth, focus groups allow six or more people to discuss their norms, beliefs, and experiences related to a given topic. The group composition and questions are carefully planned to create a nonthreatening environment conductive to revelation and disclosure. As the discussion unfolds, various opinions are quickly uncovered. Participants are allowed to ask questions, pursue related topics of interest to them, and lead the discussion in unexpected directions, revealing important information that may otherwise elude the researcher (Kitzinger 1995). In Texas, I learned a great deal from the exchange between people unfamiliar with WIC and those who had experience with the program. Many families expressed interest in enrolling in the program after learning from others that WIC offers more than nutritious food. Program administrators had not realized that nutrition education and health checkups were valuable to many families and had promoted the program as a source of free food.

Focus groups also were appropriate for this project because I needed to learn how people talked about the program. Because focus group participants talk with peers in an informal setting, they use everyday vocabulary, jokes, and culturally appropriate forms of disagreeing. In Texas, focus groups revealed how people talked about the program's benefits and barriers, allowing us to construct questions for surveys and advertising messages using vocabulary Texas families understood.

As with all data collection techniques, focus groups have important limitations that must be respected. The quality of data generated is highly dependent on the moderator's skills and ability to interact with discussants. Results can be misleading if some discussants are allowed to dominate the discussion and others fail to share their views. Also, focus group results should not be quantified. While it is fine to report that an issue was raised in a specific number of groups, it does not make sense to report how many individuals shared a certain point of view because not everyone has an opportunity to answer each question. Also, because focus group research relies on a small, nonrandom sample, results cannot be generalized to a larger population. Finally, the researcher cannot prevent participants from sharing what has been discussed during the interview, raising ethical questions about confidentiality and the topics that can be covered.

FOCUS GROUP RESEARCH: A BRIEF HISTORY

Social scientists have conducted group interviews since the early 1900s, but the development of the technique we know as focus groups is usually credited to sociologists Robert Merton and Paul Lazerfield, who worked together at Columbia University during the 1940s. Initially, they used focus groups to evaluate radio broadcasts, but during World War II they expanded their use to develop and test a variety of military training and propaganda materials and explore other war-related social issues (Morgan 1998a).

For approximately thirty years after the war, focus groups were used almost exclusively by commercial marketers. In addition to testing advertising concepts and messages, they used focus groups to study consumer opinions of commercial products; identify the need for new products and services; identify reasons people buy products; and pretest advertising messages. In most instances, focus group research was conducted by practitioners working for marketing research and advertising firms. Because many of these researchers were psychologists, they experimented with group discussions to obtain a deeper understanding of consumer motivations than those revealed in individual home surveys (Goldman and McDonald 1987). Unfortunately, few academics used focus groups during this time, so the method was over-looked in the scholarly literature and business curriculum until the late 1980s (Morgan 1998a).

The rapid growth of focus groups toward the end of the twentieth century came from many sources. The publication of several textbooks and man-uals, including the reissue of Merton's original methodology (Merton, Fiske, and Kendall 1990), stimulated widespread interest in commercial marketing and other fields. In public health, focus groups were first used in international social-marketing projects and then spread to the United States as social mar-keting became popular. Other applied social researchers found them useful for giving disenfranchised populations a voice in program-planning deci-sions, and focus groups soon became a standard practice for eliciting con-sumers' views about health and disease, for planning program services, and developing campaign messages. As qualitative research gained increased respect within academia, university-based scientists also embraced focus group research (Morgan 1996). David Morgan (1996) was a leader in dissem-inating focus group research techniques to sociologists and other social scien-tists and Richard Krueger (1998a, b, c) demonstrated the value of focus groups in evaluation research. By the 1990s, community-based participatory researchers discovered the value of focus groups for conducting needs assess-ments and program evaluations (Krueger and King 1998).

Today focus groups are widely used throughout the social sciences. Commercial and social marketers continue to rely on them to explore the effects of films, television programs, and advertising messages, including health education messages. Political scientists use them for planning political campaigns, marketing politicians, and evaluating mock trials to anticipate how a jury will decide a case. Nonprofit organizations rely on them to evalu-ate program services and assess staff morale (Kitzinger 1995). While focus groups are used by academics in many stand-alone studies, they are even more commonly used as part of mixed methodologies, as we did in Texas. In fact, they are especially effective as an initial step in identifying factors to be explored in surveys and for developing and pretesting questionnaire items. For anthropologists, focus groups are well-suited for identifying cultural norms; understanding people's perceptions of a given topic (e.g., their percep-tions of health and illness); eliciting the vocabulary used to discuss a topic; identifying factors that influence decision making; stimulating debate about controversial issues; and generating ideas on how to change behavior or design other types of program interventions.

FOCUS GROUP RESEARCH: THE PROCESS

One of the most important phases in focus group research is the development of a research plan. According to Morgan (1998b), an effective plan includes:

- goals and objectives
- a time line
- the size, number, and composition of groups
- a recruitment strategy
- the time and location for the interviews
- the moderator and comoderator
- the recording equipment that will be used
- a budget and list of personnel and other resources needed

In Texas, the research team and I worked with WIC administrators to determine the project goals and a time line for completing the work in the seven months available for the study. We decided that WIC participants would feel most comfortable talking in small groups of six to eight people. Compared to larger groups, small groups give each participant more time to relate their experiences and are less intimidating, which can be important when interviewing people with limited incomes and formal education. Larger groups would have been better if participants were more accustomed to sharing their opinions in a group setting or were less involved in the subject and expected to generate a broader range of relatively short responses during the interview.

Like most focus group researchers, we used a purposive sampling strategy to ensure that we received a variety of views and our results captured the range of experiences and attitudes about the program. We also thought carefully about how to segment people into groups that would feel comfortable talking with each other. For example, we segregated teens because they are much more comfortable talking with their counterparts in homogeneous groups than when placed in groups that contain adults. In most cases, we put people together who had similar experiences (e.g., had never participated in WIC), making it easier to analyze results. But in a few instances, we purposely combined people with different views in order to see how they influenced each other, such as when program participants explained WIC services to those who had never used the program.

The downside to placing people in more homogeneous groups is that the total sample size grows exponentially with each criterion used to segment people into groups. As illustrated in the sampling matrix below, the use of three segmentation criteria—age (teen/adult), language/ethnicity, and participation status (enrolled, eligible but not participating)—required us to conduct 32 focus groups. If another criterion had been added, such as urban or rural residence, the sample would have doubled to 64.

| | Enrolled | | Nonparticipating eligible | |
	Teens	Adults	Teens	Adults
Spanish-speaking Hispanics	2	2	2	2
English-speaking Hispanics	2	2	2	2
Anglo/White	2	2	2	2
African-American/Black	2	2	2	2
Total	8	8	8	8

Such large sample sizes are usually impractical and unnecessary. Only rarely would insights be generated in the last ten or fifteen interviews that had not emerged in previous discussions. For this reason, focus group researchers usually analyze the data as it is collected and use a strategy called "sufficient redundancy" or "theoretical saturation" to determine the number of interviews they conduct. According to this strategy, researchers compare each new focus group discussion with previous interviews to determine if new ideas or themes have been introduced and if the ideas differ from those of other subgroups or segments. In Texas, if the second interview in a subgroup within the sampling matrix yielded valuable new information, additional interviews were conducted and compared with previous interviews to determine when the discussions became sufficiently redundant and had saturated the insights we could gain from them.

A related strategy is to compare results from one subgroup with those in another group in hopes of finding the expected differences are not as great as anticipated so that the groups could be combined in the future. For example, when we learned that English-speaking Hispanics, African-American, and Anglo participants shared similar views and were comfortable talking in a group together, we were able to eliminate ethnicity as a segmentation variable and reduced the number of groups needed to twenty-four.

Although our recruitment goal was to have six to eight people attend each group, we did not expect everyone invited to show up, therefore, we recruited ten people for each interview. To minimize the no-show rate and subsequent response bias, we established a set of reminders and provided incentives for participation. In determining how much to pay participants ($40), we estimated their time, transportation, child care, other possible costs, and the "going rate" at the time. While we were able to provide cash incentives, gift certificates, or phone cards, gifts of items related to the discussion topic are also effective in enhancing participation. Another valuable incentive is the opportunity for participants to be experts and contribute ideas to a project that helps their community. Disfranchised populations, in particular, have few opportunities to share their opinions so it is important to emphasize the importance of the project and the valuable role they will play when describing the project to potential focus group discussants.

Most focus groups are conducted with people who have never met and are unlikely to interact in the future, giving them the safety that accompanies anonymity. While this was the case for most of our groups in Texas, we found that some teenagers were nervous about coming alone and allowed them to bring a friend, as long as the friend met the segmentation criteria for the group (e.g., teenager currently enrolled in WIC). We did not conduct focus groups with people who were members of existing groups, although occasionally this practice is used if it is extremely difficult to get strangers together.

WIC staff members acted as gatekeepers in our recruitment plan, inviting program participants to sign up if they were interested in attending a focus group. Researchers used the sign-up sheet to call people, screen them for eligibility, and assign them to the appropriate interview session. To recruit people not enrolled in the program, we included an invitation in a mail survey of Medicaid families eligible for WIC, explaining the study and giving them a space to provide their contact information if they wanted to participate.

With respect to recording the interviews, we rarely had access to video equipment and could not afford commercial focus group facilities with videotapes, so usually we relied on tape recorders to produce verbatim transcripts of each interview. We also used a comoderator in each group to record nonverbal communication and discussion highlights in case the tape recording failed.

The moderator's ability to make participants feel comfortable is essential for success. It is important to find a moderator with the right balance of expertise, experience with the research topic, and the linguistic and personal traits needed to interact with the focus group discussants. In projects conducted with oppressed populations that distrust outsiders it is usually best to train community members to facilitate the interviews. In addition to creating the safety needed for a candid discussion, this approach transfers valuable skills to the community and empowers its members.

In the Texas WIC project, our budget included funds for moderator fees, participant incentives and other costs (e.g., child care or transportation), refreshments, audio equipment, audiotapes and batteries, transcription fees, data analysis, and reporting. As explained below, we were able to use community resources and did not have to pay for recruiters or site rental.

Compared to individual interviews, focus groups require a great deal of logistical planning. It is particularly important to select the right time and place. Most adult group discussions last 1½ hours, while interviews with youth are usually shorter—45 to 60 minutes. When determining the time to hold a group, we had to consider work schedules, transit problems and travel time, child-care issues, popular TV viewing habits, and other cultural practices, such as religious observances and customs. The times most convenient for our study participants were mid-morning and early evening.

In selecting places to hold focus groups, we considered the advantages and disadvantages of commercial focus group facilities, health department meeting rooms, libraries, restaurants with private dinning rooms, private homes, and other community settings. We asked ourselves these questions: Will participants have difficulty getting there, finding it, or parking? Is the setting free from unpleasant associations or experiences that might bias their conversation? Will participants feel comfortable there? Will they be able to hear each other? Can they see each other and the moderator? Does the room offer privacy and a quiet place to record the conversation? Is the room free from interruptions? Is there a rental fee? Depending on the community, focus groups in the Texas study were conducted in health department meeting rooms and restaurants. We avoided the WIC clinic because of the potential for bias and interruptions, but occasionally we used space at other community program locations or at libraries.

The next major task in planning focus group research is to prepare a question guide. We followed the steps outlined in Richard Krueger's (1998a) guide, *Developing Questions for Focus Groups:*

- assemble the research team
- agree on the objectives to be achieved
- determine the background information needed from each participant
- prepare a list of topic areas to be covered
- write open-ended questions for each topic
- prepare probes or follow-up questions
- order the questions to create a logical flow
- prepare transitional statements between questions
- take a break and then come back and eliminate unnecessary questions

Perhaps the most difficult part of this task is to limit the number of questions that can reasonably be covered in the allotted time and to keep each question simple, clear, open-ended, and carefully focused on the research objectives.

The research team (moderator, comoderator, and any other assistants) typically arrives at the research site at least an hour before the group convenes to arrange furniture (usually discussants are seated in a circle), set up the taping equipment, hang directional signs to assist participants in finding the room, prepare refreshments, and handle any last-minute problems that arise. Examples of problems that had to be solved in Texas include: replacing a defective tape recorder, finding a new room when a broken air conditioner interfered with the quality sound on the audiotape, finding a new room after discovering a scheduling conflict, and persuading program staff to give up access to the room during the interview.

I believe the best overall approach for managing focus groups is to treat participants as if they have come to your home for a party. To make them feel like special guests in the Texas study, the moderator greeted participants as they arrived, introduced them to other members of the research team and participants, and helped them get seated. The comoderator or assistant helped them fill out paperwork (consent forms, supplementary questionnaire, etc.), offered them refreshments, and answered questions. If a participant brought an unexpected guest or appeared to fit poorly with the rest of the group (e.g., was high on drugs, had a disruptive personality, or did not have the characteristics designated for that segment), the comoderator informed them they were special in some way and escorted them to another room for a personal interview.

Once the focus group interview begins, the moderator takes charge. After a brief introduction and carefully crafted explanation of the study, the moderator guides the discussion. Effective moderators keep participants focused on the research topic, as well as pushing them to move beyond what has already been covered. While they often follow the interview guide, good moderators know when to permit the conversation to move to another related topic in order to put discussants at ease and/or allow unexpected lines of inquiry to emerge. Skilled facilitators also probe vague or incomplete responses and stimulate debate. They prevent individuals from dominating the conversation and draw out opinions from shy participants. Finally, they keep track of time to ensure that all the key questions are covered and a brief closing statement can be made.

Occasionally, moderators use special techniques or exercises to draw out specific information and focus participants on each other (Kitzinger 1995). They may have participants sort cards, make lists of flip charts, role play, create metaphors, complete sentences, or write scripts (Debus 1992). These techniques can be especially valuable when exploring sensitive topics because they enable participants to share ideas without having to claim them as their own views or relate embarrassing experiences.

The comoderator is typically responsible for room arrangement, monitoring recording equipment, taking notes on nonverbal communication, helping resolve problems (e.g., late arrivals or disruptive participants), and assisting with other logistical issues (greeting participants, distributing incentives, or ensuring members have reviewed and signed consent forms). The comoderator rarely participates in the conversation but may give the closing summary.

Analysis starts during the group discussion as the moderator and comoderator listen for themes to emerge and note contradictory ideas. Immediately after the session is over and participants depart, they review highlights of the session and make notes about key themes and topics to explore in future discussions.

How the data is handled after the interview varies greatly depending on the complexity of the research topic and budget and time constraints. In Texas, our focus group interviews were transcribed verbatim and entered into a computer for a thorough analysis using Strauss and Corbin's (1990) constant comparative method. A codebook was developed for use in marking sections in the transcript that dealt with specific research topics (e.g., rude treatment by WIC staff, embarrassment to accept governmental help, or confusion about eligibility requirement). At least two researchers read and coded each transcript and then compared results to identify and resolve any discrepancies. The software program Ethnograph was used to enter codes into electronic files and then extract the coded passages so they could be sorted into folders by code/topic. The passages in each folder were then reviewed by two researchers who summarized key themes, noted majority and minority views, and marked passages worthy of quotation. After working independently, the researchers met to compare results and resolve differences before determining which information to include in the final report.

In smaller, less complex studies focus group researchers may forego computer analysis and follow a simplified set of steps. In her *Handbook for Excellence in Focus Groups*, Mary Debus (1992) makes the following recommendations:

- Listen again to the tapes and/or reread the transcripts
- Group findings according to key research topics or questions
- Compare ideas expressed in each group and identify the positions or ideas that emerged about each topic area
- Sum up each of the different positions
- Pull out quotations that best represent each position
- Reread the summary notes and transcripts
- Identify constant threads or patterns that emerged about each topic
- If possible, expand upon the basic themes with comments about how they relate to other findings. For example, describe the majority and minority viewpoints or how specific subgroups of participants differ from others.
- Prepare a global synthesis of findings focused on the study's objectives. For each research objective, summarize the key findings and discuss their implications for action.

Regardless of the level of complexity or time devoted to analysis, analysis should be systematic, verifiable, and focused on the study's objectives (Krueger 1998c).

The project culminates in a report that summarizes and synthesizes the results. In talking with administrators who commission focus group studies, I have been impressed by the variation in their reporting preferences. Some appreciate a very detailed report with numerous quotations to make the consumers' voices come alive. Others prefer a short report that simply summarizes key findings and recommendations. For the Texas project, our report included:

- title page (names of all researchers, the organization that sponsored the study, the date and location it was prepared)
- table of contents
- executive summary

- background statement (problem being addressed and general purpose of the study)
- research objectives
- brief discussion of the methods employed (description of the number of groups conducted in each segment, the size range of groups, recruitment procedures and sources of participants, summary of questions or topic areas covered in discussions, moderator characteristics and qualifications, and general discussion of the procedures used)
- detailed findings (often organized by research objective or key topic)
- conclusions and recommendations
- appendices (topic guides, screening questionnaires, more detailed description of research methods used to collect and analyze the data, numerous tables and statistical findings that we feared could intimidate some readers)

We also presented our findings orally, first to a select group of WIC administrators and later to a larger number of staff. These sessions gave us valuable feedback on how staff interpreted study results, highlighted points we needed to clarify, and gave us an opportunity to explore the implications of our study findings for programmatic decisions. Fortunately, we were given an opportunity to incorporate what we learned in these sessions into the final version of the written report. When the report was finished, we facilitated a series of sessions in which the staff used the results to make marketing decisions about how to increase program participation. This marketing plan served as the blueprint for a marketing intervention that included service delivery improvements, policy changes, development of staff training and consumer education materials, and a media campaign (Bryant et al. 2001).

YOUR PROJECT

You may complete this project alone, but the exercise will be far more productive and a lot easier if you work with at least one other student. A team approach will allow you to practice both the moderator and comoderator roles, enable you to more easily conduct multiple groups, and give you someone else with whom you can compare results during data analysis.

Your first task is to select a topic of interest that a small group would be comfortable discussing for about an hour and a half (e.g., students' opinions of student health service; ways to improve food choices on campus; reasons students do not use condoms and their recommendations for increasing condom use). Clearly state your objectives and then determine the procedures needed to realize them. Decide who you need to interview and how many focus group interviews you should conduct with each subgroup or segment in the study population. For purposes of this project, you probably won't have the time or resources to conduct more than one group for each person on the team, but it is a good learning experience to consider the number that would be required to explore the topic thoroughly.

Once you have the sample in mind, think carefully about an appropriate location to conduct the interviews—one that is convenient and comfortable for participants. Be sure to visit the location before the interview to be sure it will serve the purpose well. Of course, you will need to reserve the room in advance so you can schedule the times and dates of each interview when you invite people to participate.

The next task is to develop a plan for identifying and recruiting people to participate in the focus groups you are going to conduct. Where can you obtain names and contact information for people you want to interview? Do you need other people to make the initial invitation, and if so, can you provide them with a recruitment script (see Morgan 1998a)? What incentive(s) can you use to make participation attractive? How should you explain the purpose of the study so that participants become interested but remain unbiased during their discussion in the interview (e.g., by telling them you are conducting a study to get people to eat more vegetables)?

Assemble your coresearchers and prepare an interview guide. I have found that it is extremely helpful to have Richard Krueger's (1998a) *Developing Questions for Focus Groups* by my side when preparing questions, writing transitional statements, and determining the best order for the guide. This initial meeting will take several hours and is likely to be difficult, so schedule time to meet again after a break to ensure that the questions are open ended, single barreled, and focused on your research objectives.

If you do not have two tape recorders and omnidirectional microphones that can pick up multiple people's voices in a group discussion, search for someone who can lend them to you. Many universities and colleges have media centers that loan them to students for projects such as this one.

Meet with your team members to decide who will moderate and comoderate each group and review the duties assigned to each. Practice asking the questions and try to imagine how the conversation might flow. Visualization can help you prepare for problems that might arise and develop ways to deal with contingencies.

Give each team member a chance to moderate a focus group (see Krueger 1998b). After each group, spend time debriefing to identify major themes, ways to improve the questions, and note nonverbal information that is important in interpreting results. This debriefing session also is an excellent time to provide each other with constructive feedback on moderating techniques.

Transcribe the tape for each group, and if possible, assign each transcript to two team members for review. Determine the most appropriate system for analyzing the data given the total number of groups, time available, and complexity of the study. Krueger's (1998c) volume *Analyzing & Reporting*

Focus Group Results gives clear, succinct advice about several approaches to this task. Once you have devised a plan, stick to it so that your analysis is systematic and you are able to describe the steps you followed.

Finally, make an outline for the report and assign team members to prepare drafts of each section. You may want to use an outline like the one we used in Texas or a shorter, simplified version. Schedule a time to prepare your findings, then select a team member to give an oral summary of the results to your class or an organization that can benefit from your study. Finally, share your results with the people who participated in the focus group interviews to get their feedback on how well you captured their views.

REFERENCES

Bryant, C. A., J. H. Lindenberger, C. Brown, E. Kent, J. M. Schreiber, M. Bustillo, and M. W. Canright. 2001. A Social Marketing Approach to Increasing Enrollment in a Public Health Program—Case Study of the Texas WIC Program. *Human Organization* 60(3):234–246.

Debus, M. 1992. *Handbook for Excellence in Focus Group Research.* Washington, DC: The Academy for Educational Development.

Goldman, A. E., and S. S. McDonald. 1987. *The Group Depth Interview: Principles and Practices.* Englewood Cliffs, NJ: Prentice Hall.

Kitzinger, J. 1995. Qualitative Research—Introducing Focus Groups. *British Medical Journal* 311(7000):299–302.

Krueger, R. A. 1998a. *Developing Questions for Focus Groups. Focus Group Kit Volume 3.* Thousand Oaks, CA: Sage.

Krueger, R. A. 1998b. *Moderating Focus Groups. Focus Group Kit Volume 4.* Thousand Oaks, CA: Sage.

Krueger, R. A. 1998c. *Analyzing & Reporting Focus Group Results. Focus Group Kit 6.* Thousand Oaks, CA: Sage.

Krueger, R. A., and J. A. King. 1998. *Involving Community Members in Focus Groups. Focus Group Kit Volume 5.* Thousand Oaks, CA: Sage.

Merton, R. K., M. Fiske, and P. L. Kendall. 1990. *The Focused Interview,* 2nd ed. New York: Free Press.

Morgan, D. 1996. Focus Groups. *Annual Reviews in Sociology* 22:129–152.

Morgan, D. 1998a. *The Focus Group Guide Book. Focus Group Kit, Volume 1.* Thousand Oaks, CA: Sage.

Morgan, D. 1998b. *Planning Focus Groups. Focus Group Kit, Volume 2.* Thousand Oaks, CA: Sage.

Strauss, A., and J. Corbin. 1990. *Basics of Qualitative Research: Grounded Theory Procedures and Techniques.* Thousand Oaks, CA: Sage.

12

Applying Visual Methods in Ethnographic Research

S. Elizabeth Bird

THE VISUAL IN ANTHROPOLOGY

Today we live in a world increasingly dominated by media images, which are supplied by television, movies, advertising, the Internet, and countless other places. In addition, media technologies are becoming ever more widely available, from cheap, portable camcorders and digital cameras, to software and hardware that makes it possible for more and more people to use media in creative ways. While visual anthropologists have long used photographic techniques to document and understand culture, new technological realities have opened many exciting possibilities for doing anthropological research, for professional anthropologists and students alike. The study of media and their role in everyday life has also gained importance in the discipline. Here I discuss a variety of visual research approaches, all of which are usually described as *visual* or *media anthropology*—the two fields that are closely related and often overlap, but tend to have somewhat different concerns.

VISUAL ANTHROPOLOGY PROJECTS

Visual anthropology, also known as the "anthropology of visual communication," has focused on three main areas. First, visual anthropologists produce ethnographic media, such as films, videos, and Web sites, for educational and commercial use. Visual anthropologists also focus on documenting culture for the benefit of research purposes, creating archives of film and photographs that may never be used commercially. The visual dimension offers a unique way of seeing culture that words alone cannot. For instance, the father/son team of John and Malcolm Collier were pioneers in photographic documentation of culture. They would take large numbers of photos and analyze them, showing, for example, how the way people arranged themselves in meetings and other social interactions displayed patterns of power and social authority. The eminent anthropologist Margaret Mead used film to document parent/child interactions in her studies of child-rearing practices; an archive of film like this may not only benefit the researcher at the time, but can offer future researchers raw material for study.

Second, visual anthropologists analyze visual materials produced by others. They might analyze a collection of historic photographs in terms of the "story" the photos can tell us. Or they may examine photographs from particular cultures in terms of how those cultures represent themselves; for instance, studies of formal photography in several African nations show distinctive ways in which people use photographs to create images of themselves. Others have studied collections of family snapshots or home movies. This kind of research is not confined to photography; anthropologists may also analyze art and are moving more into the study of media forms like movies and TV, overlapping with media anthropologists.

Finally, visual anthropologists are becoming increasingly interested in how visual methods can enhance research. They may use "photo elicitation" techniques, often in conjunction with other ethnographic methods. For instance, researchers have given cameras to children to photograph their schools from their point of view. They found that seeing "through the eyes" of those directly affected can offer unique insight into people's experience. A student in one of my classes worked with a community whose members felt threatened by encroaching development. She traveled around the community with residents, asking them to show her what to photograph to capture the spirit of the community. People showed her important landmarks, such as giant trees under which people had traditionally met, and other significant spaces and places whose meaning she never would have been aware of. With residents' help, she developed an exhibit in the community center, which featured their photos, as well as old photos people brought in, accompanied by quotations from residents. It was seen as a valuable assertion of community, created by and with the residents themselves.

This kind of approach also can be used with video techniques. Researchers have given video cameras and training to non-Western people, as Terence Turner did in his famous work with the Kayapo of Brazil, who learned how to document both their culture and their struggle against development. They used footage shot of negotiations and other events to make their case to the government and to gain attention and sympathy through the news media. Others have used similar approaches with young people in urban America, allowing them to document their own lives. Richard Chalfen and Michael Rich (2004) employed "video intervention assessment," giving young asthma patients camcorders to record their lives. Using the data, they found that "patients' issues . . . and value systems varied significantly from those of their physicians," opening the door to more effective intervention and treatment programs.

In a slightly different type of photo elicitation, research participants are asked to respond to photos shown to them by the researcher. The photos may be contemporary; for instance, a researcher might ask people to look at photos of their community, family, or an institution and talk about them. The visual stimulus offered by the photo is often useful in drawing out thoughts and commentary that would be difficult to elicit through words alone. This method is especially helpful in jogging memories when old photos are used, such as in an oral history project.

Creative visual techniques have been used by anthropologists in a wide variety of contexts, from academic to commercial. Video or Web diaries may be used to allow participants to document their daily lives as part of a community study. They are also used by anthropologists working for businesses interested in how to develop and market better products, where consumers are asked to visually document their use of electronics, household items, or other products.

MEDIA ANTHROPOLOGY PROJECTS

While for many years anthropologists tended to ignore the media, now we are learning that in Western and non-Western cultures, the media are playing an increasingly important role in informing us, entertaining us, and shaping the way we look at the world. To understand culture, we need to understand how people learn the values, roles, and beliefs of that culture— how do people learn appropriate gender roles, for example? While of course we learn our culture through schools, families, churches, and so on, we also learn it through the media. During the last twenty years or so, we have seen the rise of media anthropology, which seeks to explore and explain that role.

Media anthropologists have approached this task in two main ways. First, they analyze and interpret media in order to help understand how the world is represented. While we do not assume that media images have a direct causal effect on people (for instance, by arguing that violent movies directly cause violent behavior), we might study violent imagery, exploring how it might contribute to cultural patterns and attitudes about violence. Anthropologists have traditionally studied myths, folktales, and other oral traditions for the same reason; the media have often now come to replace or supplement this kind of traditional storytelling. Thus, for example, we might ask how other cultures are portrayed in American media, or how Americans are portrayed in other countries' media. Do media promote stereotypical understandings of race, ethnicity, or gender? I have written about how Native Americans are consistently portrayed in very predictable and formulaic ways by looking at a range of popular culture, from advertising and greeting cards to TV and movies. Others have done similar studies; anthropologists Lutz and Collins (1993) examined *National Geographic* magazine to learn how it perpetuated certain ways of seeing "exotic" peoples.

However, media anthropologists have begun to work most in the area of ethnographic audience reception of media. Content analysis of media can only take us so far because we cannot assume that everyone interprets media in the same way. In fact, research shows that people respond to media in very different ways. For instance, I have studied the different ways that American Indians and white Americans respond to media images of Indians. Others have looked at how Western media may be interpreted in surprising ways in other cultures; for example, the 1980s action hero Rambo became an important symbol of resistance for Australian Aborigines. This kind of research involves not only analysis of the media text itself, but also ethnographic work such as observation, interviews, and focus groups.

Other related questions might include how media can play an important role in maintaining cultural identity. For instance, there is a thriving trade among Indian-Americans in "Bollywood" videos and DVDs, which people watch and talk about with families and friends. More generally, anthropologists have become interested in how media are incorporated into everyday life. How do people get their news, and how do they form their opinions? How much time do they spend with media very day? Do they feel influenced by advertising images? Are more people becoming active media producers, making their own videos and Web sites? There has been a growing interdisciplinary interest in fan communities—people who unite over their interest in a particular TV show, movie, or star and often produce their own stories and other products. I will discuss Internet fan groups in more detail in chapter 13, Constructing a Virtual Ethnography; however, it should be noted that media-inspired fan activities do not only happen virtually. A student in one of my classes recently completed a participant-observation study of a group of people who are active fans of the *Star Trek* franchise. While they did communicate electronically, much of their activity happened in real-time meetings, where the relationships formed went well beyond the TV show itself.

It is probably apparent that these kinds of studies are not characterized by a specific methodology, but rather are questions that may be answered in many ways; later I will offer some specific ideas for approaches and methods that might be appropriate to answer some of these questions.

LEGAL AND ETHICAL ISSUES

Depending on the kind of project you choose, ethical and legal questions may become especially important in visual research. Content analysis of existing media is not a problem within the context of a class paper or presentation. However, if you create a public Web site or other more widely available forum using these images, you could face legal issues. You cannot take images from other sources without permission, and so you should carefully check copyright and ownership for any images you reproduce.

Your own images can be used freely, with one important proviso. You should always obtain written permission from those in the photo who are recognizable. This is not only a legal requirement (to avoid invasion of privacy issues), but also an ethical issue; people have the right to know what is being done with their image. In any project using photos of people, you should design a brief consent/release form—your college may well have a standard form you can adapt. You should make it clear how you intend to use the image, and you should not change that use without obtaining further permission. It is also a good idea to obtain permission for use beyond the class context so that you could use the photos in a public setting. And if you create a widely available resource, such as a Web site, you should make that intention clear to participants. No matter what people have signed, you also have an ethical duty not to use the images in ways that are demeaning or in a context that is inappropriate.

Questions may also arise about your freedom to photograph people without their permission. There are some legal gray areas here—it is usually considered legal to photograph people in a truly public setting, and permission is not required for crowd shots or similar public situations. However, if you wish to feature an individual in a photograph, it is both polite and legally careful to request permission, and not to persist if people decline. This is one reason why it is often wise to pick a topic or a setting where you are already known and trusted.

YOUR PROJECT

In choosing your project, an important point to consider is whether it requires significant technical expertise, such as video editing, and whether you have access to the necessary equipment. You are strongly advised not to attempt a project that requires you to learn a new technology—you will have enough to do simply planning and carrying out the research! With that in mind, I offer some suggestions about possible types of projects:

OPTION 1: Make a short video that documents a community, cultural event, family, or individual

If you have access to a digital camcorder and basic editing software, this is not as difficult as you might expect; a presentable video of 10–15 minutes can be produced with a home camcorder and the simple editing software packaged with standard Apple computers (IMovie) or Windows XP (Movie Maker). More sophisticated editing is possible with professional programs like FinalCut Pro or Adobe Premiere, but the learning curve on these is much steeper. And editing is very time-consuming—each minute of final footage may take an hour of work. However, the key issue here is not so much the technology, but rather your research question. Traditional ethnographic films may involve months of close study and many hours of filming. They often take the classic ethnographic approach of collecting a great deal of information and then analyzing and editing it to produce a coherent film. You do not have that time, either to film or edit, so it is important to focus from the beginning. For instance, you might decide to document how your family spends Thanksgiving, or some other holiday. The idea is fine, but lacks focus. Rather, you could ask, "How can I show the importance of Thanksgiving in creating a sense of unity among my family?" This is an interesting anthropological question, extending beyond the specifics of your family, and it helps you decide what to film. For instance, you could include footage of family arriving from around the country or region. Take the opportunity to interview them about why it is important to travel to Grandma's house every year. You might set up your camcorder during dinner, filming conversations, interactions, and so on. Uncle Bob tells the same story every year—how does that contribute to the sense of family? Are there particular foods your family always eats? Film and talk to the cook as s/he prepares the meal, and ask about the significance of the food. Are there special activities the family does on Thanksgiving—watching football, following shared religious activities, playing board games?

The project will be much more manageable if you plan your shooting schedule ahead of time. In fact, many documentary makers produce a "script" or "storyboard" before they start filming, mapping out the sequence of events/interviews that should be included. This is strongly advised since it will help you to know what you want to film and avoid shooting hours of footage that would have to be searched and edited. When you edit, you can decide whether to include such features as voice-over or written narration, music, or an interview with an "expert"—in this case, perhaps a specialist in family communication, kinship, or traditions. Depending on the topic, the incorporation of still photos can be effective; in the Thanksgiving project you could include old family photos of past holidays. To get a truly ethnographic feel, it is often useful to include minimal narration, allowing your interviewees to speak for themselves. Video can be a powerful way to enhance life history or narrative research.

It is probably apparent that in choosing a topic, you would best be advised to choose something with which you are already familiar. At the very least, you should spend time familiarizing yourself before you start filming; otherwise, you will not know what to film, what questions to ask, or who to ask. A group of students in one of my classes made an excellent video about a local community arts program for "at-risk" children, for which they filmed interviews with children, teachers, and administrators. The finished product told a coherent story about shared goals of empowerment described by both teachers and children. The students did not begin filming until they had spent about three weeks visiting the program, during which they developed the theme as it emerged through interaction with the participants. Other projects have included a documentary on the social meanings of Chinese food, done by a Chinese student, and a short piece on the significance of a local landmark, done by a student who was already doing active ethnographic research in the neighborhood. Remember, the specific topic isn't important, but your final product should tell a story that has something to say about culture.

OPTION 2: Create a photo essay or display

This can be approached in a way similar to a video, except that the story is told with still images. In spite of the old cliché that "a picture is worth a thousand words," photos do not speak for themselves, except in an aesthetic sense. As an anthropology student, you are not trying to create a purely artistic product; the challenge of the ethnographic photo essay is organizing words and pictures to create a coherent story. Thus, the narration/captions and "framing" of the photos are key. There are many potential formats for a photo-based project. Programs like PowerPoint offer creative ways to tell a photo story—using quite sophisticated animation, music, narration, and sound effects—and can be set up to play automatically. Photos might also be used to create a Web site, an exhibit board, or simply a written piece with pictures. The photos you use may be documentary images you took yourself, photos collected from or taken by informants (as described earlier in the chapter), or any combination of these. A display might include commentary by you and/or your informants. As with a video, it is important to plan your project carefully.

OPTION 3: Photo (or art) elicitation projects

While these may result in a very visual final product, like a video or photo essay, they may not. For instance, you may decide to work with informants to have them document their lives through video, still photography, or art work, such as drawing. You could ask a group of people to take a particular number of photos that capture their sense of their campus, department, workplace, dorm, club, or neighborhood. Or you could have individuals with

illnesses document their experiences visually. Your project would be to analyze the photos to describe how the place or phenomenon is seen through
their eyes, perhaps supplemented by interviews. The final product could be a
fairly traditional research paper, probably illustrated with some of the images,
or it could be a more visually based display, as described above. In one project
I saw, a student made a video about the life of a Buddhist monk in the United
States. While he filmed and interviewed the monk himself, he also lent the
video camera to him, asking him to document his life through his eyes. Some
of the resulting footage was included in the video, adding a powerful new
dimension to the story.

OPTION 4: Media analysis projects

Here you start with a question, such as, "How do TV toy commercials
teach lessons about appropriate gender behavior?" In this case, you are analyzing images rather than creating them. For instance, in observing toy commercials you might notice that boys are associated with strong, primary
colors, loud noises, action, outside scenes, and competitive play, while girls
are associated with pastels, soft voices and music, inside and domestic scenes,
and cooperative play. From these observations, you could draw some conclusions about what kind of behaviors and looks are culturally desirable for each
gender. If you have access to older commercials, or those from other countries (collections have been made commercially and are available in many
college libraries), you could study change over time or across cultures. In any
event, you need to approach your topic in a systematic way. For instance,
how was your sample obtained? Did you include *all* of the episodes of a TV
show, or use one in ten? Did you use one issue of a magazine to characterize
its advertisements, or sample one issue a month for a year? There is no defin-
itive "right answer," but you need to explain what your data base was. Simi-
larly, you need to define your terms. For instance, if you are counting "violent
acts" on a TV show or movie, you must offer a definition. Is an aggressive
shove defined as a "violent" act in the same way as a stabbing?

Alternatively, you may not be counting specific things, but rather exploring themes that emerge. Your final product would likely be a paper, but if you
have the expertise, you could also consider creating a video following the model
of Jean Kilbourne's *Killing us Softly* series. In this series, which is often available
in college libraries, Kilbourne analyzes advertising images with a technique
used in a wide variety of videos produced by the Media Education Foundation.

OPTION 5: A media response study

Rather than analyze the images, you might study a group's response to
them. Again, no single method is mandatory; media scholars have studied
audience response through surveys, unstructured interviews, focus groups, and
virtual ethnography, all of which have been discussed in detail elsewhere in
this book. The specific method should be appropriate to the research question.
For instance, you might be interested in how people respond to a specific
movie or TV show. Having people watch the item followed by a focus group

discussion could work quite well. It is often useful to have a general discussion about immediate responses before moving into specific topics that interest you. As an example, I once conducted separate focus groups of American Indians and Anglos following their viewing of a TV western series. I was interested in their responses to depictions of Indians. The Anglo groups discussed many aspects of the show, but never touched on that topic until I raised it late in the process, while the Indian groups raised it immediately. Quite apart from the differing opinions of the two ethnic groups, this clearly told me that for Indians their representation is much more significant to them than it is for Anglos.

However, you might be more interested in general questions about how people use the media. Where do they get their news? Which sources of information do they find most credible? In this case, observation, individual interviews, or even surveys might be useful. Sometimes your questions might not be directly about the media, but may "back into" the topic. For instance, you may be interested in whether advertising influences people's buying decisions. However, since most people deny such influence, a series of questions could be developed about buying habits, which allows the respondent to reflect upon their decisions and may well result in references to advertising or other media. My book, *The Audience in Everyday Life* (Bird 2003), contains several audience response studies using different methods; it might be helpful as you decide on a research question.

Media and visual anthropology approaches are becoming an increasingly important area of the discipline. They are relevant and useful in research involving health, education, cultural identity, and many other topics. They both acknowledge the power of the media to create and influence culture, as well as the ability of people to use media to document and enrich their lives. Your project can allow you to let your creativity shine, as well as conduct meaningful cultural research in today's media world.

REFERENCES

Bird, S. Elizabeth. 2003. *The Audience in Everyday Life: Living in a Media World.* New York: Routledge.

Chalfen, Richard, and Michael Rich. 2004. Patients Teaching Physicians through Visual Illness Narratives. *Visual Anthropology Review* 20(1):17–30.

Lutz, Catherine A., and Jane Collins. 1993. *Reading National Geographic.* Chicago: University of Chicago Press.

A FEW SELECTED READINGS FOR FURTHER INFORMATION

Alfonso, Ana I., Laszlo Kurti, and Sarah Pink, eds. 2004. *Working Images: Visual Research and Representation in Ethnography.* London: Routledge.

Askew, Kelly, and Richard R. Wilk. 2002. *The Anthropology of Media.* Malden, MA: Blackwell.

Bird, S. Elizabeth. 1999. Gendered Representation of American Indians in Popular Media. *Journal of Communication* 49(3):61–83.

Collier, John, and Malcolm Collier. 1986. *Visual Anthropology: Photography as a Research Method.* Albuquerque: University of New Mexico Press.

Lovejoy, Tracey, and Nelle Steele. 2004. Engaging our Audience through Photo Stories. *Visual Anthropology Review* 20(1):70–81.

Turner, Terence. 1992. Defiant Images: The Kayapo Appropriation of Video. *Anthropology Today* 8(6):5–16.

13

Constructing a Virtual Ethnography

S. Elizabeth Bird & Jessica Barber

A RESEARCH PROJECT

For some years now Bird has been studying the role of the media in the contemporary United States. Today we live in a media-saturated world; the media do not merely affect culture—they are actually embedded in our culture. They provide us with many of our shared cultural references, and it is through the media that American culture is moving so quickly across the globe.

As an anthropologist, Bird's main research focus is not on the effects of the media—which are difficult, if not impossible, to measure—but on how people relate to various media. She has studied the audiences of supermarket tabloids and television news programming and explored how people respond to media images of American Indians. In the past, she used familiar methods (such as observations, in-depth interviews, and focus groups) to investigate how people use the media in their everyday lives. But the research on the representations of American Indians led her into a new kind of media ethnography.

Bird wrote an article about how white and American Indian viewers responded to the television series *Dr. Quinn, Medicine Woman,* which regularly featured Cheyenne characters. She concluded that white viewers tended to accept the rather stereotypical portrayal of the Cheyenne precisely because it fit with the way mainstream culture had come to understand how Indians *should* behave. Indian viewers, on the other hand, found these same stereotypes demeaning.

Bird was surprised one day to receive an e-mail from a woman who had read her article and explained that she was a member of an e-mail discussion list devoted to *Dr. Quinn;* she requested permission to post the article for the members' comments. Bird agreed and then subscribed to the list in order to read and respond to those comments. Fascinated by the careful, lengthy discussions that followed, Bird began to realize that this electronic fan group could provide a way to understand how at least some people use the Internet to discuss their favorite television show and to communicate in the most basic sense—to make connections with people that go beyond the context of the show. Bird began several years of "virtual ethnography," in which she observed and participated on the discussion list, interviewed members, and asked them to respond to her interpretations of their community. She learned a great deal, not only about the role of the Internet in media fan culture, but also about the ever-growing role of the Internet in our culture as a whole.

It is important to remember that "virtual ethnography" is not so much a method in itself, but is often a way of applying in a new context the various methods you have studied in other chapters in this book. It is possible to use observations, interviews, life histories, and so forth in the form of structured chat room experiences. You may be surprised at how much electronic communication parallels "natural" communication, although you will probably also learn how different it can be. Bird, for example, carried out a remarkably intimate ethnography of a group without ever seeing a human face or hearing a human voice, a strange experience for an anthropologist.

VIRTUAL ETHNOGRAPHY AS A RESEARCH TOOL: A BRIEF OVERVIEW AND HISTORY

Bird's research is one study among many that has found electronic communication to be an exciting new way to understand contemporary culture. Her purpose was to add another dimension to her previous studies of media use, although she found herself becoming interested in the development of this e-mail group as a "community."

The concept of community has long interested anthropologists, who have often been especially concerned with communities having a geographic base—the villages or territories of the traditional peoples who were the focus of anthropological research until relatively recently. At the same time, anthropologists have always found it productive to study associations that are not strictly place-bound, such as societies and organizations that unite people with common interests, even in small societies. As more anthropologists study complex societies and become involved in the multidisciplinary concerns of globalization, we find that people's associations are increasingly varied, and may not be place-bound. Our social networks can include families that may be widely dispersed or involve people who share hobbies, employment, religion, or any number of common experiences.

Nonplace communities develop norms and institutional memories based on common experiences, such as a "community" of physicians or Baptists. Virtual communities are essentially an extension of this principle, the main difference being that they develop around computer-mediated communication and that social interactions take place online. The focus of much research in this area tends to be an examination of the difference made by this new communication format: How are virtual and "natural" communities similar and how are they different? We know, for instance, that the existence of a technology can actually make a specialized community possible. While some fans of *Dr. Quinn* might have corresponded or shared their enthusiasm through more conventional means, Bird's research suggested that such a deep commitment would not have been possible without electronic communication. Indeed, many respondents told her that their fandom was a purely private, internal feeling until they discovered other fans through the Internet. Many researchers have thus taken community formation as a central question to be asked through virtual ethnography: What *is* a virtual community, how does electronic communication make new kinds of community possible, and how does it facilitate existing ones? A brief review of some of these studies points to questions you might want to consider in beginning a research project of your own.

One assumes that national identity is already one type of community, but in the "real world" it may be hard to maintain once people become geographically dispersed. How might the Internet affect that process? Daniel Miller and Don Slater (2000) found that in Trinidad, for example, the Internet has become the most popular medium for national community maintenance. Nearly the entire population of Trinidad has Internet access and uses it primarily to keep in contact with other "Trinis" located around the world. The two researchers were participant observers of both the "real" and the "virtual" Trinidad, carrying out an ethnography of e-mail discussion lists and contextualizing their data with archival research. They saw "virtual Trini" communities as a method of cultural maintenance and a chance to "lime," a popular Trinidadian pastime roughly equivalent to "hanging out" in the United States. The Trinis were able to reassert and publicly practice their Trinidadian identities, even in the absence of substantial place-bound communities outside the home country. Other researchers have shown how even people who no longer have a significant geographical home (e.g., the Assyrians) have been able to use the Internet to create a sense of identity among a widely scattered population. The Internet is increasingly being used around the world by indigenous groups to maintain identity, argue for their rights, and get the word out to people in their own and other nations.

Other virtual communities are formed on the basis of common interest, such as BlueSky, the pseudonym for a MUD (multiuser domain) studied by Lori Kendall (2002). It was made up primarily of computer programmers and systems administrators and used almost exclusively during business hours as a diversion and information source. This online community shared characteristics with off-line communities, insofar as its members shared various attitudes and behavior patterns. But in this case, computer communication was the very reason for the community to be in existence. BlueSky members were predominantly male, middle-class, technically literate professionals and students. The members avoided anonymity and were overtly hostile to those who tried to practice anonymity and identity manipulation. Studies of other online interest communities show that, like off-line communities, each one has its own norms about communication, personal identity, gender participation, and so on.

In addition to community formation, education has been a topic of great interest to ethnographers. They have traditionally evaluated programs ethnographically by studying the culture of schools. Online communication opens up new possibilities for ethnography, just as it is transforming education itself. For example, the Pueblo program is housed in Arizona's elementary schools, where it has become the basis of linkages among students in the United States and in other countries. Online courses and "virtual schools" can also pose interesting questions about how learning takes place most effectively.

Some researchers have pointed out that e-communication often mirrors natural communication in such areas as gender—predominantly female groups tend to favor a collaborative, nurturing style, while mainly male groups tend to be more argumentative. Yet the virtual environment also allows participants to play with gender identity, as well as with other aspects of identity, such as ethnicity, age, and sexual orientation. Researchers are trying to find out how communication changes when we know so little about the person with whom we are communicating. More broadly, they are asking whether people's own senses of identity are likely to change in situations where they can become anyone they choose.

Researchers have used analytical techniques such as social-network analysis to look at the interconnections between groups of users and the information flow inherent in an electronic environment. For instance, it is possible to study the intricacies of information flow through the popular game "six degrees of separation" in which a public figure is chosen and a series of links between that person and another public figure (or even oneself) are mapped, showing the unlikely connections in a society based on social networks. This game was played long before the advent of electronic communication, but studying it virtually allows us to understand the importance of access to technology and the social networks opened up by that technology. For example, with the development of wireless technology and related software, "six degrees of separation" has evolved into "seven degrees of separation," or 7Ds. Today, users of the Internet are realizing the potential of linking related sites and sources of information into a cache that others can access. This type of sharing has practical uses (e.g., for emergency services during times of crisis) as well as serving as a hub for foragers of a given topic.

A relatively recent Web form that has become very popular is the Weblog, or blog, in which individuals post their comments and activities, often linking to other blogs or Web sources. These can be studied in terms of how they help people connect with others and provide a way to construct one's identity online.

Finally, an aspect of virtual reality that is huge in some people's lives is online gaming, which offers significant ethnographic opportunities. At the simplest level, we might work with people who play traditional games like poker online, often practicing for games in the "real world." At its most complex, we have massively multiplayer online role-player games (MMORPG) such as Everquest, which can involve hundreds of players connected online all over the world. These games raise intriguing questions about the relationship between online and off-line realities as players take on complex identities and use real money to buy virtual items needed for the game—often using online sites like E-bay.

Life online is becoming simply another part of life in the twenty-first century. Online communities may replicate many of the features of other nonplace-based communities, but they also make available new possibilities and new kinds of connections. Virtual life offers exciting potential for online ethnographies; indeed, the challenge for the student ethnographer is to decide where to start.

CONDUCTING A VIRTUAL ETHNOGRAPHY: THE PROCESS

The Internet is a virtual world, with any number of potential points of entry and any number of questions that might be interesting to explore. Before you begin, you need to think carefully about what you're interested in and why it would make sense to study it electronically. It is important to think about one question in particular: Are you interested in studying a phenomenon about which people communicate on the Internet, or are you interested in studying the nature of electronic communication itself? These concerns are, of course, related, and may come together during the course of an extended research project, but they do require different approaches, at least at the outset. For example, Bird once worked with a student who was a recovering alcoholic and had rejected the spiritual dimensions of Alcoholics Anonymous. He still needed support from other recovering alcoholics and found that some like-minded people had created e-mail groups to share their concerns. While participating as a member, the student used a discussion group to locate people from around the country and then interviewed them through e-mail. His main concern was to understand why some people rejected the AA approach; he elicited a range of opinions, producing an interesting paper as a result. Along the way he touched upon the emerging role of electronic communication in creating a virtual community, although that aspect of the matter had not been his focus.

On the other hand, another student was interested in how and when a sense of community arises on the Internet. She participated in two e-mail groups; one was largely informational and was concerned with issues of relevance to librarians. The other was a support group for mothers of children with disabilities. She found that while the first group was active and lively, it was primarily an exchange of objective information and did not encourage the sharing of personal data. In fact, if people became interested in getting to know each other personally, they would move "off-list" to "talk" privately. On the other list, the prime purpose was to create a nurturing community, and the discussion was deeply personal. The student examined the communication strategies, such as rule-setting, that each group used; her focus was not on what she could learn about librarians or mothers of disabled children, but on how each group used electronic communication to achieve its particular aims.

For a paper in a course on media anthropology, Barber looked more generally at patterns and perceptions of Internet usage in an online group. She used both survey research and participant observation, and after familiarizing herself with the group's rules of conduct, she posted a message describing her project and asked for volunteers. Participants were asked questions to determine their level of Internet use, which was based on the number of hours online, the number of sites visited, and their perception of themselves on a scale of low to high involvement. She discovered that users with approximately equal numbers of site visits and total online time often rated their use differently. A self-described moderate user might actually spend far more time online than someone who self-identified as a heavy user. Barber's research therefore focused on developing norms of Internet usage, rather than on the nature of Internet communication as such.

As anthropologists, our first responsibility in conducting research is to be fair and honest with the people we study; we must never lie to them, invade their privacy, or betray their trust. We should not abandon basic ethical principles even when we are conducting research among people we never see. We should be very skeptical of the suggestion that because the Internet is a public place, the norms of privacy do not apply. A simple content analysis of a public Web site is not ethically problematic, and it is probably acceptable to quote messages posted on public message boards. But in the latter case, it is probably *not* appropriate to attribute those quotes even to an online pseudonym. When studying online communities with defined memberships, where people are addressing their comments to a particular audience, researchers owe the participants the same courtesy as those they study in the natural world. That is, the members should be informed of your presence, of your intentions, and of your resolve to avoid using real names, e-mail addresses, or other information that could identify them. Since most of these groups have formal rules and expectations of behavior, the researcher would be well-advised to read and follow them. One researcher, for example, studied a breast-cancer support group whose members were interested in being active participants in her research. By offering drafts of her work for comment and requesting permission to use quotations, her interest in the group was legitimized for the members. She had followed their established procedures of open sharing and acknowledged their right to determine the way in which their comments were used. Bird used the same approach in her research and found that presenting herself in this manner actually opened up interesting possibilities for true collaboration with the respondents.

We must always keep in mind that electronic communication is stripped of all but the written word. Electronic attempts to represent gestures, facial expressions, and tone of voice are crude at best and are easily misinterpreted. Moreover, the gender, age, and ethnicity of a person to whom we are "talking" can easily be concealed from us. Imagine having developed a detailed life history of a fascinating old man who tells a gripping narrative of growing up on an Indian reservation, only to find out that "he" is actually a twenty-five year old white woman with a vivid imagination and a library of books on native life. Learn to be critical, to evaluate virtual sources carefully, and avoid making claims of certainty that cannot be backed up by your methodology.

YOUR PROJECT

Choose from among the following suggestions to develop an online research project of your own. Whichever project you select, please make sure that your final report contains not only information about what you found out about the particular topic, but also some of your personal reflections on the process of doing ethnography online.

OPTION 1: How does electronic communication help create a sense of ethnic or national identity?

Choose a group in which you are interested. Locate Web sites, e-mail discussion groups, usenet groups, and so on. You might simply observe, perhaps doing a content analysis of an ethnic Web site, to find out how Irish or Cree identity is defined on the Web. Who created the site? What kind of image is the site attempting to create? Does it incorporate a guestbook or other opportunity for feedback? How does such a mechanism contribute to the mutual development of ethnic identity? Is ethnic pride dependent on demonizing or denigrating other ethnic groups, and if so, how is this goal accomplished? On the other hand, you might prefer to participate as well as observe. Lurk on an e-mail list or usenet group and look for ways people discuss ethnic identity. Then join in, although you should avoid disrupting the group with your own research agenda. Conduct interviews with selected members.

OPTION 2: What is the nature of virtual communities?

Do your own study of any kind of online community—a professional or interest group, an extended family listserv, a support group, a political activist group, a blog, or a multiplayer game. The possibilities are endless. Think about the questions discussed above: How are rules of conduct made and applied, and how is order maintained? What are the norms of anonymity? Do members extend their relationship outside the virtual environment? How significant is the community in people's lives? You might focus on particular techniques: participant observation might be the best way to look at rules and community-building strategies, while interviews might be more effective in finding out how members feel about the community.

OPTION 3: How is society impacted by time spent online?

If a person spends six hours a day at her computer, what does this activity replace? Would she be reading, writing letters, or socializing in person? What happens to couples and families when individuals spend a great deal of time online? Can online interaction actually transform a shy person into a more sociable individual? There are many ways to approach these questions, and you should refer to other chapters in this book for ideas. For example, you could conduct online life histories, asking people to write or talk about their lives in detail, with special emphasis in this case on how the computer may have changed their lives. Or you might use online diaries, in which people are asked to record their thoughts at particular times of day. Your focus might be the family, a couple, or even one individual, producing a detailed, intimate portrait of that person's interaction with technology.

OPTION 4: How is differential access affecting our society?

Internet technology is touching the lives of not only dedicated users, but also those with limited or even no access to the online world. You might explore the impact of the so-called "digital divide" that separates those with easy access from those without. Do teenagers who can only access the Internet for thirty minutes a day in a school media center use it differently than those with access in their own rooms at home? What are the educational impacts of easy access? How is fluent computer and Internet literacy related to questions of social class or status? Such questions might best be explored through a combination of virtual and natural ethnography—for example, conducting interviews online combined with observing behavior at home.

OPTION 5: What impact is the Internet having on education?

How does using the Internet as a teaching medium change the interaction between students and teachers? How do online student discussion groups contribute to learning? It is very likely that you had at least some of your own educational experiences online; use this opportunity to develop your ethnographic skills while thinking more deeply about your own learning processes.

OPTION 6: How is the Internet affecting the way we consume and become informed?

Many people do almost all their shopping online, as well as surf for news and other information. E-bay and other auction sites have offered ways for individuals to make a living by buying and selling. This kind of project offers opportunities to interview people off-line to discuss their consumption habits, as well as looking at the actual sites. Does it make a difference if people get their news online, rather than from newspapers or TV? Do or do not the many sources available make us better informed?

OPTION 7: How does the technology affect the very nature of communication?

In this case, the emphasis is not so much on the content of people's communication, but on the act of communication itself. When we don't know who people are, we can take on many identities. We can certainly present ourselves differently in various "real" social situations (a process sometimes referred to as "style shifting"), but how does this process change when the medium itself allows us to communicate as if we were of a different racial category or a different gender? Does the fact that we cannot see faces or respond to body language affect the nature of language and communication? What is special about the language of online communication, which can include emoticons, acronyms, and many special features adapted to the virtual world?

REFERENCES

Kendall, Lori. 2002. *Hanging Out in the Virtual Pub: Masculinities and Relationships Online.* Berkeley: University of California Press.

Miller, Daniel, and Don Slater. 2000. *The Internet: An Ethnographic Approach.* New York: Berg.

A FEW SELECTED READINGS FOR FURTHER INFORMATION

Bird, S. Elizabeth. 2003. *The Audience in Everyday Life: Living in a Media World.* New York: Routledge.

Gabrial, Albert. 1998. Assyrians: "3,000 Years of History, Yet the Internet Is Our Only Home." *Cultural Survival Quarterly* 21(4):42–44.

Hakken, David. 1999. *Cyborgs@Cyberspace? An Ethnographer Looks to the Future.* New York: Routledge.

Hine, Christine. 2000. *Virtual Ethnography.* London: Sage.

Jones, Steven G., ed. 1999. *Doing Internet Research: Critical Issues and Methods for Examining the Net.* London: Sage.

Markham, Annette. 1996. *Life Online: Researching Real Experience in Virtual Space.* New York: AltaMira.

Wilson, Samuel M., and C. Peterson Leighton. 2002. The Anthropology of Online Communities. *Annual Review of Anthropology* 31:449–467.

14

Developing an Electronic Ethnography

Alvin W. Wolfe & Guy Hagen

A RESEARCH PROJECT

Ethnographic observations by practicing anthropologists studying the operations of health and human service agencies in the Tampa Bay area revealed a common need by these agencies for useable, readily accessible information to support the functions of planning, monitoring, evaluation, management, and budgeting. Individual agencies typically gather as much information as possible given the limitations of their own resources of personnel, time, and money. The results are often disappointing, and the process is very inefficient. Both the ethnographers and the agency staff were hard-pressed to learn who is doing what for whom with what resources and with what effect. To address this common problem, Mary Rust, a planner with the city of Tampa who had earned an MA in anthropology at the University of South Florida, approached Alvin Wolfe, one of her former professors, with a proposal to develop Human Services Information System (HSIS). Rust, Wolfe, and several students convened a planning workshop, which was attended by representatives of more than twenty-five agencies. The workshop participants agreed on a number of points: that the need for information is vital to their ability to carry out their duties; that they intended to meet that need; that the system should ultimately serve the widest feasible range of functions; and that its organization should have the form of a consortium of agencies.

It is difficult for an entire human services system to organize for collective action. The system of services for children and families in the Tampa Bay metropolitan area, for example, consists of more than a thousand firms or official agencies and several thousand less formal programs providing hundreds of types of services to hundreds of thousands of people. Each political unit (city, county, state) wants to keep control over its own agencies and programs, so political forces inhibit the expenditure of public funds for cooperative endeavors that crosscut these boundaries. Moreover, there is little profit in the provision of human services, so the system is not structured by market principles of supply and demand. As a result, the human services system is almost unmanageable because of the complexity of the system itself. Its overall structure resembles a network rather than a hierarchical bureaucratic organization, even though it is composed of hierarchically structured subsets. Even as a network, it is not beautifully symmetrical like the web of a healthy spider, rather it is asymmetrical, with dense clusters and gaping holes—the infamous "holes in the safety net," or the equally infamous "cracks through which clients fall." Nonetheless, there is some kind of whole in operation, and that whole can be grasped by using the electronic and network analytic tools made available to us by engineering and mathematics.

Because human beings stand behind all the entities in these complex systems, we as anthropologists realized that the people involved in them connect organizations to one another; the people themselves are in turn connected to one another by their common involvement in the organizations. In developing the HSIS, we were able to employ mathematical techniques to help us make sense of these heretofore bewildering networks, a process we call electronic ethnography. Just as earlier ethnographers learned to use mapping instruments, still cameras, audio recorders, movie cameras, and video equipment, so modem electronic ethnographers must learn to use current technology and the mathematical analysis that supports it. The social-network analysis that produced the HSIS took advantage of computers to augment traditional ethnographic techniques, allowing for the analysis of larger communities and more complex structures than would be possible using traditional manual techniques. Computer analysis also enabled us to probe the nature of an "electronic community" whose members are not defined by common physical location, but rather by common interest (in this case, the provision of human services in a large urban area). The HSIS is a device for mapping how communication takes place across this dispersed (and, on the surface, chaotic) community, whose members deal with each other through e-mail and other electronic media rather than in face-to-face interactions. The

HSIS was first presented in a paper by Wolfe, Rust, and Patricia Sorrells delivered at the annual meeting of the Society for Applied Anthropology in 1980.

ELECTRONIC ETHNOGRAPHY AND NETWORK ANALYSIS AS TOOLS OF ETHNOGRAPHIC RESEARCH

Traditional ethnographers described cultures that were expressed through communications among a few thousand persons. For example, Raymond Firth's classic study was conducted on Tikopia, a Pacific island with a population of 1,300 in 1929; even if everyone on the island communicated with everyone else, the total number of relationships would only have been about 845,000. By contrast, ethnographers who work in modem societies confront numbers of a vastly greater magnitude. The population of the United States alone is 280,000,000 according to the 2000 census. Moreover, modern communications media make it possible for these vast numbers of people to share information instantaneously. Even as long ago as 1980, 150,000,000 people worldwide saw and simultaneously experienced the Super Bowl. In that same era, half the households in the United States—almost 100,000,000 people—watched the television miniseries *Roots*. The scale and scope of communication has increased greatly in the ensuing two decades. In this milieu, old-fashioned ethnography cannot do a complete job.

Technology has enabled unprecedented new levels of communication and interaction among human populations. New communities, cultural norms, and elements of language have been facilitated by the growth of the Internet. Complex interest groups ("chat" and "news" groups) form around shared interests, and dense webs of electronic communication enable long-distance interactions in ways never even imagined until very recently. Web pages are electronic representations of companies, communities, and individuals. There are an estimated 800 million Web pages today, with approximately one million pages being added every day. ClickZ.com, advertising itself as the world's best source for such statistics, estimates the worldwide Internet population to be over 1.08 billion in 2005, growing to over 1.8 billion by 2010. Over 84% of American workers use the Internet every day, and over 62% of American adults are "online." Countless people participate in online discussion forums, interactive Weblogs ("blogs"), and bulletin boards; 90 million Americans have participated in online groups according to the Pew Internet & American Life Project. Over 82 million people globally use "instant messaging" technology to "chat" in groups in real time. All these developments make up a world that ethnographers must cope with. Social scientists are just beginning to adapt methodologies to explore this electronic frontier, and ethnographic analysis must keep pace.

Since the beginning of ethnographic fieldwork, the preparation, colla-tion, indexing, and storing of field notes has been among the most important of activities for researchers, for only if such details are carefully attended to can the relevant information be retrieved when needed. Surely it was such tasks as organizing the information derived from observations of hitherto unknown cultures that led anthropologists to conceptualize culture as a com-plex whole, divisible into various domains and levels, yet integrated through relations among those domains and levels. As anthropologists took into account more of the internal variability within traditional cultures that used to be stereotyped as "simple," their informal methods of handling data were strained. The matter was complicated when they began dealing with the dif-ferentiation and specialization of modern societies. For a long period in the middle of the twentieth century, the major statements about complex societ-ies were derived from the macro-level data sets of economists, political scien-tists, and sociologists, while anthropologists and other ethnographers tended to provide only "local color." We believe that ethnographers can and should do more.

It may yet be within our capabilities to do holistic ethnographies of complex systems analogous to what used to be done in traditional cultures. We assume that culture must be described not only in terms of the locally accepted standards, but also with respect to variances from those standards. It will come as no surprise that the amount of data necessary to record not only the norms but the variations as well is massive. Nevertheless, we should not be dismayed or discouraged. Technological advances have enabled new data processing tools that can be used to surmount these challenges, including the introduction of new levels of computing capacity. Today's microprocessors are approximately 100,000 times faster than the earliest processors. Industry experts predict that computing power will continue to double every eighteen months. Within twenty years, individual computers may be more powerful than all the combined computing power currently available in Silicon Valley. Moreover, data storage becomes more efficient because of increased capacity of each unit as well as distribution among units.

In addition to rapidly and efficiently handling masses of data, computer programs can now model the complex relations among data domains and levels. Database-management systems incorporate methods for handling large sets of data that are logically organized to satisfy a variety of users' requirements. Instead of relying on sequentially organized records, whose relations derive basically from the fact that they draw certain attribute values from common domains, modern databases can be hierarchical or relational in organization. If they are hierarchical, they originate in a root and the records branch out in one-to-many relations, toward terminal records, as seg-mentary lineage systems or bureaucracies do in social life. On the other hand, record structures may have a network form, wherein each record may be related directly to several other records—a very complicated architecture that, alas, models the complexity of most sociocultural phenomena.

To illustrate how the data of a reasonably complex system can be organized, we can take a look at the schema for the HSIS (see figure 1). Each box represents a table (or record type); for example, the "firm" record has information about an agency. The lines represent direct hierarchical linkages creating a set of tables, one table relating to others in one-to-many relations. Many-to-many relations, on the other hand, occur when one firm operates programs at several sites or one site houses the operations of several facilities. The database permits easy retrieval of information in either direction on the network. From data so structured, it is possible to retrieve the specific information desired and to have that particular report printed in the format desired. Instead of some kind of generalizing statistical statement—that so many thousand services were performed by some number of agencies—one can make a more descriptive statement closer to the reality of the situation, preserving the variation among agencies or firms, programs, clients, and so forth, as well as preserving information about their relationships. An excerpt from such a report is shown in table 1.

It is important to note that such a database is not conceived as fixed. In addition to storing and retrieving data, users may continuously insert, delete, update, and amend data as the system that is being modeled changes. We are dealing with a system open to exchange with the environment and therefore offering management capabilities beyond its own narrow limits. Feedback from component to component provides for maintenance of levels of flow and for making adjustments within the system. There is also the potential for feedforward, in that predicted future conditions might influence the state of the system, an anticipatory quality obviously useful for planning and forecasting.

Such schemas can model cultural structure, and computer programs can provide the windows through which an ethnographer of a complex society may view different domains. The richness of ethnographic detail transcends the aggregation of raw data, our traditional way of viewing information storage. Rather, such a system offers the capability of looking back through aggregate information over the course of time while viewing complex relationships on multilevel plans at the same point in time. Such capabilities offer flexibility for decision makers. Patterns emerge and overviews are feasible; planned change may be designed based on the small picture as well as the large. Database-management systems that were originally designed to meet the needs of business and government enterprises can now be used to help achieve the holistic perspective of anthropological studies of culture.

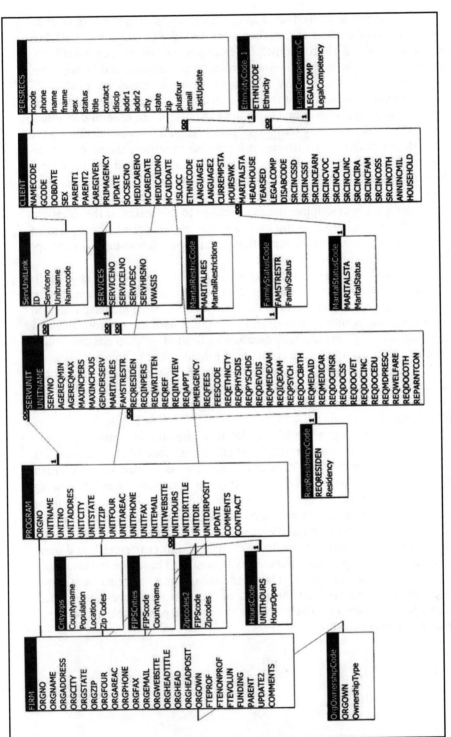

Figure 1 Types of Records (Tables) Related in HSIS Database

Table 1   Report produced by the Human Services Information System

Department of Anthropology, University of South Florida, Tampa, Florida 33620

Program: Agency for Community Treatment Services HSIS
Database No: 12100
4211 E Busch Blvd
Tampa, FL 33617-5916
813 9886096
Type and Funding: Non-profit, Incorporated
(Voluntary) FEES

Program: ACTS, Adult Residential Detox
6806 N Nebraska Ave
Tampa, FL 33604
813 2389505
Program Services: alcohol counseling services
detox serv for drug abuse
residential trtmnt alcoholism

Program: ACTS, Agcy for Comm Trtmt Svcs
4211 E Busch Blvd
Tampa, FL 33617-5916
813 9883533
Program Services: alcohol abuse educa/info serv
alcohol counseling services
drug counseling services

Program: Adolescent Group Home, ACTS
3806 W M.L.King Blvd.
Tampa, FL 33614
813 8700578
Program Services: residential trtmnt alcoholism
residential trtmnt drug dpndn-

Program: Adolescent Receiving, ACTS
8620 N Dixon Ave
Tampa, FL 33604
813 9314669
Program Services: alcohol counseling services
detox serv for alcoholics
detox serv for drug abuse
drug counseling services

Program: Agency for Community Treatment Services, ACTS
4612 N 56th St
Tampa, FL 33610
813 2464899
Program Services: juvenile counselling
psychological assessment
psychological therapy

Program: Alcohol Community Treatment
4403 W M.L.King Blvd
Tampa, FL 33614-7604
813 8791649
Program Services: alcohol counseling services
internships
residential trmnt alcoholism
transitional serv-alcoholism

Program: Dependency Group Home, ACTS
3812 W M.L. King Blvd.
Tampa, FL 33614
813 8702236
Program Services:
foster care – dependency
group home – pre-dlnquent youth

Program: Halfway House ACTS
4403 W M.L.King Blvd
Tampa, FL 33614
813 8759645
Program Services:
internships

Program: HARP, Residential Svcs, ACTS
8702 Stark Road
Seffner, FL 33584
813 6216051
Program Services:
resid.care,long term,mental r-

Program: Homeless Day Center, ACTS
6220 N Nebraska Ave
Tampa, FL 33604
813 2376630
Program Services:
shltr-newcmrs,travlrs,homeless

Program: Outpatient Counseling ACTS
1815 W Sligh Ave
Tampa, FL 33604 -5811
813 2376630
Program Services:
alcohol abuse educa/info serv
alcohol counseling services
drug counseling services

Program: Outpatient Counseling, ACTS
4211 E Busch Blvd
Tampa, FL 33617-5916
813 9883533
Program Services:
alcohol counseling services
drug counseling services

Program: Pinellas Domiciliary
3575 Old Keystone Road
Tarpon Springs, FL 34689
813 4612881
Program Services:
alcohol counseling services
internships
residential trtmnt alcoholism
transitional serv-alcoholism

Program: Youth Outpatient, ACTS
8620 N Dixon Ave
Tampa, FL 33604
813 9314669
Program Services:
alcohol counseling services
drug counseling services

Program: Youth Overlay Services, ACTS
3806 W M.L.King Blvd.
Tampa, FL 33614
813 8700578
Program Services:
alcohol counseling services
drug abuse ed/info serv
drug counseling services

NETWORK ANALYSIS AND ELECTRONIC ETHNOGRAPHY: THE PROCESS

The first step in the process is to identify a personal network by preparing a new spreadsheet document in order to record the network under study in a matrix format. In other words, the software helps to create a table in which members of the network are listed simultaneously as row labels and column labels. Matrices are the most common format for storing and manipulating network data. In order to find out who communicates with whom, it is necessary to survey the members.

The number of individuals in a network is its size (represented by n). People will have differently sized networks depending on how socially active, influential, or popular they are. In addition to size, a network may be characterized by its density, which is the proportion of active links in a network to the maximum possible links. Another characteristic of a network is its prestige factor. Not all connections in the matrix will be reciprocal. Sometimes one person lists another as a contact, but the latter does not necessarily list the former. Individuals who are cited more frequently than others are said to have prestige. In the HSIS, for example, individuals with high prestige were the ones most likely to have access to important information required across the network.

YOUR PROJECT

This project entails the construction of a simple network database. You will explore an "ego network" of connections within a small group of individuals and will use simple network-analysis techniques to identify social and qualitative characteristics of that group and its members. The requirements for this project are limited to tools that should be available to most students: a computer with a spreadsheet program (e.g., Microsoft Excel, Lotus, Appleworks) and an e-mail account. More ambitious students might want to explore the UCINET network-analysis software that is available at http://www.analytictech.com. Depending on your personal interests, we present two options for your project. If you are primarily interested in augmenting traditional ethnographic techniques, you may explore your own personal network of friends and family. If you are interested in exploring the electronic medium, you may collect data on e-mail communication among your friends.

As noted above, the first step is to prepare a spreadsheet. Make a list of the people you communicate with most frequently (between ten and twenty individuals) and enter them into the database. If you are exploring an e-mail network, work from your e-mail program's contact list. Imagine that your network includes you, your professor, and nine friends. The resulting matrix might look something like table 2.

Table 2 Sample Network Matrix

	you@university.edu	prof@university.edu	friend1@apple.com	friend2@msn.com	friend3@yahoo.com	friend4@hotmail.com	friend5@cs.com	friend6@aol.com	friend7@networks.net	friend8@insna.org	friend9@whitehouse.gov
you@university.edu	0	1	1	1	1	1	1	1	1	1	1
prof@university.edu											
friend1@apple.com											
friend2@msn.com											
friend3@yahoo.com											
friend4@hotmail.com											
friend5@cs.com											
friend6@aol.com											
friend7@networks.net											
friend8@insna.org											
friend9@whitehouse.gov											

Any cell that contains a "1" indicates that a network connection exists between individuals whose rows and columns intersect; "0" indicates a lack of connection. For purposes of this example, a network connection signifies that frequent communication (e-mail or otherwise) exists between members. Since we need not be concerned with people who send e-mail to themselves, put a 0 in cells where the row and column labels are the same.

Next, contact each individual in the network. Provide each member with a copy of your list and ask each of them to indicate every individual that they have regular communication with (or each individual who is on their e-mail contact list). The resulting filled-in matrix might look something like table 3.

You can now calculate the density of your network by using the spreadsheet's *sum* function. First add the total number of links in each column and then add up the total of these values. The result will be the number of links in the network. Divide this number by the maximum possible links (calculated with the formula $[n \times (n - 1)]$. Results can range from 0 (lowest density) to 1 (highest density). How might you explain the density pattern that characterizes your network?

Table 3   Complete "Ego Network" Matrix for Ego and Ten Contacts

	you@university.edu	prof@university.edu	friend1@apple.com	friend2@msn.com	friend3@yahoo.com	friend4@hotmail.com	friend5@cs.com	friend6@aol.com	friend7@networks.net	friend8@insna.org	friend9@whitehouse.gov
you@university.edu	0	1	1	1	1	1	1	1	1	1	1
prof@university.edu	1	0	1	1	0	0	0	1	1	0	1
friend1@apple.com	1	0	0	0	1	1	0	0	0	1	1
friend2@msn.com	0	1	1	0	1	1	1	1	0	0	1
friend3@yahoo.com	1	0	1	1	0	0	0	0	0	1	0
friend4@hotmail.com	1	1	0	1	1	0	1	0	0	1	1
friend5@cs.com	1	0	1	0	0	1	0	1	0	1	1
friend6@aol.com	0	1	1	0	1	0	0	0	1	0	1
friend7@networks.net	1	0	0	1	0	0	0	0	0	1	0
friend8@insna.org	1	0	0	1	0	1	0	0	0	0	1
friend9@whitehouse.gov	0	0	1	0	0	0	0	0	0	1	0

Your first calculation in the density analysis—the total number of links per column—is also your measure of prestige. The individual with the highest score is the one with the most prestige. How might you explain the patterns of prestige that you find in your network?

You may conclude your analysis by constructing a sociogram, a visual graph of the network that will help you clarify its characteristics. There are a number of powerful, free software packages for visualizing social networks, such as yEd (http://www.yworks.com), Visone (http://www.visone.info/), GraphViz (http://www.pixieglow.com/graphicviz), and NetDraw (http://www.analytictech.com). These can be invaluable tools for mapping network relationships, and can serve as simple tools for exploring and understanding social structure. Sociograms representing very large networks such as the HSIS will, of course, be extremely complex. But for the purposes of this project, there is a relatively simple method: start by placing labels for the individuals in your network around a circle. Draw a line between each pair of labels that are connected (i.e., represented by a "1" in a cell at either the row-column intersection or the column-row intersection, which may be different depending on the prestige factor). Here is a simple sociogram based on our example:

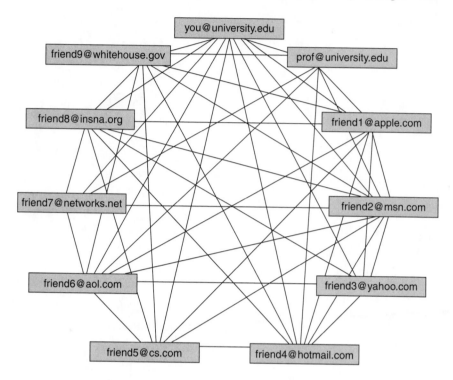

Draw a sociogram of your own network. Does the graph suggest anything interesting? Are the density and prestige calculations revealed?

A FEW SELECTED READINGS FOR FURTHER INFORMATION

Horrigan, John, Lee Rainie, and Susannah Fox. 2002. *Online Communities: Networks That Nurture Long-Distance Relationships and Local Ties.* Pew Internet & American Life Project (http://www.pewinternet.org/).

Wilson, Samuel M., and Leighton C. Peterson. 2002. The Anthropology of Online Communities. *Annual Review of Anthropology* 31:449–467.

15

Composing Autoethnographic Stories

Leigh Berger & Carolyn Ellis

The students in my "Writing Lives" class stare at me expectantly. We are about to discuss Carolyn Ellis's *Final Negotiations: A Story of Love, Loss, and Chronic Illness*. The book details the loss of her partner, Gene Weinstein, and also describes her approach to writing. I open today's conversation by throwing out a question: "What was the purpose of this book?" I am met by a full minute of silence.

"Well, Professor Berger," Dan, one of my more talkative students, ventures, "I think that Ellis wanted to make sense of the death of her partner, Gene."

I nod while replying, "Okay, good. Any other feelings about the purpose of this book?"

Carrie raises her hand and says, "It seems like it was partially to make sense of his death, but she also interpreted what happened from a social science perspective and used what other social scientists had to say."

I smile. "Great point. But why would she want to connect social science to the death of her partner?" Another few moments of silence. This time, there doesn't seem to be anyone with the courage to try a response, so I ask a follow-up question: "What is Carolyn Ellis's job?"

"Social scientist!" several students respond simultaneously.

"What do social scientists do?" I ask.

"Study people and society," Dan replies, running a hand through his closely cropped, dark hair.

"How?" I inquire.

"They observe things," Jennifer, another student, explains as she leans forward. "You know, some go hang out with people for a while and take notes on what goes on."

"That's called ethnography," I interrupt her, writing the word on the board. "But if ethnography usually involves studying other people, what is Ellis doing?"

"Some sort of combination of ethnography and autobiography," Erin, one of my quieter students, pipes up.

"Excellent," I encourage her. "Exactly! And that is called autoethnography." I write this word on the board below "ethnography." "Carolyn Ellis is using her own experience as a starting point for studying how death and chronic illness are experienced, and she is writing in a more literary way to draw readers into those events." I am cut off by a hand going up in the back of the room. "Yes, Chad?"

"But why is that not just a memoir or something—I mean, how does her experience get classified as social science?"

"Good question. Would you say that death and illness are important to our society? Are they events commonly experienced by people?"

There is agreement as students nod and murmur, "Yes."

"Well, couldn't Ellis have gone out and conducted a statistical survey about how people deal with death and loss instead of using an autoethnographic method?" A few students nod while others shake their heads "no." To clarify, I ask, "Why didn't she do that?"

"Well, getting statistics is fine, but I don't think that was her goal," Carrie says thoughtfully. "I mean, statistics give important information about how many people experience something, but wasn't Ellis's purpose to have readers feel what she was feeling?"

"Or feel their own losses," Dan throws in.

I reply, "Well, if we accept that as one of her goals, let me ask if, while reading this book, you connected to her story."

"Yes," Dan says. "It made me think about my grandfather's death, actually. Even though he had cancer, not emphysema, there were still a lot of similarities. Because my grandfather was sick for so long, I remember that I felt relieved when I knew it was almost over, but then that made me feel guilty— like Ellis describes. Reading this also made me realize a lot of the things my grandmother must have gone through because she took care of him."

Carrie's green eyes mist over with tears as she says, "Ellis really described a lot of the feelings I had when my mother died. My mother had diabetes for most of her life, and little by little she began losing control of different functions. Ellis was really good at describing how your feelings go back and forth between wanting the person to finally be in peace, but not wanting to lose them."

"For those of you who were reminded of your own losses, did the book also give you new ways of thinking about or dealing with those deaths?"

"Definitely," says Carrie. "It made me understand that other people also felt what I did. Like I wasn't alone, and it helped me feel less guilty about the times I wanted my mother's life to finally end."

Erin added, "I haven't experienced loss of a loved one yet, but I'm still glad I read this work. I think I'll be better prepared now when I do."

The class is quiet and contemplative for a few seconds. Finally I say, "What I'm hearing is that this story provided a window into loss that resonates with your own knowledge about how the world works and helps you anticipate future experience. And it also opened new possibilities for understanding illness and death. Do you agree with that assessment, Chad?"

Chad nods and says, "Yeah, but . . . I'm still wondering. How can this be scientifically valid?"

"The goals of autoethnography are not validity—or accuracy—in the traditional sense of the word. Instead, autoethnographers attempt to communicate emotional truth." I try to think of a way to explain this clearly. "In autoethnography, it is the job of readers to determine if they think the story is honest and if it rings true to their experiences. The whole idea of an autoethnography is to show readers ways they are similar to and different from others in the world. If Carolyn Ellis's book moves us to consider the experience of loss, if it makes us question the ways we can relate to her story, and the ways we might not, then we are learning about the social world. And," I add, "don't forget that Ellis is trained as a social scientist. She looks at the world through the lens of that expertise. So even when using her own experiences, she is analyzing and drawing conclusions as a social scientist and giving readers insights into social processes."

"But I'd still want to know if her experiences are generalizable," Chad says. "That's what we learned to ask in my methods class. I mean, it was just her experience. She didn't select a sample or anything, or even talk to other people about their experiences for comparison."

"I think her work *is* generalizable," Carrie replies thoughtfully. "But she's thinking of generalizability in a different way from most social scientists. She's not thinking of it from a sampling point of view, but from an audience perspective. I mean, you can see from our responses to her story that we've experienced some of what she did."

"I think she'd say our experience resonated with hers," says Erin, brushing some of her red hair behind one shoulder.

"And remember, her goal is to evoke experiences from readers, to open up conversations about them, not to accurately represent the mean experience," I remind them, very happy with the conversation we're having. "I think I see that happening today, with Carrie and Dan discussing how Ellis's work reminds them of their experiences with loss. Ellis provides a description of what's possible, not what's typical, and then she asks the audience to compare their experience with hers and with others, talking about how they're similar and different. So in essence you, the reader, become a social scientist, analyzing and drawing comparisons."

"Cool," says Pete, speaking his first words of the semester.

I glance at the clock. "I hate to do this, but we should also discuss the other piece you read for today, which is a paper based on my two-year ethnography of Dalet Shalom, a Messianic Jewish congregation. We can continue to talk about autoethnography as it applies to this paper." As the students shuffle through readings, I ask, "What makes the Messianic movement unique?"

Jim, who hasn't spoken yet today, answers, "They're essentially both Jewish and Christian."

I nod and say, "Yes. They consider themselves Jewish, and observe Jewish holidays and celebrations, but they believe Jesus—Yeshua—is the Messiah."

"Is Yeshua really the Hebrew pronunciation of Jesus?" Jennifer asks.

"Yes," I reply. "So they are a group who lives on the boundary between Jewish and Christian, and this makes them controversial not only within the Jewish community, but also within the mainstream Christian community. How is that for complicated?" The students chuckle in response. "Now, in what ways would you say this is similar to Ellis's work?"

"It's written like a story, too," Carrie explains.

"Yes, good. How else?"

"Well, you talk a lot about your . . ." Erin searches for an appropriate word, "feelings about what's going on and talk about your own experiences as a Jewish person."

I am pleased that Erin is speaking so freely today. "I do. My starting point for understanding Dalet Shalom is my own feelings and reactions. So, what makes this work similar to Ellis's is its use of autoethnography. What makes it different?"

"Ellis's work focuses more clearly on her own story about the loss of Gene. Yours is about you, but its main focus is on a religious congregation." Dan leans back in his chair.

"Yes. Essentially, what's going on in this piece is two parallel journeys. We have my exploration of this Messianic congregation, but at the same time I show how I am also on a quest to examine my own questions of Jewish identity and spiritual experience. Why do you think I chose to use a narrative technique to write about my study?"

Jim raises his hand and says, "Well, it's pretty hard to describe religious experience in an objective way. How would you explain what faith feels like without using a story?"

"Good point, Jim. Think about your own experiences of spirituality, or maybe the experiences of others you know. Religious systems themselves are stories—the Bible, Native American traditions—they're all based on storytelling. Also, Messianic Judaism is evangelical, so the congregation worships in a highly emotional way and most people there express having a personal experience with God. Narrative autoethnography is a style that naturally lends itself to accessing the personal and emotional." I pause. "I think some of you are lost," I say, looking at a few students who furl their eyebrows and look around as if they have no notion of what's going on. "I think we need to step back and really think about what autoethnography is." I glance at the clock. "Unfortunately, we're out of time. How about next time we pick up with a discussion of the history of autoethnography so you can clearly understand these issues." Looks of relief cross many faces. "See you all then. Have a good afternoon!" I call after them as they rush for the door.

I gather my notes and head to my office. On the way, I stop at Carolyn Ellis's office and knock on the door. "Come in," her voice calls. As I enter the room, Carolyn turns around and smiles.

"Do you have a minute?" I ask.

"Sure." After moving some piles of books out of my way, she beckons me to sit in a black recliner next to her desk.

"I just got out of class. We were discussing *Final Negotiations* and one of my papers about Dalet Shalom," I explain.

"Really? Any interesting reactions?"

"A few were able to connect your story to their own experiences of loss. Most of them seemed to understand the purpose of autoethnography, but some were clearly confused. One student wanted to know how this was considered social science. And they asked about validity and generalizability. We ran out of time, but I told them I want to discuss the history of autoethnography next time."

Carolyn looks contemplative as she responds. "You could always give them a written history and description of autoethnography that they can read. In fact, I have something I wrote for my classes." She rises and rummages through one of her file cabinets, pulling out a paper and handing it to me. Looking down, I see "A Brief History of Autoethnography."

"Thank you," I say. "This may be just what I need."

"Then I'd probably give them a list of articles about autoethnography."

"I thought of that already," I respond.

"And maybe a few more autoethnographic stories," Carolyn continues, "and ask them to use these as models for writing their own experiences. You could give them 'There Are Survivors,' where I focus on my own experience. And I just happen to have an outline of steps to follow for writing personal narratives," she adds as she rummages through her file cabinet, producing a yellowed sheet of paper. "Here you go," she says, handing the paper to me.

"And I could give them a piece from my dissertation on the Messianic congregation," I say, "where I wrote about others but included myself as a character. I'll also write an outline of steps to follow for that kind of writing."

"Good idea," Carolyn says, beaming. "The only way they're really going to learn about autoethnography is to write it themselves."

"That certainly was true for me," I respond. Carolyn smiles a knowing smile as I get up to leave.

I immediately read Carolyn's paper on the history of autoethnography and copy it for my students. The next day I hand it out to my class and I review the paper as they read. Here is the paper:

A Brief History of Autoethnography

Autoethnography is an autobiographical style of writing and research that connects personal and cultural experience. Autoethnographers not only observe the world around them, but also examine their internal perceptions and feelings about their place in that world. Usually written in the first-person voice, autoethnographic works can take various forms: poetry, short stories, fiction, novels, photographic essays, and social-science prose. These accounts include characters, action, dialogue, and emotional response. Autoethnographers ideally use all their senses, their bodies, movement, feeling, and their whole being to learn about others.

The term "autoethnography" has been around since the 1970s. Like many terms used by social scientists, the meanings and applications of autoethnography are now so varied that it is hard to provide a precise definition. Autoethnography is linked to the feminist movement and the social-scientific questioning of relationships between researchers and subjects. Many feminist writers advocate making the researcher's presence, values, and biases known in the writing of research and embrace the idea of research based in personal experience. The distanced, "objective" voice of the (usually) white, male researcher no longer seemed to address the issues that were being raised by newer ethnographers who were increasingly members of racial and ethnic minorities, lower-class, and/or citizens of the third or fourth world. As a result, many social scientists questioned the ways ethnography had traditionally been carried out and written about.

Autoethnography encourages ethnographers to develop a relationship with those studied, to treat them as coresearchers, to share authority, and to assist participants to author their own lives in their own voices. Readers, too, take a more active role as they are invited into the author's world, asked to respond to and discuss the events being described, and are stimulated to use what they learn to reflect on, understand, and cope with their own lives.

Essentially, autoethnography opens a dialogue among the researcher, participant, and reader. In the sharing and cocreation of stories, the goal of this conversation is for the researcher and participants to understand one another better and for readers to interpret and form opinions about what they are reading. Autoethnography invites readers to accompany the author on a journey and to add their own emotions and reactions as they travel into worlds of new discoveries and possibilities.

"That helps, but I'm still having trouble," Chad says after reading about autoethnography. A few students who haven't been participating, nod in agreement. "Are there other things we could read like this that might help us understand autoethnography better?"

"Well, yes, glad you asked. I just happen to have a short list here for those of you who want to read further." I hand out the list:

Readings on Autoethnography

Berger, Leigh. 1997. Between the Candy Store and the Mall: The Spiritual Loss of a Father. *Journal of Personal and Interpersonal Loss* 2(4):397–409.

Bochner, Arthur P. 1994. Perspectives on Inquiry II: Theories and Stories. In *Handbook of Interpersonal Communication*, 2nd ed., ed. M. Knap and G. R. Miller, 21–41. Newbury Park, CA: Sage.

———. 1997. It's About Time: Narrative and the Divided Self. *Qualitative Inquiry* 3:418–438.

Denzin, Norman K. 1997. *Interpretive Ethnography: Ethnographic Practices for the 21st Century.* Thousand Oaks, CA: Sage.

Ellis, Carolyn. 1995. *Final Negotiations: A Story of Love, Loss, and Chronic Illness.* Philadelphia: Temple University Press.

Ellis, Carolyn, and Arthur P. Bochner, eds. 1996. *Composing Ethnography: Alternative Forms of Qualitative Writing.* Walnut Creek, CA: AltaMira.

———. 2000. Autoethnography, Personal Narrative, Reflexivity: Researcher as Subject. In *Handbook of Qualitative Research*, 2nd ed., ed. Norman Denzin and Yvonna Lincoln, 733–768. Newbury Park, CA: Sage.

Kiesinger, Christine. 1998. From Interview to Story: Writing "Abbie's Life." *Qualitative Inquiry* 4(1):71–95.

Richardson, Laurel. 1994. Writing as a Method of Inquiry. In *Handbook of Qualitative Research*, ed. Norman Denzin and Yvonna Lincoln, 516–529. Thousand Oaks, CA: Sage.

"The reading will help, but I think one of the difficulties you're having in understanding autoethnography is that you haven't experienced writing one yourselves," I say, delighted that I am prepared. "So, I've come up with two possible assignments you can choose from. The first is to write a personal narrative similar to the style of Ellis's *Final Negotiations*. The second is to write about others, but include yourself as a primary character, as I did in my work on Messianic Judaism."

I begin handing out the assignment. "Each assignment begins with a brief story to remind you of the two approaches. The first is an excerpt from a story Carolyn wrote about the death of her brother, Rex. Mine is another piece from my ethnography of Dalet Shalom. Following each story are step-by-step instructions for each assignment. Let's read them over now. Then you can decide which one you want to do."

"There Are Survivors": Telling a Story of Sudden Death
by Carolyn Ellis

Rex was scheduled to arrive in Tampa today, Friday, January 13, 1982. Although I was supposed to meet him at 4:30, his plane was just ready for take-off from Washington when I called the airline at 3:45. Since I had invited several friends to dinner, I was glad for the extra time.

"Hey, what you doing?" my older brother, Art, asks when I pick up the ringing phone. I am surprised to hear from him, and, in spite of the lightness of his words, detect worry in his voice. Rather quickly he asks, "Has Rex gotten there yet?"

"No, his plane has been delayed. Why?" Already I feel alarmed.

"Oh, someone called Mom and said a plane had crashed, and she thought they said something about Tampa. I just wanted to reassure her that Rex is okay. You know how she worries."

Although he says this nonchalantly, I tense up because I feel how hard he is working to normalize this conversation. Then I speak from inside a numb fog. "Where did they say the plane was headed?"

"Well, she thought they said it was coming from Tampa to Washington."

"Then that can't be it," I responded too quickly, adrenaline now starting to pump. We breathe.

Into the silence my brother says, "But there was confusion because they said it was Flight 90."

"That's his flight number, but Mom probably just got the number wrong." Yes, that's the explanation, I assure myself.

"No," he says, "I just heard the number myself on the radio."

"Did they say Air Florida?"

"I don't know, just that it had crashed into the Potomac."

"Oh, God. I'll call the airline and call you right back."

Flashes of lightning go off behind my eyes. My breathing speeds up, yet I am suffocating. As I dial, my hands shake, and I say aloud over and over, "No, please, God." Struck by the triviality of my everyday concerns, I remember how rushed I had felt getting ready for Rex's arrival and how important that had seemed. Now, if he is only alive, nothing else will matter. Of course he is, I admonish myself. Calm down. Mom has this all messed up. But then how did Art hear the same flight number?

I get a busy signal a couple of times before an Air Florida agent responds, "Air Florida, may I help you?"

The familiar greeting comforts me. See, there's nothing wrong, I reassure myself. "Yes, I want information on an arrival time."

"Certainly. What is the flight number?" he asks cheerfully.

"Flight 90."

Now his voice takes on a business-like quality as he quickly replies, "We cannot give out information on that flight."

"What do you mean you can't give out information on that flight?"

"We can't give out information on that flight," he repeats.

My heart pounds as I calmly ask, "Did an Air Florida plane crash today?"

"Yes."

"Was it going from Washington to Tampa?"

"Yes," he says, seeming relieved to answer my questions.

"How many flights do you have going from Washington to Tampa today?"
"Two."
"When were they scheduled?"
"One this morning. One this afternoon."
"Did the one this morning make it?"
"Yes."

"Thank you very much," I say softly and hang up the phone, my heart pounding.

Art answers on the first ring. "There was a crash," I say, "And it sounds like it was Rex's plane."

"They are saying now there are survivors," says my brother, and I feel hope. He continues, "I'm going to Mom and Dad's. They're pretty upset. They're going to be more upset."

"Okay, yes, go. We'll keep in touch."

Now I am alone, in shock, adrenaline rushing through my body. Numb on the outside, my insides are over-stimulated. I tumble through blank space. "Please, God, no," I hear myself moaning deeply from my gut. I move quickly to turn on the television. "Flight 90 crashes." It rings in my ears. "There are survivors in the water being rescued. Look, another head." This is not a movie or an instant replay. I sit, my arms wrapped around my body, and sway back and forth twelve inches from the TV, breathing deeply and groaning. My eyes are glued to the rescue of the victims from the Potomac, and I search frantically for Rex. "He has to be there," I say out loud. In a daze, I am conscious of myself watching the TV as part of the scene. Reality becomes hazy, and more multilayered and boundary-less than usual.

A car approaches and I know from the familiar sound that it is Gene, my partner, and Beth, his daughter, home from shopping. When I rush to the door, the fog lifts suddenly and the slow-motion scene I am in slips into fast-forward. "What's wrong, honey?" Gene asks as he steps through the door, drops his packages to the floor, and embraces me.

Quietly and desperately, I say, "My brother's plane crashed."

"Oh, my God," he says calmly. "Do something!" I want to yell. "Make it okay." But I say nothing. His body quivers; his embrace tightens. It feels good to be held and to have told someone. Not just someone. Gene, my anchor. He will know what to do and how to think about what has happened. My body slumps against his. "Oh, my God," he says again.

"It doesn't seem real," I say.

"Death never does," he replies. "But it is." Death? Why is he talking about death? It's just a crash. I cry quietly.

Then like a shot, I remember. "The TV. I've got to get back to the TV. There are survivors," and I break free from his embrace. That's right—he doesn't know there are survivors. That's why he's talking about death. "I'll see Rex being pulled from the river," I say loudly, fists clenched in the air. "Then I'll know he's all right. He had to make it. He's tough. There are survivors," I repeat.

Beth and Gene don't watch the instant replays of the people floundering in the icy water. Why do they sit silently at the kitchen table? They should be helping me look for Rex. They must not believe me. But they don't know him like I do. He can get himself out of anything. Any minute his head will appear. I continue rocking back and forth with my hands clasped together, periodically putting my face against the television screen to get a closer view. But I cannot find my brother in the Monet-like dots and lines. Hope and desperation alternate—hope when a new survivor is sighted, desperation when it is not Rex. There must be more survivors. "Rex, pop out of the fucking water!" I scream.

The announcers talk about the hero who just died saving others. "That must be Rex," I say, feeling proud. "He would do that. That's what he was like." Was? Why am I using the past tense? "He's not dead," I say. "I know he isn't." But if he has to be dead, I want him to be the hero. But then I will be angry that he could have saved himself and didn't. Why aren't Gene and Beth responding to me? They sit, silent, sad, watching me. He's not dead. Quit acting like he's dead. Of course he's not dead. Not my brother. I continue watching what are now the same instant replays of the same people being pulled out of the same river. Twelve people have survived. Then they announce seven. Then there are five. And one dead hero.

At my parents' home, the people came. Three to four hundred of them. They occupied my parents and validated for me how important Rex had been. I became the greeter, letting them in, hugging, listening to them marvel at how I had changed, and then directing them to my parents, who sat side-by-side in their matching Lazy-Boy chairs. Offering their sympathies, men looked sad and stoically held my father's hand and kissed my mother. Women were more likely to cry openly with my mother and often with my father, sometimes falling into sobs into my parents' arms. Older people comforted, while the younger ones stammered about not knowing what to say. That would come with experience. My mother cried continually and my father wiped tears constantly. I was the dry-eyed director, who craved and feared collapsing into my parents' embrace.

Everyone came bearing food. The smell was sickening. Knowing exactly what to do, several community women took over the kitchen. They served big meals to whoever was there, ignoring that no one ate much. Later in the week, it would take hours to throw away all the uneaten food: green beans cooked with hamhock; whole Old Virginia hams—the real ones, salty, strong, and fat; green and red Jell-O salads embedded with nuts and coconut, made in circular tins with globs of Miracle Whip filling the middle hole; apple pies made quickly from canned apples with dough crisscrossed on the top and too much cinnamon added; sweet pound cakes, chocolate layer cakes with chocolate icing, and yellow cakes with white frosting; big, fluffy white loaves of Wonder Bread; gallons of sweet tea in pickle jars that still tasted and smelled of pickles. Years later, I would find containers of instant coffee—the family size—and CoffeeMate and hundreds of plastic utensils still bundled in plastic wrappers in the cabinets.

Part of the role of greeter was to record who had brought what so that thank-you cards could be sent. My sister and I took turns keeping records. Sometimes I wanted to scream, "What a waste of time and energy!" Other times I was glad for the task and respected the final ritual of acknowledgement.

Mixed in with the mourners came the florists with the flowers we had requested not be sent. Donations for my parents' church also poured in. "What can we do?" everyone asked. "Write some thank-you notes," I wanted to say, but didn't. It was not their job. "Then go help throw food away," I thought, but again I said nothing. Proper etiquette dictated that you wait until people insisted—or better yet, just did something. I had never been involved in a funeral before, but I intuitively knew the rules. They were an extension of the small-town etiquette that I had lived the first twenty-two years of my life in.

I helped my mother make up a list of pallbearers. "They should be his best friends," she instructs. "It can't be relatives. They have to be men. There must be six." This is not the time to argue for women pallbearers. This is for my mother.

YOUR PROJECT: WRITING THE SELF

The excerpt from my autoethnography shared above shows how I reveal my innermost thoughts and feelings during an especially tragic and emotional moment—finding out that my brother has died in a plane crash. I take you into the immediacy of the moment. The first part of the story is told in the present. I invite you to be there with me as I hope for life and then come to the realization that my brother is dead. In the next segment, I take you into my parents' house, the day before the funeral. Now I am the greeter for those who come bearing food and sympathy. I tell this part of the story to you in the past, to provide some relief from the intense emotional immediacy of the first segment. In this second section, I become the observer, the ethnographer who shows you the small-town rituals of death and funerals, as I rediscover them for myself.

The story focuses on my emotional experience of my brother's death. In addition, this piece looks at the reaction to sudden death, media images of accidents, corporate response to tragedy, the juxtaposition of hope and facing reality, family communication in times of tragedy, and small-town responses and rituals surrounding death.

Keep the following points in mind as you carry out a similar project. First, think back to an event that was particularly emotional for you or think about one you are currently going through. Type out or write down all you can remember about the experience. Try to remember conversations that you had and reconstruct them as best you can to show how you are feeling. You may become emotional as you do so. Remember that you will not actually be in the experience and trust that you can bring yourself out of the emotionality whenever you need to. Continue writing for a few days. Your memories and feelings will stimulate other memories and feelings.

If possible, talk with others who are part of this episode and ask them what they remember. As you talk to and listen to them, you will remember other events. With their permission, record or write down these stories. Make sure to secure the permission of other characters you include, if possible. If not, think deeply about the ethical implications of writing about those who have not given permission and do not know you are including their stories in your story.

Finally, read through all your notes and think about how you want to tell this story. It is important to figure out which part of the story you want to tell, since you can't tell everything. It is important that the story be evocative and engaging, inviting readers to enter the story or to think about their own.

Using your notes, write your story. Be sure to include vivid descriptions of the scene and of your thoughts and feelings. Use dialogue. This is the time to try to look at the story from outside the experience. Think about your writing. Think about what the story means. Think about what a reader can learn from the story, in addition to finding out about your experience. What social processes are revealed in your story? Make sure you develop them, but do so narratively. The emphasis should be on *showing*, not *telling*.

Reread your story and share it with others for feedback. Take that feedback into consideration in preparing a final draft, and write a conclusion that analyzes the story and discusses what can be learned from it. With your instructor's approval, consider reading the story aloud to the class.

Messianic Judaism: Searching the Spirit
by Leigh Berger

I stand with my head bowed during a worship service at Dalet Shalom Messianic Jewish Congregation, thinking about my ethnography and the two years I have spent with these congregants. Messianic Jews identify themselves as Jewish, carrying out Jewish rituals and celebrations within the context of a belief in Jesus (Yeshua). Messianic Jews are not accepted by mainstream Jews because of their insistence that Yeshua is the Messiah; they have a conflicted relationship with mainstream Christians because they believe that Christianity's understanding of the Bible is misguided. Simultaneously defining themselves as Jewish while believing in Yeshua places Messianic Jews in an undefined borderland. I am fascinated by this boundary existence, in part because I can understand being frustrated with mainstream Judaism and desiring a highly emotional practice of religion.

My thoughts turn to my own ambivalence about being Jewish, and I wonder how much of that feeling is rooted in the context of my familial history. I always felt like I was born with a mark of shame on my soul. As though deep within me—already present at conception—was a reminder of faces and bodies pressed tightly into train compartments headed for Auschwitz. As though the genetic mass within my mother's womb, dividing and subdividing, already felt the twinges of comprehension that, from that moment on, Judaism would become a constant reminder of victimhood.

What do my memories of life with my parents tell me? I am half of their union. Half of my father, half of my mother. I am half of both their happiness and sadness. Half of each of their minimal Jewish loyalty. As a family we marked our Jewish identity three times a year: Yom Kippur, Hanukkah, and Passover.

And now I am surrounded by people worshiping in an evangelical style, but with loyalty to Jewish identity and ritual. The congregants at Dalet Shalom express their Jewishness with passion and emotion, but within the context of belief in Yeshua, the figure not accepted as the Messiah by mainstream Jews.

I am pulled out of my internal reflection by the voice of Dalet Shalom's rabbi, Aaron Levinson. "Just relax and receive the Lord. Don't try and fight it, just receive." A quiet melody swirls around us, and I slowly sway back and forth. "Open your heart and receive the Lord. Anyone who hasn't yet received Yeshua, but who would like to now open your heart to him, please come forward." There is a pause, and I open my eyes, wondering if this invitation is directed toward me. I think I am the only person there who hasn't accepted Yeshua as their savior. Suspended in the interval, I am uncomfortable with my own resistance, wishing a deep spiritual experience could move me into complete belonging. Since much of my interpretation is shaped by my role as semiparticipant, I wonder if conversion would allow me full participation, thereby profoundly altering the ethnography that I write.

"Rabbi! Rabbi! I had a vision!" shouts a woman to my right. "I've been questioning my belief and what I should do, but today I had a vision. There was a man in a white robe, sitting on a throne. And as I came closer, I sensed two more people on either side of him, also in white. I felt them all reach out for me, and it was so peaceful. Just peace. And I knew that it was the Messiah."

"Amen!" congregants call out while clapping.

"Hallelujah!" others yell.

I close my eyes again. What would it be like to "receive" the Lord? I turn this thought over in my mind and begin to imagine a white-robed Jesus, looking much like he does in millions of artistic renderings. I imagine his hand reaching toward me, reaching and waiting for my acceptance. I try to imagine my own salvation: what would happen if my own hand reached back to Him? Would the hand be inviting? Would I feel safe, secure, and unburdened?

I know I have a deep desire for spiritual fulfillment. The urge for it has always filled me like a hunger, causing me to seek it out continually, but without complete satisfaction. At Dalet Shalom, I love the feeling of joining in praise and worship, of having Rabbi Levinson ask about my emotional well-being, of how it feels when congregants invite me to sit with them during services. However, I feel estranged by their belief in biblical literalism, by their intolerance of homosexuality, and by their insistence that there is only one correct way to worship. Because of those disconnections I wonder if it would ever be possible to convert to Messianic Judaism. I want the intense emotional energy of Dalet Shalom and the warmth and caring among members. I want the moments of transcendence offered by the singing and dancing and the link to the sights and sounds of my heritage.

Toward the end of the service, Rabbi Levinson asks us to repeat a prayer, but offers a condition: "Please do not repeat the prayer if you have not recognized Yeshua. It is very important to only say these words if you believe in Yeshua, because it is a contract with the Lord! It is urgent that you decide to live in light rather than walk on a dark path to Hell." He begins the prayer.

I remain silent. But a moment later I am reconnected when Rabbi Levinson covers his head with his *tallit* and performs the Aaronic benediction in Hebrew *a capella*. "May the Lord bless thee and keep thee. May the Lord cause his countenance to shine upon thee. . . ." This ritual strikes me deep within my soul, the Hebrew words gliding over the familiar melody, binding me in a breathtaking moment to the generation that came before me.

That night, I have a dream about my grandfather. After his death seven years ago, he would frequently appear in my dreams, but I have not dreamed of him in many years. He is standing in the kitchen of the south Florida condo where he and my grandmother lived for most of my life. I enter the room and he smiles warmly at me. His startlingly blue eyes light up, and he brushes some of his soft white hair away from his forehead.

"Grandpa?" Contrary to real life, in the dream I feel like I am physically much smaller than he and I have an impression of him towering over me.

He continues to smile at me, and somehow I know that he is leaving to walk to synagogue, like he does every Friday. Both he and my grandmother were religious Jews who attended synagogue regularly and followed the Jewish dietary laws of keeping *kosher*. My grandfather holds up a hand, as though waving good-bye to me.

"Grandpa? I need to ask you. . . ."

But he is slowly turning away from me, until I can no longer see his face. I desperately want him to turn back around, to answer my questions. I awake from the dream with a start, confused for a moment about where I am and what has happened. I realize that I have been dreaming and I smile at the memory of my grandfather. "I miss you," I whisper into the dark room and close my eyes again.

I have had this dream because of my research, because he and my grandmother were observant Jews, and because I have been questioning my own religious beliefs. I wonder if my grandfather's turning away symbolizes my feeling that I have rejected part of my Jewish identity. After all, I am not an observant Jew, and now I'm studying a congregation of people who are considered traitors among the majority of Jewish Americans. What would I have asked my grandfather if I hadn't lost his attention? What was the comfort he got out of his faith? What was his conception of God? Maybe his overlooking my questions symbolized how difficult they are to answer. Maybe he was trying to tell me that not all questions *can* be answered.

Memories and dreams such as this continue to surface during my fieldwork, ghosts of my past woken up by my insistent probing. The more I travel into the Messianic world, the more I realize I have embarked upon a parallel journey of self-exploration.

YOUR PROJECT: WRITING THE SELF AND OTHERS

The portion of my ethnography shared above shows how I both describe Dalet Shalom and simultaneously reveal my own internal feelings and memories. I connect my discoveries of Dalet Shalom to my own life and experiences, using myself as a vehicle for exploring Messianic Judaism. Since we have no way to systematically examine concepts like God or the afterlife, we must study them by looking at how people talk about and describe their religious experiences to themselves and others. I open religious belief by showing the interactions between the lives of my participants and my own accounts of my life and experiences as a Jewish woman. Keep the following points in mind as you carry out a similar project.

Choose a religious congregation or other formal gathering that you wish to observe. It can be either one that is new to you or one with which you have some personal experience. Find out times of services and/or gatherings and meetings. Call the group and be prepared to explain that you are observing as part of a class assignment. If they will only welcome you if you promise to become a full-fledged member, respect their position, but find another group to study. In any case, make sure you have permission to observe (it will be useful to have it in writing, particularly if your school requires you to file a formal informed consent application) and then plan to attend at least two of the meetings.

Take a notepad with you when you go to the service/meeting unless you have explicit permission to use either audio- or videotape. Try not to spend the entire meeting, however, taking notes. It is better to write down your descriptions, feelings, and reactions immediately after the meeting. Some questions you might want to ask yourself include: How/why did you choose this particular group to observe? How did you feel emotionally during the service/meeting? Why do you think you felt this way? Did you understand what was going on? Why or why not? How do the activities at this meeting compare with others that you have observed or participated in? Is this a group you could become part of? Why or why not?

Look over your notes and put together a narrative account of your observations (both of the group and its meetings and about your own reactions). The narrative should have a clear beginning (in which you set up your history with this topic, your decision to choose this group, and a basic description of who they are and where they are located), a middle (in which you describe the scene, people, and activities), and conclusion. In the conclusion, reflect on whether or not you could be a member of this group. Explain why or why not. If you have selected a group of which you are already a member, explore whether or not playing the role of observer made you more or less committed to the group. What did you learn about ethnography? What did you learn about your own emotions and perceptions?

16

Participating in an Ethnographic Field School

Tim Wallace

As you have learned, the ability to carry out ethnographic research, one of the hallmarks of professional anthropology and other social sciences, consists of a set of skills that even beginning students can master. Ethnographic research skills can be effectively utilized in many settings outside of traditional communities, including business, education, and health care. It is with good reason, then, that all undergraduate and graduate programs in anthropology (and an increasing number of programs in other fields) require coursework in ethnographic methods. Most methods courses require some hands-on experience, but there are obvious limitations imposed by other demands on students' time. So if you really want to find out what ethnography is all about and how to do it, it is a good idea to attend an ethnographic field school, which will give you time to focus your attention on a single set of learning activities without the interference of other coursework assignments.

WHAT IS AN ETHNOGRAPHIC FIELD SCHOOL?

As I use the term, "ethnographic field school" means an intensive, extended stay in a locale significantly different from the student's usual surroundings, during which time the program's director combines instruction in ethnographic methods with the conduct of an actual research project. That project may be either independently conceived and carried out by each student under the supervision of the director, or it may be a group project with all the students contributing to a common final product. In some cases, the students' research will be integrated into the director's ongoing research in the area in which the school is held. Ethnographic field schools all require students to practice taking organized field notes and/or keeping formal field journals and to submit these documents along with the actual product(s) of research. Field schools also give some form of university credit; the normal load is six credits for a four-to-six week program.

Beyond these basics, however, there is considerable variation in what field schools have to offer. Variation is due to differences inherent in the research settings, the theoretical interests of the program director, the educational backgrounds of the student participants, and the degree to which other languages must be learned. Some schools have structured activities involving frequent contact with the participants, while others are more loosely structured and expect that students will be able to work independently most of the time. Most field schools have some kind of home-stay component; in some cases, it may be merely a brief overnighter, with students living mainly in dormitories, hotels, or community buildings; but in other cases, the student may board with a local family for the duration of the school. Some programs last for an entire academic semester while others last for a few weeks (usually during the summer).

There are other kinds of field schools that can be interesting and valuable to anthropology and other students. For example, there are archaeology field schools in which students assist the project director in excavating and analyzing a dig. There are field schools that are essentially guided study tours of famous or important heritage or ethnic sites in which the program leader is mainly a lecturer to students in a mobile classroom. There are still other field schools whose purpose is mainly language study. But my remarks in this chapter are directed mainly toward an understanding of the true ethnographic field school as described above.

LEARNING OBJECTIVES OF
ETHNOGRAPHIC FIELD SCHOOLS

All ethnographic-field-school programs try to provide opportunities for a student to learn ethnographic research skills, to learn something about the culture of the community under study, and—perhaps most important—to internalize the psychological "right stuff" one needs to do the job of an ethnographer. In a real sense, field schools give a student the opportunity to be an apprentice ethnographer.

There are some concrete skills that are part of the learning package. I emphasize the following skills in my own seven-week ethnographic field school in Guatemala: designing a field research project; selecting appropriate research methods or data-collection techniques based on a realistic appraisal of the field site; defining and utilizing appropriate sampling procedures; developing daily and weekly research goals; writing field notes and keeping a journal; coding field notes; carrying out systematic observation techniques; understanding ethical issues involved in fieldwork; conducting both formal and informal interviews; working effectively with informants and translators; developing appropriate rapport-building devices; carrying out community and cognitive mapping; understanding how and when to use rapid appraisal techniques; understanding time-allocation study techniques; surviving and overcoming culture shock; using laptop computers for simple research tasks; analyzing ethnographic data; and writing effective research reports.

It is very important for students to become competent participants in the local culture. Participation opens them to listening and observing the culture in which they find themselves—a key skill to develop in ethnographic research—so they can build rapport, gain the confidence of the local people, know what kinds of questions to ask, and of whom to ask them.

By way of preparation, it is usually a good idea to have taken a course or read books and articles about the culture you will be visiting and working in. Most students in my program will have done some background reading and other library research before arriving in the field so they can hit the ground running as soon as they enter the site. Since the program lasts only seven weeks, it is important that they have some knowledge and understanding before they get to the school. Some field schools in fact build specific ethnographic, topical, or language courses into their orientation programs.

Two Examples of Ethnographic Field Schools

My field school is an intensive seven-week summer training program in Guatemala in which students from my own university (North Carolina State University) and other universities around the US and the world gather to learn what ethnographic field research is all about and how to undertake their own independent fieldwork. I have had applications from students in Asia, Africa, Europe, and North and South America. In 2005 one of the participants was a Canadian, while another was from London. In 1999 one of the students was an undergraduate from a university in Medellín, Colombia, and another was a graduate student from Japan. Since my first field school in 1994, over 150 students have participated. I have also led workshops for professional colleagues interested in organizing ethnographic field schools of their own. Often students from colleagues' universities participate in my program, and sometimes my students participate in theirs. We encourage our students to find the program that best fits their academic and intellectual needs and interests.

There is a maximum of thirteen students for each session of my field school. The first third of the program consists of formal classes, fieldwork exercises, and informal discussion sessions. By the end of the second week, all students have selected a topic, written a research project outline, and begun their ethnographic data collection. By the end of the program, each student will have completed an independent project. A twenty-page preliminary written report must be completed before departure.

Throughout the program each student lives with a local family, which I consider to be a vital component in their training. My students consistently tell me in their program evaluations that the home-stay was the single most valuable aspect of the program. The home-stay is not simply a place to sleep and eat. The families have been carefully chosen ahead of time for their interest in and enthusiasm for providing the students with a safe, friendly environment for learning about the community. The families are as excited about having the students stay in their homes as the students are to find out what the local people's real home life is like. The families are their first key informants and collaborators who help them get the most out of their ethnographic experience. Many of the families are quite interested in the students' research and are even anxious to help them in their work. Students are able to depart with an appreciation of what it takes to do ethnographic fieldwork, not only because of what they have learned in the classroom, but also from their experience of doing fieldwork on their own. Collaboration with their home-stay families helps them get involved quickly and intensively with the local community so they can do their independent project. In the long run, what the students learn experientially on their own has more lasting value than what they learn in class.

Another field school takes place in Barbados and is directed by George and Sharon Gmelch of Union College in Schenectady, New York. Their program, however, is three months long and offered in alternate years, instead of seven weeks and annually like mine. All the Barbados program students are from Union College. The program is well-known on campus, students are easily recruited by word-of-mouth, and former participants play a key role in the recruitment and orientation of new students. Nearly all the students are anthropology majors and have had several appropriate courses in preparation for their experience abroad. In addition, in the semester prior to departure, the selected participants are required to sign up for on-campus orientation sessions, read books on the Caribbean and related topics from a prepared bibliography, and interact with former field-school students. All the students are undergraduates, and the total group of participants is relatively small, so students have frequent one-on-one access to the program directors. Because the Barbados project lasts for three months, it is possible for participants to build strong relationships with their research subjects. They can develop more detailed projects, deal with culture shock, and develop a high level of competency in ethnographic data-collection skills. Moreover, since English is the language of Barbados, it is possible for the students to begin interacting with local people immediately.

A week-long on-site orientation in Barbados includes some classroom work on ethnographic methods (including detailed discussion of writing field notes) and the completion of some warm-up ethnographic fieldwork exercises. After this orientation, the students are assigned to their home-stay families. The students live in separate communities spread around the island, and each one completes an independent research project. Each student must submit a preliminary report before departure. During the three months, the directors visit each student in his or her community at least once a week. The students rarely interact with each other, except on weekends; most of their week is taken up with their own projects. The directors expect the students to make themselves and their purpose known to members of the community, to develop a network of acquaintances and friends, and to become integrated as much as possible into the life of the community. Although the directors are always available to mentor the students, the latter are expected to test their own ethnographic wings and work on their own as much as they can.

ADVANTAGES OF PARTICIPATING IN A FIELD SCHOOL

The presence of an on-site program director is a real asset to the participants. A good field-school program director is one who is more a mentor than a teacher. In the long run, the only way to learn ethnographic methods is to do actual ethnographic research. A teacher can never do the learning for you, but a mentor can be there for you when you need a word of encouragement, advice about handling a sensitive subject, a suggestion about how to work with a difficult informant, an idea about how to organize one's data for the write-up, or tips on coping with culture shock.

The director/mentor can play a decisive role in helping students understand that culture shock is a natural part of the learning process. No matter how familiar the setting may be, the immersion into the local culture that is required in an extended piece of ethnographic research can be an unsettling experience, and when it hits students can be confused and upset—perhaps even ashamed that they are doing something wrong. The mentor helps them handle the shock of living in a new setting and plays a key role in getting them back to normal. For example, a few years ago one of my field-school students spent about $1,000 in telephone calls to an intimate friend back home. I suspected that this student was trying to cope with severe culture shock. Rather than criticize the student's costly coping strategy, I decided to change the home-stay to a more nurturing family. As a result, the student felt more comfortable in the community and more confident in conducting the research. After graduation, this student told me that the field school had been the most important and meaningful aspect of the entire four college years. In general, the positive experience of completing an interesting and useful research product convinces students that culture shock, while distressing, need not be fatal. Having a mentor around makes it a bit easier to find out that they have the "right stuff" to be an ethnographer after all.

STUDENT COMMENTS ABOUT THE LONG-TERM VALUE OF A FIELD SCHOOL

In addition to the concrete skills students develop as participants in field schools, there are also positive, long-term outcomes (such as learning how to cope with culture shock) that are just as important, even if they are intangible, personal, and sometimes difficult to describe. For example, one undergraduate wrote me about the impact of the Costa Rica field school:[1]

> I had traveled a lot in the military, but I was scared when you dropped me off with my host family that first rainy night when we arrived. . . . Going to Costa Rica reminded me that there is a world out there. I think about people from where I live who have no conception of different places. They live in their reality and there is no other for them. I guess the field school experience has made me want to remain outside a small cultural bubble. I wish sometimes I was a millionaire so I could go on a field study somewhere different every year.

Another undergraduate wrote:

> I have become much more culturally sensitive since the trip, and I feel as though I understand much more the importance of and need for diversity throughout the world. My research at [Manuel Antonio National Park in Costa Rica] secured my decision to pursue environmental education and awareness, and because of the trip I am planning to live outside the U.S. at some point for an extended period of time, hopefully to study environmental awareness and protection. Living within a different culture, although brief, helped me to surface and develop many of the passions and interests that I needed to grow on a personal level. I discovered both positive and negative aspects of myself and my ability to relate to other people, which helped me to focus on personal improvement and identification.

A final example comes from another undergraduate who wrote me to say:

> Amazingly enough, I believe that I experienced a hefty dose of culture shock coming home from Costa Rica. I had a hard time easing back into air-conditioning and hot showers once I realized they were truly luxuries! The field school taught me so much about the world, and quite unexpectedly, about myself. Quite honestly, I don't think that my family and friends knew how to react to the new, wiser, and more anthropologically confident me. Working in the field gave me a greater appreciation for what classroom learning provided, and motivated me to continue my interests in tourism. The program made me more aware of other people and places. It gave me the capabilities to bridge different perspectives to foster greater understanding and positive change.

ANOTHER PRACTICAL REASON FOR A FIELD SCHOOL

There is also a good financial reason to participate in an ethnographic field school. It is a good place to find out whether you are psychologically suited to be an anthropologist. If, by the end of the program, it turns out you are not so inclined, you will save lots of money and time by refraining from studying anthropology as an undergraduate major or in a graduate program. The field school gives you an opportunity to find out what ethnographic fieldwork is really like. Not all students end up convinced they should stay in anthropology and make a career of conducting ethnographic research. One very good student switched her major to journalism shortly after returning to campus. She had done well in the field, but decided that anthropology was not the best match for her talents. She was neither the first, nor will she be the last, anthropology major to change programs after attending a field school.

Students are understandably anxious about their dedication to and skill in cultural anthropology, but having doubts about one's ability to do fieldwork are not at all uncommon. In a book entitled *Fieldnotes*, anthropologist

Roger Sanjek (1990) presents evidence of how even the most famous ethnographers experienced such doubts; in their private notes, they wondered why they were in the field at all. Michael Agar (1996), author of *The Professional Stranger*, expressed the same fears about his own fieldwork. I, too, was terrified of doing my dissertation research and got angry with my professors because I thought they had not trained me well enough. I thought I had learned precious little about how to do such basic tasks as writing field notes, interviewing, taking genealogies, analyzing coded data, mapping, and taking censuses. Fieldwork is a challenge that can be overwhelming if one has to face it alone for the first time. I therefore decided to organize a field school that would be open to both beginning students as well as to graduate students on the threshold of their own independent research.

I have learned in my years of directing a field school that students feel more comfortable testing their wings when they know that someone with experience is available for advice and guidance. Fear of rejection and fear of failure are two normal emotions that both apprentice and professional ethnographers confront when they enter the field to do research. But in a field school, these fears can be assuaged in a reasonably comfortable, supportive atmosphere. In this kind of program, students not only have a mentor available when a problem arises (or even when it is only anticipated)—they can also find support and encouragement from other participants who are going through the same process of adjustment and learning.

In the end, though, doing ethnographic fieldwork is fun, and when it all comes together in an interesting and useful product, it can be exhilarating. In the field school you can share both your failures and your successes with everyone else in the program. When you get home you will find you have been changed for the better, even if the changes are invisible to all but you and those closest to you (including, perhaps, your professors). The other people who attended field school with you, however, will understand what has happened to you, since they shared that time and had similar feelings. You will never forget the people with whom you went into the field, for they have shared with you a very important moment in your life—the moment when you became a real ethnographer.

SOME CONCLUDING ADVICE

By participating in an ethnographic field school, undergraduates can see what kinds of skills are needed to be an anthropologist. Graduate students can also benefit by gaining hands-on experience prior to undertaking their own independent thesis or dissertation research projects. Even post-doctoral professionals can participate in these programs as refreshers or as a way to learn new and innovative techniques. What unites all students who participate in an ethnographic field school is the opportunity to test themselves in a cross-cultural setting under the tutelage of an experienced mentor who provides structure and lots of encouragement and support when the going gets tough. The mentor-student interaction process is a vital component of all ethnographic field schools and is an important reason for their popularity.

If you are interested in the possibility of joining a field school, the first place to look is your own university. If it does not have a program of its own, it may be able to help you locate programs elsewhere; in some cases, financial support may be available for students wishing to participate in such a program. Another good source of information is *Anthropology News*, the monthly (except June, July, and August) newsletter of the American Anthropological Association (AAA), which has a "Career Development" section in which field-school opportunities are announced. You can also contact the AAA directly and request information from the program assistant in charge of keeping a list of field-school programs. The AAA office is located at 2200 Wilson Boulevard, Suite 600, Arlington, VA 22201; the phone number is 703-528-1902, and the Web site is at http://www.aaanet.org. The newsletter of the Society for Applied Anthropology also regularly publishes field-school information (http://www.sfaa.net). Announcements also appear on various anthropology listservs. Ask your instructor which ones he or she thinks are most appropriate for you to monitor, or ask him or her to keep track of some of them for you. Recently the National Association for the Practice of Anthropology published an entire issue devoted to ethnographic field schools (Iris 2004). Five field schools are profiled in this issue, with commentary from student participants.

When you identify a program that interests you, it is essential that you speak in person to the program director. Since s/he will be the main person you will be dealing with in the field, be sure to interview him or her in as much detail as possible; find out about how the program is structured, how much mentoring you will receive, whether a home-stay is part of the program, how many credits you will be earning, what kind of product you will be responsible for submitting, and how much access you will have to the director. Be sure also to clarify all logistical matters: all costs (including airfare), insurance, inoculations (if needed), and passport and visa requirements. Do not be afraid to ask for as many details as you think you need to make an informed decision. On the basis of all this information, you can make a reasonable decision about whether the program suits your needs and interests. If you want further suggestions, advice, or information, you may also contact me at tim_wallace@ncsu.edu. I also have a Web site at http://www4.ncsu.edu/~twallace.

NOTE

[1] As of 2006, I have led thirteen field schools: two in Hungary, six in Costa Rica, and five in Guatemala. Currently the field school functions at Lake Atitlán, Guatemala; students are housed

with Maya families. Nevertheless, student comments from Guatemala are similar to those who studied in Costa Rica. Many past program participants have been so involved in their work and the people they work with that they have returned to visit, intern, or find employment.

REFERENCES

Agar, Michael. 1996. *The Professional Stranger: An Informal Introduction to Ethnography*, 2nd ed. San Diego: Academic Press.

Iris, Madelyn, ed. 2004. Passages: The Ethnographic Field School and First Fieldwork Experiences. *NAPA Bulletin 22*.

Sanjek, Roger, ed. 1990. *Fieldnotes: The Makings of Anthropology*. New York: Cornell University Press.

A FEW SELECTED READINGS FOR FURTHER INFORMATION

Gmelch, George, and Sharon B. Gmelch. 1999. An Ethnographic Field School: What Students Do and Learn. *Anthropology and Education Quarterly* 30(2):220–227.

Wallace, James M. Tim. 1999. Introduction: Mentoring Apprentice Ethnographers through Field Schools. *Anthropology and Education Quarterly* 30(2):210–219.

Contributors

Michael V. Angrosino is Professor of Anthropology and Religious Studies at the University of South Florida where he teaches courses in applied anthropology, qualitative methods, and comparative religion. His publications include *Opportunity House: Ethnographic Stories of Mental Retardation* and *The Culture of the Sacred: Exploring the Anthropology of Religion*. His current projects include the ongoing ethnography of deinstitutionalized persons with mental retardation and chronic mental illness and a study of the evolving role of hospital chaplains.

Yvette Baber is the Director of the Dr. Carter G. Woodson African American Museum in St. Petersburg, Florida. She has taught African-American history and anthropology at the post-secondary level and has conducted research on the impact of education policy on urban students, and on community development issues such as youth development and education.

Roberta D. Baer is Professor of Anthropology at the University of South Florida. Her research interests include medical and nutritional anthropology. Her current projects focus on the cultural aspects of diabetes in Mexico and cross-cultural aspects of folk illnesses.

Jessica Barber has earned her MA and is currently enrolled in the doctoral program in Applied Anthropology at the University of South Florida.

Leigh Berger continues to observe and study how people form and experience religious beliefs. When not writing and reading about spirituality, she tries to discover the cultural norms of the toddler's world through interaction with her two-year-old son.

S. Elizabeth Bird is Professor of Anthropology at the University of South Florida. She is the author of *The Audience in Everyday Life: Living in a Media*

187

World, as well as two other books and over fifty articles and reviews in the areas of media anthropology, folklore, and popular culture.

Kathryn Borman is Professor of Anthropology and is affiliated with the Alliance for Applied Research in Education and Anthropology at the University of South Florida. She has extensive experience in the field of educational reform. She is currently working on a national longitudinal evaluation of comprehensive school reform. Other research projects include "Understanding Factors that Sustain Science, Technology, Engineering, and Mathematics (STEM) Career Pathways," "Effects of College Degree Program Culture on Female and Minority Student STEM Participation," and "Assessing the Impact of the Urban Systemic Initiative."

Carol Bryant is Professor and Codirector of the Florida Prevention Research Center at the University of South Florida. She is currently developing and evaluating a community-based social marketing approach for bringing about social change. This framework teaches communities to conduct research to understand their members' needs and design programs that will enable them to realize their aspirations.

Constance P. deRoche went to Nova Scotia to do the doctoral fieldwork on which her chapter is based, and has been teaching there ever since. She is currently Professor of Anthropology at Cape Breton University. She has done research on work, organizational culture and change, and community economic development, as well as on media stereotypes. The areas in which she teaches include qualitative research methods, societal problems, science and society, work, and organizational culture. She has always enjoyed designing hands-on pedagogical projects.

Carolyn Ellis loves to write stories, experiments with form, thinks about qualitative methods, and is an observer of how people feel and consider emotional experience. She enjoys teaching and writing as a Professor of Communication and Sociology at the University of South Florida. When she's not working, she can be found at her cabin in the mountains of North Carolina, walking in the woods with her two dogs, engaging in intense relational conversations, and traveling with her partner Art. Her most recent book is a novel set in a classroom entitled *The Ethnographic I: A Methodological Novel about Autoethnography.*

Bill Goddard earned an MA in Applied Anthropology from the University of South Florida. His thesis drew from the study reported in the chapter in this book. He currently works at the Muskie Center at the University of Maine where he conducts research on programs aimed at providing alternative career opportunities for students who have had difficulties in their high school academic careers.

Guy Hagen earned his bachelor's degree in anthropology and computer science from the University of Minnesota and his master's degree in applied urban anthropology from the University of South Florida. He is currently President of Innovation Insight, Inc., a research consulting firm that specializes in qualitative and quantitative research methodologies as well as social network analysis.

Amy Fox McNulty earned a BA from Middlebury College and an MA in Applied Anthropology from the University of South Florida. She currently works as a Project Associate for Formative Evaluation Research Associates in Ann Arbor, Michigan. She has conducted a wide range of evaluations for nonprofit organizations in the areas of education, youth development, and community foundations.

Serena Nanda is Professor Emeritus of Anthropology, John Jay College of Criminal Justice, City University of New York. She writes widely on gender, India, and the teaching of anthropology. She is the author of *Cultural Anthropology*, 9th ed. (with Richard Warms), *Neither Man nor Woman: The Hijras of India*, 2nd ed., *Gender Diversity: Crosscultural Variations*, and *American Cultural Pluralism and Law*, 3rd ed. (with Jill Norgren). She is currently working on a book about artistic representations of the West by non-Western peoples.

Laurie J. Price is Professor of Anthropology at California State University East Bay (formerly Hayward). She teaches ethnographic methods, medical anthropology, theory, applied anthropology, and is currently developing a course on the anthropology of food. Her research and applied work center on health issues, both in the United States and in Ecuador.

Ellen Puccia is currently completing her doctoral dissertation in the applied anthropology program at the University of South Florida. Her research focuses on sex workers in Costa Rica.

Nancy E. (Lange) Redfern-Vance was born in Anderson, Indiana. She spent most of her childhood and teenage years in Japan where her parents taught and did missionary work. She graduated from Itazuke High School and returned to the United States to attend college. She earned her bachelor's degree in nursing from the University of Michigan. After the birth of her two sons she attended a nurse-midwifery program at the University of Mississippi Medical School and was certified as a nurse-midwife. During her midwifery career, she delivered more than 1,400 babies. After earning a master's degree in nursing administration from the University of Florida, she completed her doctorate in applied anthropology at the University of South Florida in 1999. She is now Associate Professor in the College of Nursing at Valdosta State University.

Martha Woodson Rees is Associate Professor and Department Chair of Anthropology at the University of Cincinnati. She earned her doctorate from the University of Colorado and has held two Fulbright lectureships, received two research grants from the National Science Foundation (including supplemental support for undergraduate researchers), and currently holds a Rockefeller Humanities Fellowship. Her research uses survey and ethnographic methods to understand regional systems and communities, as well as individual and household interactions within those systems. She has conducted fieldwork in Mexico on topics such as indigenous technologies, migration, and women's work. She has also been conducting research on Latino migrants in the United States.

Cheryl Rodriguez is Associate Professor of Africana Studies at the University of South Florida. Her primary research interests are in the areas of black women's activism, housing issues, social inequality, community ethnography, and urban community development.

Gerry Tierney is Associate Professor of Anthropology in the Behavioral and Social Sciences Department of Webster University, where she teaches courses in cultural anthropology, applied anthropology, women's studies, and criminal justice. She has taught anthropology in Austria, Japan, and Thailand. She is interested in qualitative methodologies and has collected life histories in Alaska and Japan. She continues to enjoy summers in Alaska and keeps in touch with the Anchorage street people she interviewed during her research in 1988.

Tim Wallace is Associate Professor in the Department of Sociology and Anthropology at North Carolina State University. He has led thirteen ethnographic field schools since 1994. His applied research on tourism has taken him to Madagascar to conduct an impact assessment for an eco-tourism project, to Hungary to study the economic effects of tourism in the post-Soviet transition, as well as to Costa Rica and Guatemala. In 2002 he was a Senior Fulbright Scholar at the Universidad del Valle de Guatemala; he returned there in 2003 as a Senior Specialist in Anthropology. He recently served as a member of the Executive Board of the Society for Applied Anthropology, and he is coeditor of the *NAPA Bulletin*.

Susan C. Weller is Professor of Preventive Medicine and Community Health at the University of Texas Medical Branch in Galveston. Her research interests include medical anthropology and formal anthropological methods. Her current projects focus on cross-cultural aspects of health and health care.

Alvin W. Wolfe is Distinguished Professor Emeritus of Anthropology at the University of South Florida. For more than twenty years he was Coordinator of Internships in Applied Anthropology, and he directed the Human Services Information System, a database management system that used up-to-date technology to help applied anthropology interns keep up with ever-changing information on local social services. He applies formal network analysis to many social situations, including a study of 600 organizations in the Tampa Bay area that serve children and families. He recently led a team in the study of welfare reform in Florida. He is Chair of the Florida Health and Human Services Board.